BARBECUE LOVER'S TEXAS

Restaurants, Markets, Recipes & Traditions

FIRST EDITION

John Griffin and Bonnie Walker

gpp

GUILFORD, CONNECTICUT

All photos by the authors.

Editor: Tracee Williams
Project Editor: Lynn Zelem
Layout Artist: Mary Ballachino
Maps: Alena Joy Pearce © Morris Book Publishing, LLC

ISBN 978-0-7627-8151-5

Printed in the United States of America

I dedicate this book to my dad, William Henry Griffin, who taught me his version of barbecuing when I was young.—John

I dedicate this book to my husband, David Miron, for his encouragement and support, as always.—Bonnie

CONTENTS

ABOUT THE AUTHORS

John Griffin is an award-winning writer and editor from San Antonio who specializes in food, wine, travel, and theater. He is the cofounder of food website SavorSA.com, and his work has appeared in *Texas Monthly*, *Spirit* magazine, the *San Antonio Express-News* and the *Sarasota Herald-Tribune* among others. He is the coauthor of *Food Lovers' Guide to San Antonio* and *Oma's Cookie Jar,* a collection of his mother's recipes.

Bonnie Walker has been a food and wine writer and freelance editor in San Antonio for 20 years. A cofounder of food blog SavorSA, as well as writer and editor, Walker is a former editor of *San Antonio Taste* magazine and was food writer for the *San Antonio Express-News* for nearly 15 years. She is the coauthor of *Food Lovers' Guide to San Antonio* (Globe Pequot Press).

ACKNOWLEDGMENTS

We want to thank all of the pitmasters, barbecue joint owners, and Texas barbecue lovers who took the time to talk with us, share their warm hospitality and stories, and serve us some exceptionally fine barbecue. Deborah Orazi, Brian West, and Cecil Flentge offered invaluable help. Ginger Robinson, Pat Sharpe, Daniel Vaughn, Lisa Rawlinson, Robert Jacob Lerma, Roger Diaz, Lance Cullison, Phillip Kent, Jenny Martinez, and Nichole Bendele each helped make our work easier. A final word of gratitude goes to all those who sent up prayers on our behalf.

Here's to sharing more brisket in the future.

My greatest thanks go to my parents, Annaliese and William Henry Griffin, as well as Linda, Annaliese, and Brigritte and their families. Support above and beyond came from Bill Steiden and my creative mentor, Carol Yeager. Mike ("You're gonna die!") Bergin and James Canter provided welcome and essential doses of humor. Of course, thanks go out to Bonnie Walker: What's next on our plates?

—John Griffin

Thanks to my family, especially my mom, Kathryn Poen, and sister, Marcia Walker, for their interest and unflagging support. Thanks also to friends whose encouragement came when most needed. Finally, thank you, John Griffin, for everything, especially for eating the eyeball in the *barbacoa*.

—Bonnie Walker

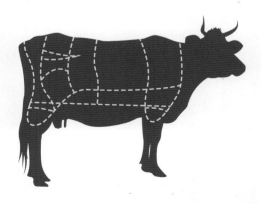

INTRODUCTION

When you start talking barbecue with folks you don't know, it's best to figure out which side of the fence they come from. If they hail from Memphis, Kansas City, or North Carolina, just tip your hat, smile politely, and pretend to listen. Your mama raised you to be mannerly, remember?

But if they're from the right side of the fence, also known as inside the Texas border, then the real talk begins.

That's because Texas barbecue talk isn't just about what you're having for dinner. It's not merely a heap of smoked meat spread out on a sheet of butcher paper with pickles and onions scattered off to the side. Texas barbecue is a way of life, and it's become so ingrained in Lone Star culture that it's practically a religion.

Listen to the awestruck whisper they use to describe a brisket that was so moist and delicious that it all but melted on their tongues while bursting with a mingling of beef and smoke flavors. Or pay attention as they reach for their inner poet to convey the sight of a pit boss emerging from billows of smoke while bearing a slab of ribs held to the bones by skin so hot that it was still sizzling from the pit. Then bow your head to contemplate the gratitude that swelled within your own chest when you bit into a sausage ring full of garlic, pork fat, and post oak smoke.

The mysteries of barbecue extend to the people in the pits. Wayne Mueller, who runs the revered Louie Mueller Barbecue in Taylor, doesn't see himself as a master. "I'm really a student of barbecue," he says. "I know I will learn something new every day."

That's one reason why Texas has such high standards when it comes to barbecue. It's also why barbecue is finally coming to be recognized in a global

food community that once looked down on pit-cooked food as not being refined enough or worthy of study. "Texas is one of the great epicenters of world barbecue," says TV host Steven Raichlen, who has authored cookbooks such as *The Barbecue Bible* and *BBQ USA*. "Its emphasis on smoked or smoke-roasted meat with only a minimum of seasonings and condiments (some of the greatest Texas barbecue joints don't even serve sauce) sets it apart from barbecue elsewhere in the US and around Planet Barbecue. I would rank Texas brisket, as epitomized by Franklin's in Austin, as one of the top 10 barbecue specialties in the world." (A more recent ranking from Raichlen listed San Antonio's the Granary 'Cue & Brew and Two Bros. BBQ Market higher than Franklin Barbecue.)

The feeling that great barbecue inspires is shared by another celebrity chef, Adam Perry Lang, author of *Serious Barbecue*. "Barbecue is such a personal thing," he says. "It is my passion, my love." The French-trained chef may be from New York, but he understands how pleasurable it is to bite into a piece of meat that has been perfumed with the right accent of smoke. Perhaps that's why the pecan he uses comes from Gourmet Wood in Fort Worth.

To Lang, the whole mystique of barbecue is primordial, something that can be traced back to man's early relationship with fire. "Fire is something you can kind of contain, but you can't dominate," he says.

Hunger is something else that has yet to be dominated, which is why the desire to drive great lengths for barbecue is so intense. But before you rev your motor to head out on the various trails through the state, it helps to understand just exactly what Texas barbecue is. This was something we kept learning over and over again, as we went to new areas and talked to different pitmasters, each with a unique and valid approach to preparing what they call barbecue.

We had originally thought Texas barbecue meant smoked meat, instead of the grilling style that the rest of the world calls barbecue. But that wouldn't be entirely right. "'Barbecue' is a slippery term," Raichlen says. "At first glance it would seem to refer to smoked beef brisket or shoulder clod, but that would leave out the baby back pork ribs at Two Bros. BBQ Market in San Antonio or *barbacoa* (Mexican-style pit-roasted steer head). It's tempting to say

meat cooked low and slow using indirect heat in a barbecue pit, but Cooper's in Llano (and many other places) uses a process more akin to direct grilling." In East Texas the hickory used in the pit tastes different from the mesquite that you'll find in South and West Texas or the post oak preferred in Central Texas, making for regional differences.

Or as Greg Gatlin of Gatlin's BBQ in Houston says, "Everybody brings their own kind of style to the Texas style of barbecue."

That brings up the cultural issues of barbecue, the history and the traditions that have been handed down through the years from blacks, whites, and Latinos alike. Stories involving Germans, Czechs, Africans, Mexicans, and Southern transplants add to the mix.

What it boils down to is this: There is no one single definition of Texas barbecue. The state is so huge that it is home to several regional styles so engrained in their areas that it's what the locals want. Try to get them to change, and you'll be facing an uphill battle.

But why would you want them to change? Why not embrace the culinary diversity that has conquered the state?

That's what chef Ernest Servantes has done. During the week he oversees the food services at Texas Lutheran University in Seguin, but on weekends he becomes a barbecue warrior. He's the pit boss of the Burnt Bean Co. competitive barbecue team with his wife, Bel, and he's spent years traveling the state of Texas in an ongoing study of how Texans eat their barbecue. His passion drives him to towns that are barely on the map, but his practical mind has also helped him form a studious approach to the growing world of barbecue competitions.

So, what's the barbecue lover's best tool to learning about both the dramatic and the subtle variations in Texas 'cue? "It's called an Excel spreadsheet," Servantes says. On it he keeps notes of every local style of barbecue he tastes, so he knows what the judges from the area might be predisposed to like. If a competition is in the South, say, he might want to consider a sauce with a touch of cumin or a higher spice level than normal. In that way, he's cooking to the crowds. It's helped earn him state championship wins as well as the top spot on the Food Network's *Chopped Grill Masters* in 2012, where he walked off with $50,000 in prize money.

Servantes isn't alone, by any stretch of the imagination. Brothers hit the trail as a way of staying in touch, bachelor parties head out together for a last taste of freedom, families pack up the car for a weekend escape. Yes, it's a male-dominated world, but you'll also encounter groups of women who plot and plan their own 'cue crawls months in advance. In other words, these are Texans from all walks of life. Or they're barbecue lovers from all over the world. And they're taking the time to make a pilgrimage to Lockhart, Luling, and now Austin to try the meats that are considered to be the best in the state, if not the world. But they don't stop there. They travel on to tiny towns like Eden and Spring, Mexia and Inez, all in search of good barbecue.

That's why an investment in a map or a navigational system that you can trust is a plus. We got lost more than a few times searching for places that seem to have disappeared, like Brigadoon, in the mist. Plan your stops in advance. This book is organized alphabetically, so the places listed are not going to be xt to each other. In the West Texas chapter, for example, Chubb's BB-Q in 'aso is a 6½-hour drive from the next place mentioned, Chuy's BBQ and 'ng in Eden.

ng your sense of humor with you, too. The major places along the bar-
rails are all independently owned. Some of them could go out of busi-
a moment's notice. That doesn't necessarily mean their barbecue was
here might have been a family crisis, a fire, or an unsuitable building, or
r opportunity might have arisen. Who knows? On a trip through South
, we discovered our first stop had recently closed down. The second place
e list was long gone. A third had closed up shop, too, but another barbe-
int had opened in its place. By the time we headed home, five places on
st had to be scratched off because they had closed their doors, and a sixth

place closed after our visit. That didn't mean we were starved for good barbecue. We merely asked the locals where they went.

Having a hearty appetite is a must. Why head out on the barbecue trail if you're only going to dine at one spot 500 miles from your home? You want to stop and experience several in a day, which means you'll be buying a lot of meat. Don't think that you have to eat all of it at one sitting, or that each person in your party has to buy a three-meat plate. Share a plate so you and your fellow travelers can dissect each slice of brisket or each rib.

As good as that meat is, it isn't the only aspect of what makes Texas barbecue special. It's the people you meet along the way. It's how they handle the day-in, day-out demands of a truly exhausting job. It's how the smoke from the pit permeates more than just their clothing. It's how their training, sometimes their lineage, is poured into the rub on that chicken or the mop on those ribs. This is their livelihood. The ones who do it right are often out of bed each morning long before you wake up, and they keep at it late into the night.

So, when you next head out on the barbecue trail with your family or your best buds, do yourself a favor. Get out of your shell or bubble. Focus on something other than the photo of that lip-smacking rib that you want to post to Instagram or Twitter. Leave your comfort zone and talk to as many people at each place as you can. At a place like Zimmerhanzel's in Smithville on a Saturday morning, you probably won't get a spare word in with any of the crew, as the line of customers usually trails around the entire dining room, but you can sit at one of the communal tables and discover just how the meal you're having fits into the bigger picture of the community.

If you're lucky, you'll find a place where you can spend some time with the men and women who work the pits. Each one has a story to tell. It might be about the lineage of the food you're getting ready to eat or about the mother who developed a butter-rich recipe for cobbler that's been a menu fixture for decades. Or it might be a story of their lives beyond the barbecue pit. Just be prepared to listen.

We won't soon forget sitting down with Kathy Braden at Burns BBQ when she talked about how her father, Houston barbecue legend Roy Burns, got his start in the business. It seems that in the early 1970s, her father needed a little extra money to buy his kids clothes. So, he set up a smoker by the side of the road and sold his meat to anyone driving by. It's what Texas food writer Robb Walsh, in *Texas Eats: The New Lone Star Heritage Cookbook,* calls "shade tree barbecue." You'll find these makeshift stands all over Texas, especially on Saturdays when church and school groups like to do a bit of fund-raising.

It seems Roy Burns had such a success on his hands that he continued selling barbecue whenever possible. He had more time for it after he got laid off. From the street corner, he moved to a food truck, and within three years he had his own place on DePriest, which is just a few blocks from where Braden's version of Burns now operates. (By the way, if you ever see a smoker in a parking lot or under a shade tree and a hand-printed sign advertising ribs or brisket plates, don't think twice. Head toward it with cash in hand.)

Perhaps you'll run into Lee Hammond at Sam's Bar-B-Que in Midland and hear tales of how his business has ridden the waves of the booms and busts that have affected much of West Texas. He's seen plenty in the past few decades, and whether things are up or down, he's managed to turn out barbecue that's true to his turf.

These stories matter. They flavor the meat as much as the smoke does. They make Texas barbecue as special as the cuts of moist brisket on your plate or that handmade sausage ring that was made with the same grind their German ancestors used when they settled Texas. And we're glad we can share a few of their tales with you.

A Short History of Texas Barbecue

BY BRIAN WEST

Although barbecue is a tradition in Texas, it is still part of the South as a whole.

Texas has a reputation as a pretty proud state. Texans love being Texans. We accept that we are part of the South. There is such a thing as Southern hospitality—and in Texas, we mean it.

We've come a long way, and our history is rich, thick, and juicy, so suffice to say that our food could have no other outcome. Our culinary tradition matches our history and our barbecue reigns supreme.

However, when it comes to brisket, no one does it better than Texas. Not everyone in Texas owns a horse, wears boots, or drives a truck, but most of us love beef and we know how to treat it.

One cannot bite into a slice of perfectly smoked brisket without experiencing culinary magnificence. When you savor the spicy-rich crust, sometimes called the "sugar cookie," you're tasting the crispy fat cap that renders on the surface melted along with the spicy dry rubs, which takes slow cooking, as long as 24 hours. Inside that delicious cap you'll be tantalized by the melted meat screaming umami, with that famous kiss of smoke and streaks of fat that have turned into something like a savory treat hidden within the meat.

Many of us like to eat barbecue, even brisket, with our hands. Maybe, just to reset the palate, it might be dipped into a thick sweet-hot Texas barbecue sauce that is always placed on the side and most of the time not needed.

Wow! Those uninitiated to eating Texas-style smoked brisket may find, after that first experience, that eating barbecue will never be the same again.

Barbecue scholars have one common school of thought on the history of Texas barbecue. It is not what legend has to say about it. It is a common belief that barbecue was developed by the Western cowboys, which is understandable when you take into account that they were cattle ranchers who consumed their product.

And it's true, they did have barbecue, but it didn't start with them. As a matter of fact, it began thousands of years before them. The discovery of fire and the knowledge to use it as a means to preserve meats is what truly gave

Chef/instructor Brian West of the Culinary Institute of America, San Antonio, includes barbecue among the subjects he teaches and leads a team of CIA students who partici- pate in barbecue competitions throughout Texas.

barbecue its beginning. Any culture wielding fire developed a rough form of barbecue, whether in underground pits or fire huts.

In Texas, several distinct periods are identified, dating from more than 10,000 years ago.

History states that the Texas Caddo Indians, who are referred to as the first pioneers, were also the first to smoke meat in order to preserve it for the long term. The next big step was in the 1600s. Spanish missionaries and sol- diers sailing across the ocean to America through the Caribbean came to what is now present-day South and West Texas. They brought with them their tradi- tion of pit-roasted *barbacoa,* which in essence is meat that is slow roasted with indirect heat. This technique slowly dissolves the collagen (connective tissue), turns it to gelatin, and makes the meat tender. However, it was not smoked nor did it pick up any smoke flavor.

The origin of the word *barbacoa* is believed by most scholars to come from the Caribbean Taino Indian word *barbracot,* which is the wooden struc- ture on which meat was roasted slowly over a grate. The Spanish morphed the word into *barbacoa,* which eventually became "barbecue."

Turning the page, settlers and former slaves from the Old South brought in the tradition of barbecuing pork and whole hog with what became the sweet East Texas barbecue sauce. This helped round out the techniques and set the stage for Texas barbecue.

But the pieces of the puzzle really came together with the arrival of the Germans, Czechs, and Eastern Europeans in the 1830s. They brought with them the old-world butcher-involved sausage making along with their techniques for smoking meat in brick-enclosed smokers. That was the first real textbook barbecue.

Finally, the cowboy comes in. When cattle ranchers and the cattle drives were running through Texas, they lowered the price of beef to 4 cents a pound, making it more accessible to the public. Theirs was a big business, and their ranch handlers were often paid in beef. With an endless supply of fresh beef, cooks had plenty of opportunity to perfect the art of barbecue and placed it in a category of its own, one that is still enjoyed and respected as it has become a staple in many parts of the South.

As the years went by, because of health regulations, meat was no longer allowed to be cooked in the earth pits. This gave rise to the cast-iron smokers and open pits. Soon barbecue became the center stage for all public events, and in this format the techniques were passed on to a larger audience, which helped refine the art with input from the masses.

Trading secrets, sharing recipes, and teaching new techniques continue to this day, making barbecue in Texas remarkably better and better.

Texas barbecue has been altered from its humble beginnings to such a culinary enchantment that it now has world recognition. In my opinion as a chef and barbecue devotee, the best thing about it is that the work is unfinished. More chefs and food enthusiasts are taking on the task of becoming pitmasters. Yes, we stand on the shoulders of giants, but modern pitmasters still see further. And because of our vision, experience, and ability to combine modern techniques with old Texas traditions, Texas barbecue is looking forward to a second gilded age.

BARBECUE CALENDAR

A list of every barbecue event across the state of Texas could make up its own book. There is a seemingly endless number of amateur cook-offs, sponsored by fire departments, independent businesses, and fraternal organizations. Then there are the events sponsored by organizations such as the Texas Gulf Coast BBQ Cooker's Association and the Lonestar Barbecue Society, who oversee their own series of cook-offs.

The entry fees for these events can get quite heady, running into the hundreds if not thousands of dollars for each team looking to score points that might lead to an annual champion status. The money is earmarked for charities that range from scholarship funds to the purchase of community medical equipment and on to those helping children in need.

Some of these associations are spread out over the entire state; others are regional. Here are a few just to show you the range of events they present:

The **Lonestar Barbecue Society** (www.lonestarbarbecue.com), founded by Glenn and Pat Nicholas, dates back to 1996. Cook-offs it sponsors include the Hog Explosion in Bandera in March, the Easter Fest in Kerrville, June's Rhythm & Ribs in Round Rock, and the Tin Star Ranch BBQ & Chili Cook-off in Fredericksburg just before Christmas. You can keep up with the group's schedule on its website, though even that comes with a warning that events are subject to a change in dates or cancellation. In other words, don't just go by what the site says; do a search or two or even place a call before heading out. It's advice worth taking with regards to any of these events.

The **International Barbeque Cookers Association** (www.ibcabbq.org) covers the state, from Driftwood to Beaumont, Kurten to Victoria. But it also has events in Louisiana, New Mexico, and even Hawaii on its schedule.

Of course, the groups also get regional. The **Texas Gulf Coast BBQ Cooker's Association** (www.tgcbca.org) of Katy handles events both large and small throughout the year. A few include the San Antonio Stock Show & Rodeo's annual Bar-B-Que Cook-Off, which draws more than 300 teams; the Freedom Fest BBQ Cookoff in Concan; the Weiser Air Park BBQ Cookoff and Fly In, a state championship event in Houston; and a members-only invitational in Montgomery.

Then there's the **Central Texas Barbecue Association** (www.ctbabbq.com), which is more active than either the North Texas Area Barbecue Cookers Association or the East Texas Barbecue Cookers Association, neither of which has a website. There was once a West Texas Barbecue Association, but it hasn't been active in recent years.

A few events go beyond the associations, attracting thousands who want to dine on brisket, ribs, and more. Some feature restaurants, rather than teams, to draw in people. Others add music, mosquitoes, and even rattlesnakes to the mix.

Here's a look at some famous Texas festivals by season:

Spring

Each April, Nacogdoches hosts its **Oldest Town in Texas Biker Rally and BBQ Cook Off** (www.ottrally .com), which is an outgrowth of the earlier Do-Dat BBQ Festival. So, you can "get your rib on," as the festival's tagline promises, while teams compete to smoke up the best ribs, chicken, and brisket around.

And who can resist a barbecue contest in the town of Mesquite, which hosts the annual **Real. Texas. Festival.** (www.realtexasfestival.com), which is also in April?

Summer

You might think summer would be too hot for adding wood-burning heat to the heat that Mother Nature dishes out, but Texans seem to like that sort of thing. So, late July brings the annual **Great Texas Mosquito Festival** (www .mosquitofestival.com) to Clute complete with barbecue and fajita cook-offs as well as a mosquito-calling contest.

Fall

Labor Day brings on several annual events, including the **Bedford Blues and BBQ Festival** (www.bedfordbluesbbq.com), which mixes music and food for three days of fun, and the **World Championship BBQ Goat Cook-Off,** a Brady tradition for 40 years.

Toward the end of September comes the annual **Gettin' Sauced** (www .gettinsauced.com), which brings barbecue sauces from around the country and beyond to Austin. Of course, man cannot live by sauce alone, so barbecue is a part of the day's fun.

Czhilispiel (www.flatoniachamber.com/czhili) is staged in Flatonia during the fourth weekend of October each year. This celebration of the area's Czech heritage includes a barbecue cook-off, but it doesn't stop there. Try your hand at the jalapeño-eating contest to see if you can stomach some real heat.

Every five years *Texas Monthly* prints its Top 50 list of barbecue joints from around the state. The article generates an intense amount of discussion among 'cue-heads who have their own ideas of who should be on the list. The real test, of course, is in the tasting, and for the last four years, the magazine has invited those 50 places each year to take part in **TMBBQ Fest.** It usually takes place around the first Sunday in November. This event has grown so large and so popular that you have to get your tickets more than a month in advance. It sells out that quickly. Check www.tmbbq.com for details.

Winter

Livestock shows and rodeos in both San Antonio and Houston occur each February and March, respectively, and barbecue competitions are a part of the fun. Each cook-off attracts about 300 teams.

For several years now, the Wine & Food Foundation of Texas (www.wine foodfoundation.org) has brought the world of barbecue to the Hill Country with its **Cowboys + Gauchos** party, which honors the links between food and wine from both Texas and South America. February is the month to look for this event.

Winter comes to a close with the **Sweetwater Rattlesnake Roundup** (www.rattlesnakeroundup.net). That's right, folks in this town catch and kill rattlesnakes that are then skinned and cooked for the crowd. If chicken-fried snake isn't to your liking, you can stick to the barbecue cook-off that's also on the schedule.

Dallas & North Central Texas

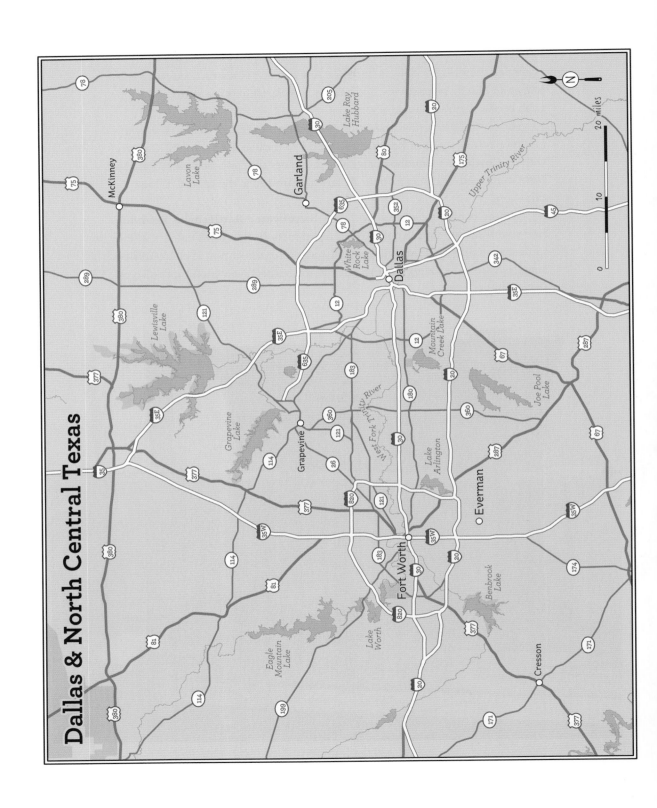

Dallas & North Central Texas

What a difference a few years can make on the barbecue scene. Before BBQ Snob Daniel Vaughn authored *The Prophets of Smoked Meat* or became *Texas Monthly*'s first barbecue editor, he wrote a piece for *D Magazine* in early 2010 listing his top 16 barbecue joints in Dallas. In the opening paragraph, he singled out what he called the ugly truth of the time: "Dallas does not do barbecue well."

More than a few people got the hint. In the intervening years, the Big D barbecue scene has blossomed in a number of different directions. Tim Byres showed, with his adventurous menu at Smoke, that barbecue was not just the realm of the hole-in-the-wall shack; it could be transformed into fine dining that anyone could enjoy. Then Justin Fourton of Pecan Lodge took mesquite, which has few fans outside West and South Texas, and showed how it could perfume perfectly moist brisket and hand-stuffed sausages that were so good that people would willingly wait in line for 90 minutes or more just for a bite. Lockhart Smokehouse brought a taste of the Barbecue Capital of Texas to Dallas. And more recently, the list has grown to include Jack Perkins's hickory-smoked meats at the Slow Bone as well as Todd David's outrageous beef ribs at Cattleack Barbeque.

These are balanced with plenty of old-school barbecue favorites, many of which are in the communities surrounding Dallas, from Garland to McKinney, Fort Worth to Grapevine. They also prove that, with the right motivation from customers and the fruitful efforts of gifted pitmasters, the region's barbecue scene can be among the state's most vital. And who knows where it will be in a few short years from now?

Angelo's Barbecue

2533 White Settlement Rd., Fort Worth, TX 76107; (817) 332-0357; www.angelosbbq.com **Founded:** 1958 **Pitmaster:** Jason George **Wood:** Hickory

For more than half a century, Angelo's has served Fort Worth exactly what it wants: fine barbecue with an ice-cold schooner of beer on the side. (The order of those two may have been reversed once or twice, but who's counting?)

It still delivers with brisket that's full of natural beef juices and pork ribs that practically beg you to rip the meat from the bone with your teeth. With your meat order, you get all three sides, cumin-scented beans in a thick broth as well as potato salad and coleslaw, both with a lively dose of celery seed for extra punch. Skip the pressed ham, unless you're going for a sandwich, though the smoked braunschweiger offers some retro appeal in that regard.

The sandwiches are big at lunch, says Jason George, who's the third generation of George men to run the place. While the braunschweiger may not be

the most popular item on the menu, it is a tradition and some people like to have it with cheese and crackers as a snack. Don't forget to order up a schooner of Shiner Bock—or Bud Light, if you must—from the tap. The frosty glass produces a tongue-tickling layer of ice shavings that float on the top of your beer and add an extra dose of relief on a hot Texas day.

All of this is served up in a vast pair of dining areas with an active hold on Texas's past. When you enter, you're greeted by a stuffed bear that's been standing guard since the 1970s. There's also a sign reminding you that the place closes at 10 p.m. in a way you're sure to remember: "All beer double price after 10 p.m." The main dining room continues the animal theme with heads of antelopes, deer, and even a gator mounted overhead, all souvenirs of hunting trips that the George family has taken over the years. It's the bear, though, that people talk about most, says Jason: "They may not remember the name of the place, but they remember the place with the bear by the front door." Closed on Sunday.

Bartley's Bar-B-Q

413 E. Northwest Hwy., Grapevine, TX 76051; (817) 481-3212
Founded: 1968 **Pitmaster:** Shane Wilkinson **Wood:** Hickory

Bartley's has had a roster of owners through the years, but each one has cared enough about this barbecue joint to keep it alive and family owned. In recent years H. L. Owens and his pitmaster, Shane Wilkinson, have done more than that. They have upped the ante by producing some fine smoked meats that have captured the attention of barbecue lovers near and far.

You might not think it's possible at first. Bartley's is in a nondescript strip mall that also houses a dance studio and a kickboxing center. Upon entering, you find a cafeteria line that takes you first to your meat order, where the abundance of meat options includes Cajun turkey, hot links and sausage, pork loin, ham, and bologna in addition to the prized brisket, ribs, and chicken.

Don't miss the Cajun turkey, which is exposed to smoke only for a couple of hours; that provides the subtlest hickory flavor beneath the natural flavor of the meat and the spicy rub on the out-side. The brisket is well-marbled and full-flavored, while the rib meat, shellacked in a sweet rub that has melted into the meat, just tears from the bone. Don't over-look the bologna sandwich, Wilkinson advises. "Some people are scared of it," he says. "They're picturing in their mind a cold bologna sandwich, but it's not that at all. It's very popular. If we give people a sample, they'll go ahead and order it."

Slide your tray down and settle into a spread of Southern favorites for your sides, including greens, fried okra, cabbage, macaroni and cheese, and two types of beans as well as your expected array of salads: macaroni, potato, and coleslaw.

That's a handmade roll with your meal. It comes from Bartley's Hometown Bakery next door. Owens's brother, Marvin, is in charge and he supplies the restaurant with a fine array of desserts, including banana pudding and a real crowd-pleaser, pecan cobbler. After you've finished off your barbecue, you can walk next door and get some *kolaches* to go. Closed on Sunday and Monday.

BBQ on the Brazos

9001 E. US 377, Cresson, TX 76035; (817) 396-4758; www.bbqonthe brazos.com; @meathisbbq **Founded:** 2013 **Founder/Pitmaster:** John Sanford **Wood:** Post Oak

The drive to Cresson, if you're coming down from Fort Worth, isn't long, but coming up from San Antonio and getting to the Texaco truck stop was

a good long haul. Fortunately, at the end of this drive was a barbecue joint (next to the Texaco store at the filling station) that we'd heard of by way of a Twitter post a few weeks earlier and didn't want to miss. We'd also heard they might run out of meat on Saturday mornings (be warned), but this was a Thursday afternoon.

The three partners running BBQ on the Brazos are led by chef/owner John Sanford, who has a varied background that does, in fact, include owning a previous barbecue restaurant, Sanford's Fort Worth Barbecue. Plus, he's done Cajun and a few stints as executive chef, opening restaurants for others.

"I didn't want to open this place. I wanted to go fishing," Sanford said after we'd made introductions. At the table, a plateful of meat had much of our attention, though Sanford is an engaging conversationalist and pretty funny, too. As he tells it, "Tornadoes hit [nearby] Granbery and a lot of people came in here. It kinda got a little crazy." That's when he got what he termed a "500-pound machine" for smoking barbecue and with his brother-in-law, Michael Warren, has been turning out some fine brisket ever since.

Like the potato salad and the banana pudding, the coleslaw isn't traditional, but it's very good, and we suggest getting at least one order of it. It was created by Michael Warren and is lightly tossed in a green dressing that tastes like a sort of cilantro pesto—and that's not a bad flavor at all to pair with smoky meat.

The "machine" is an Ole Hickory rotisserie, and Sanford said that while the gas-fired aspect of the contraption is handy for some, he tossed the manual aside and essentially uses it as a wood-fired barbecue pit. "A lot of people don't know you don't have to

use all the bells and whistles," he said. He also has a wood-burner outside as well. "I can put some flat-out magic out of her."

We didn't have meat off the old wood-burner, but the Ole Hickory put out BBQ on the Brazos's highly recommended brisket. With a coarse, black crust and melting fat, and a beefy aroma that promised it would taste good, it didn't disappoint us. The pork ribs had a slightly pebbly crust with an appetizingly dark red color tinged slightly with black, and a meaty, tender texture that makes that good pink meat nearly irresistible.

Sanford said he's particular about the sides, and because we respect well-made side dishes ourselves, we kicked around our relative approaches to potato salad and coleslaw. BBQ on the Brazos's potato salad seemed made without mayo, but it's well worth adding to your meal. We didn't have a chance to try the corn bread salad, but we will on our next visit.

The final touch to lunch here was the banana pudding, made by Sanford's wife and working partner, Kathryn Warren.

"Just imagine there's bananas on this," she said. They'd run out of bananas, but we got the last scoop of the pudding, which had a texture more like banana fluff. It was lovely and cold and topped with crumbled vanilla wafers and whipped cream. You'll want some. Closed on Sunday.

Cattleack Barbecue

13628 Gamma Rd., Dallas, TX 75244; (972) 805-0999; www.cattleack
bbq.com **Founded:** 2010 (catering), 2013 (storefront takeout)
Pitmaster: Todd David **Wood:** Hickory, Post Oak

Cattleack Barbecue was originally for takeout only one day a week—Friday.
Owners Todd and Misty David thought that would be good enough to drum
up some interest in their barbecue catering business. It did. It also generated
so much foot traffic to their storefront in a nondescript industrial plaza that in
early 2014 they added Thursday hours as well.

A few people, men mostly, can be found waiting for the doors to open,
and within minutes the line will stretch out the door. To help you stay patient
while you wait, grab a free Shiner from the ice chest near the door and forget
everything but the meal before you. There are no tables or chairs, but since we
were first in line the morning we were at Cattleack, we nabbed a little bench
outside, where we sat down to attack our stash of meat. Others ate in their cars
or off the roof of their truck or just drove off.

Before you can place your order, Todd David will likely hand you a taste
of whatever he's cutting, such as brisket or his massive beef ribs. That should
convince you right then and there that when someone knows what he's doing,
a gas-fired Ole Hickory smoker can be effective.

The beef short ribs on the bone run about 1½ pounds each and are a house
specialty. They are rich; the fat is marbled and melted throughout the silky-
tender meat. The pork ribs have a well-blackened crust, as does the brisket.
The ribs are pull-apart tender; the brisket has a healthy red smoke ring and

again, that melted fat basting the tender meat. We
got both a bit of the lean and the marbled, and both
met the mark.

If you're a sandwich lover, don't miss the Todd-
father, featuring brisket, pulled pork, and sausage
all piled on a bun before being topped with barbecue sauce and coleslaw. Yes, you can pick this
up with your hands, but whether your mouth is
large enough to bite into all three meats at once is
another matter.

Among the house specialties is the Que-T
Pie, a brisket empanada with a buttery crust, served very hot. Try at least one,
or take a dozen home for a party—they're good.

On the walls you'll find photographs of some celebrated pitmasters from
across Texas, including Alan Caldwell of Fargo's in Bryan, Tootsie Tomanetz

Pendery's World of Chiles & Spices, a Fort Worth Gem

When in Fort Worth, make plans to stop at **Pendery's World of Chiles & Spices.** Open the door to the vintage residence that houses the business at 1407 8th Avenue, and the scents alone will pull you in.

Pendery's does have barbecue rubs, which can be found on a wall in the room to the right of the entrance. But they also have the spices that go into just about any rub you might wish to develop. Roam around and enjoy the collection, the books, and other culinary supplies as well as spices and herbs. There are spice blends custom-made for fish and seafood, chicken, beef, or lamb. Cinnamon quills, exotica such as frankincense gum resin, or things of beauty such as the Murray River apricot flaked salt will be hard to put down.

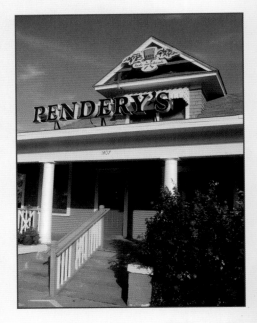

Chiles—whole, powdered, or in blends—are a major part of Pendery's business. When family member DeWitt Clinton Pendery arrived from Ohio to join the firm in 1870, he developed a lively interest in chiles. "The health-giving properties of hot chile peppers have no equal," he said, according to the company website. In this respect, he was ahead of his time. But his love for chiles was also culinary. A particular blend that he called "chiltomaline" is made of chile pods, cumin, oregano, and other ground spices. It seems to be a forerunner of the chili seasoning we can buy in supermarkets today. Chili's longevity, history, and great flavor are why this "bowl of red" was named the Texas state dish. Some choose to disagree. A blogger recently suggested a new state dish take the place of chili. His suggestion was—you guessed it—brisket.

Pendery's spices, once delivered by "horse-drawn stagecoach," are now available online at www.penderys.com. Or call (817) 924-3434.

of Snow's in Lexington, Roy Perez of Kreuz Market in Lockhart, and Justin Fourton of the nearby Pecan Lodge. It's obvious David would like to be considered among their ranks. As word continues to spread about Cattleack, his beef could just place him there. Open Thursday and Friday until sold out.

Hutchins BBQ

1301 N. Tennessee St., McKinney, TX 75069; (972) 548-2629; www .hutchinsbbq.net **Founded:** 1978 **Pitmasters:** Tim Hutchins, Adolfo Espino, Octavio Jaimes **Wood:** Pecan, Hickory, Mesquite

Man 1: These rolls is good.

Man 2: Told ya.

Man 1: Yeah, everything's good at this place.

That's the kind of conversation Tim Hutchins loves to overhear at his barbecue joint. It shows that paying attention to details like house-made rolls and jalapeño corn bread pays off in high praise from his customers. They also rave about the ribs, with their lightly sweet rub and a perfect give that lets you sink your teeth into each one without having the meat slip off the bone. The brisket is cut marbled or lean to taste, so you can get some of that fine bark that seals in all those meat juices.

Can't decide what meats to get? Hutchins offers an all-you-can-eat option so you can sample whatever's in the pit, including pulled pork, ham, and turkey. There's also fried catfish, which gives Hutchins a connection to barbecue joints in the eastern part of the state. You can scoop up your own side dishes, which include macaroni and cheese, broccoli salad, macaroni salad, flat beans with bacon, and corn, in addition to—you guessed it—beans, potato salad, and coleslaw. Folks who dine in can also help themselves to a dessert bar that includes peach cobbler, banana pudding, and soft-serve ice cream.

While you're enjoying your meal, take a look at the historic photos that line the walls of Hutchins BBQ. Unlike the so-called authentic replicas that fill too many chain barbecue joints, these prints offer a fascinating glimpse of a bustling McKinney long before it was subsumed into Dallas's sprawl. You can also find an article from the local paper detailing how Hutchins had a pit fire in 2012 that forced it to close for several months. Tim Hutchins, who took over the restaurant from his father, Roy, used that time to remodel and expand the dining area. He and his general manager, Dustin Blackwell, were able to keep their staff paid during the time they were closed, which meant that all of them returned when Hutchins reopened. "We had all of the same people come back—and that was a blessing," Blackwell says.

Though Hutchins has been a fixture on the scene for several decades, the pit isn't resting on its laurels, which has included landing on the 2013 *Texas Monthly* Top 50 list. "Tim and me, we're always going down to Austin to see what's happening there," Blackwell says, citing Franklin Barbecue and La Barbecue as being among the places they frequent. "We're always trying to get better—and we have gotten better." And that's why their meats, not to mention those rolls, are winning over customers all the time.

Lockhart Smokehouse

400 W. Davis St., Dallas, TX 75208; (214) 944-5521; www.lockhart smokehouse.com; @DallasLockhart **Founded:** 2011 **Pitmasters:** Tim McLaughlin, Will Fleischman **Wood:** Post Oak

A younger generation of a noted family from the barbecue heartland has been making some noise in Dallas's Bishop Arts District.

Spreading the word of good pit-smoked meat is a noble occupation, and from what we saw at Lockhart Smokehouse, it makes business sense as well. Co-owners Jill Grabowski Bergus and her husband, Jeff Bergus, teamed up

with seasoned pitmasters and their staff hit the 2013 Top 50 best barbecue joints named by *Texas Monthly* magazine.

Jill Bergus comes from the Schmidt family, which owns Kreuz Market in Lockhart. The Dallas restaurant sells sausage from Kreuz, and it has the "no sauce, no forks, no kidding" attitude and signage that further states their heritage.

Another thing that gave us a personal sense of vindication: The restaurant's pair of dispensers for iced tea are labeled "unsweet" and "unsweet, too." After all—sugar packets!

As do some barbecue joints, Lockhart might run out of meat by the time you get yourself through the doors—like, at 2:15 p.m. on the day we showed up. Happily, it was hardly a desolate shell. The music was at a moderate blast, customers were availing themselves of drinks at the (full) bar, and the staff was running around cleaning up the place for the dinner trade.

After chatting a bit with Jeff Bergus, something magical happened: meat. And, not only was a sampling on its way, I was invited to the pit room to meet Tim McLaughlin, pitmaster. McLaughlin offered a short demo on how to tell if a brisket is done by holding it in the air and gently waving it back and forth. The impressive mass of crust-coated meat responded by gently bending with the movement. "If it's stiff when you do this, it's either overcooked or undercooked," McLaughlin said. He also demonstrated how to cut it. These are things he teaches at a Smoke Camp that he presents each month. His own teacher? The famous Roy Perez, pitmaster at Kreuz Market.

Heading out to one of the pub tables near the entrance to the bar area, we slapped down a beautiful stack of meat on butcher paper and started with a slice of truly moist turkey, its rub hinting at warm Mexican spices—and no overload on the cumin. The pork ribs came from the "skinny end," another pitmaster secret. "The skinny end has less bone," McLaughlin says. They were excellent. The brisket, if it was the same one waved in the air, showed no ill effects, the good, black crust of seasoning soaked with melted fat, tender slices from the meaty interior, and best of all—no fork needed. For the Berguses, doing Dallas was a good idea and well-executed. Not only that, it is fun. Go ahead and join the crowd.

The owners of Lockhart Smokehouse have opened a new location in Plano at 1026 E. 15th St., sharing property with the Sutton Place furniture store. For hours, map, menu, and more, visit their website.

Longoria's BBQ

100 Christopher Dr., Everman, TX 76140; (817) 568-9494; www
.longoriasbbq.com; @Longoriasbbq1 **Founded:** 1995 **Founder:** Fred
Longoria **Pitmaster:** David Longoria **Wood:** Post Oak, Pecan

If your barbecue trail takes you to Longoria's BBQ in the Everman area of Fort
Worth, it will seem an almost relaxing drive if you have braved the Dallas free-
ways. Even the neighborhood where this family restaurant is located seems
calm, and the restaurant itself had just a few lingering customers during a lull
in business around 3 p.m.

Longoria's caters parties, and those appear to be an important part of its
business. But walk-in customers are catered to as well, judging by a friendly,

helpful staff that waited patiently,
offering answers to questions as
customers scanned the menu.
This menu takes plenty of depar-
tures from the traditional barbecue joint, though its smoked meats
come off an indirect-heat pit, says
the personable young manager,
Takaeus Flowers, who agreed to
sit down and talk while we opened
our paper-wrapped packages.

Flowers disappointed us only
when we asked for a recipe. He
kept his smile but shook his head
and said that his boss (and pit-

master), David Longoria, had turned away the Food Network's Guy Fieri after
finding out that he would be asked to share the restaurant's famous brisket
sausage recipe for *Diners, Drive-Ins and Dives*.

The brisket is smoked and sliced at Longoria's, and we recommend ordering it—it's moist with an ample amount of smoke and cut into generous slices.
It's also ground, cooked, and served as a burger, too, which we found excellent—leaner and denser than your everyday burger, but still tender and full of
beef flavor. You can also buy the raw, ground brisket by the pound—and pick
up some of the sausage and spicy chorizo to take home as well.

We didn't get a taste of the brisket jerky—and should have taken some
along to fuel the ride home. But we did enjoy a rib sandwich, a burger bun
packed with a couple of staunch pork ribs, on the bone, served with sauce on
the side. There just isn't a better way to get pure, perfectly smoked and slightly

chewy pork rib meat in your sandwich than having it come on the original bone. And it does make an impressive presentation.

Tacos, Frito pie, a tossed chicken salad, hot dogs, and tamales on the menu just tell us that Longoria's 18 years in business has given them the flexibility to bow to customers' wishes. It might be the only place we have seen a bologna sandwich for sale in a long time, and we hear that it has quite a following. Longoria's has a real family feel—and judging by articles and awards on the wall, it has had its share of recognition. Our takeaway: Everybody's Texas hometown should have a barbecue joint like Longoria's. Closed on Sunday.

Mac's Bar-B-Que

3933 Main St., Dallas, TX 75226; (214) 823-0731 **Founded:** 1955
Pitmaster: Billy McDonald **Wood:** Hickory

Billy McDonald is proud to say that Mac's Bar-B-Que is "family-owned, family-operated, and that's a family member fixing the food." He is the family in Mac's, which his father started in 1955, and he's the person who will be carving for you the meats that he smoked that day using indirect heat at a consistent temperature of 275°F. His brisket doesn't feature any rub on it and nothing has been injected into the meat, so what you get is beef at its purest. It's his cooking technique that turns out cuts that are fork-tender and delicious in a way that speaks to the tradition used. This is old-school brisket with no apologies needed.

Ribs are a big hit here, but they were gone by the time we arrived, about an hour before closing. By way of an apology for running out, McDonald offered his rub recipe for those beauties (page 230). We ended up with some mouthwatering ham and a sausage with plenty of snap that loved Mac's tomato-based sauce with a lively blend of sweet and tart spices. What you may notice about all of these meats is the judicious amount of smoke flavor each has. It is present, but it is not overwhelming. That's precisely the way he wants it, because he wants the quality of his meat to be the focus of your meal.

Mac's is open for only a few hours each weekday. Part of the reason for that is, "in this area of Dallas, they roll up the streets at 6,"

according to McDonald. And part of it is that a lot of work goes into that process. "I'm the guy who gets up at 0-dark-thirty in the morning and comes in by 6 a.m. to get the ashes out of the pit and, by 7 a.m., get the fire built, all the while getting ready to open," he says, adding that cleanup after closing and catering events add even more hours to his workday. "Barbecue is a 24-hour deal."

That was the work ethic McDonald developed from assisting his father and learning the business. "I grew up in the '60s here in Dallas when everyone had to make what they served that day," he says. "Today, society is frozen this and frozen that . . . You can buy pre-smoked briskets and just heat 'em up for your customers—we call that the pizza oven specials."

At Mac's, the sides are served in separate bowls and include everything from green beans and slaw to pintos and fried okra. The french fries are considered some of the best in Dallas—and for good reason, McDonald says. They're made by hand, not out of a freezer bag. His coworker, Debra Schultz, who handles everything from the baking duties to running the register, peels the potatoes while McDonald slices them up before frying. You can't get a fresher taste than that. Also, if Schultz has pumpkin pie on the menu, don't miss it.

Ham is often overlooked on barbecue menus, but when it's done right, as it is at Mac's, it's a genuine pleasure.

The dining area is clean but fairly nondescript except for a few historical photos near the order line. One features President Franklin D. Roosevelt passing by Joe's Barbecue, which was the forerunner of Mac's. Another shows the original Mac's, which had been 4 blocks away on Exposition, until the operation moved to its current location in 1982.

The future of Mac's isn't clear. McDonald doesn't see another generation taking over the place after him. "Barbecue is hard work, too hard for some folks," he says. Closed on Saturday and Sunday.

Meshack's Bar-B-Que Shack

240 E. Avenue B, Garland, TX 75040; (214) 227-4748 **Founded:** 2009
Pitmaster: Travis Mayes **Wood:** Pecan

The word "shack" in the title says it all. This is not a barbecue joint with any sort of physical refinement. The menu is painted on the wall. The food comes in a Styrofoam container. The side dishes are limited to potato salad and baked beans. (Do you really need anything else, except for some sauce and maybe a slice of bread?)

The focus here is on the meat—pecan-smoked brisket, ribs, and sausage, to be precise. That's where owner Travis Mayes lavishes his attention, and it has paid off handsomely. Meshack's often makes lists of Dallas's best restaurants, even if you have to eat your order in your car or, picnic-style, on the hood.

The name Meshack's has a lengthy tradition in the Dallas area. It was the name of a small chain created by James Meshack, whose daughter Donna is married to Mayes. "No, it's not Meshach from Shadrach, Meshach, and Abednego," Mayes says, referring to the biblical story of the three men who survived the fiery furnace. After James Meshack died, the Mayeses kept the Garland location running for a few years. It eventually closed, but they started it up again in 2009 to great acclaim and long lines.

The brisket boasts a thick black bark and an appetizing smoke ring, while the meat itself is tender, displays a complementary layer of pecan smoke, and features a small, well-rendered layer of fat. The housemade sausage has plenty of black pepper and garlic mixed in the grind, while the casing has the right attractive snap. The ribs may be the best of all, given their sweet-spicy rub, the thorough infusion of smoke, the give when you bite into them, and the way a little of Mayes's vinegar-based sauce adds a whole new dimension.

Meshack's signature dish is called Da Jasper, and it is a sight to behold. It's a double helping of chopped beef and sausage on bread. If yours is too moist to pick up, just scoop it up with a spoon or fork. The sandwich was named in honor of Jasper Parker, a longtime customer who "kept adding more things to his sandwich," Mayes says. "Every week he'd say, 'Put a link of sausage on that' or 'Put some more chopped beef on there.'" In time, the perfect combination was reached, and it's been pleasing customers ever since.

You will want to get to Meshack's early. They sell out often, and when they do, that's it until tomorrow. Closed on Sunday and Monday.

Off the Bone Barbeque

1734 S. Lamar St., Dallas, TX 75215; (214) 565-9551; www.offthebone
barbeque.com **Founded:** 2007 **Pitmaster:** Dwight Harvey
Wood: Pecan

Off the Bone advertises itself as a "gourmet" barbecue experience—and the
menu shows evidence of this. Don't worry about barbecue becoming weird
when that term is applied, though. Dwight and Rose Harvey have built a restaurant that also pays attention to the basics: good smoked meat, a varied
menu, interesting side dishes, and some terrific chocolate chip pecan cookies.

After retiring from the corporate world seven and a half years ago, Harvey
says he wanted to set up a business of his own, something that could be passed
on to the couple's kids. He credits his wife's father for guiding him to the barbecue restaurant business.

The barbecue, says Harvey, is a "kind of Texas, Louisiana" style. That's a
tip to the fact that sweetness, from sauces to meat, will be more prevalent here
than it is in barbecue styles from other parts of the state.

Harvey uses pecan wood, and briskets are cooked in the low, slow style.
They are given a dry rub first, then a
mop as they are cooked in an Oyler
rotisserie smoker for 12 to 14 hours.
That brisket comes out with a blackened crust and is fork-tender. If you
don't want sauce on it, let the staff know
at the time you place your order.

On baby back ribs, the sweetness
complements the natural flavor of pork
and lets some of the smokiness through.
If you like the sweeter style, go for the
pulled pork, piled on rolls with a dousing of sauce, and some of the honey
spiced baked beans. The coleslaw,
dressed with a touch of blue cheese, is
different, but in a savory good way. Also
consider the deep-fried, spicy corn on
the cob (see the Deep-Fried Corn on the
Cob recipe on p. 238). "That was one we
just kinda tripped over," says Harvey.
"I was at the farmers' market and got a

case of corn. My wife was going out of town and I wasn't sure what to do with it, so I told the guys, 'Let's just shuck it and drop it in the deep-fry.' We did, and added some spice to it and people just love it."

We didn't try every dessert on the menu—cakes and cobbler sell by the order or by the whole cake or whole cobbler. The chocolate chip pecan cookies, however, we did try as we waited for our food order. These are excellent—have one as an appetizer, but be sure to buy another for dessert. Closed on Sunday.

Pecan Lodge

2702 Main St., Dallas, TX 75201; (214) 748-8900; www.pecanlodge.com **Founded:** 2010 **Pitmaster:** Justin Fourton **Wood:** Mesquite

For several years Pecan Lodge was situated in a tiny booth inside the Dallas Farmers' Market, where it built a fiercely loyal clientele of barbecue lovers who

were willing to wait in line for hours to get a taste of their brisket, beef ribs, or any of the sausages they stuff and smoke using mesquite in an indirect-heat pit. This was a place that advertised itself as being open only a few days each week, and the hours were listed as running until 3 p.m. But pay no attention to that. The sold-out sign often appeared before 1 p.m., leaving dozens of would-be customers without a taste of anything at all.

Then, late in 2013, word got out that owners Justin and Diane Fourton would be moving their home to the Deep Ellum area. How this will affect the barbecue we can't begin to gauge, but we recommend you check Pecan Lodge's website for up-to-the-minute news and hours. Then plan on showing up at least an hour before opening, because you won't want to miss out on some of the finest meats being smoked in Texas today.

All of this may seem a little strange. The Fourtons are just in their 30s. Their background was in corporate America before they started up a catering company. Justin picked up his barbecue skills from his grandparents in Abilene, which helps explain his use of mesquite, as opposed to the hickory and pecan woods that are more prevalent in the Dallas area, according to the Pecan Lodge website. But nothing in that outline explains why, as if by magic, their business has been able to produce meats that are this good and why so many people are willing to give up half a day just for a paper boat filled with smoked meat.

Of course, being lauded as one of the top four barbecue joints in the state during the 2013 *Texas Monthly* roundup helped get the word out and caused those lines to snake even further through the market's indoor area. But it didn't make Fourton's beef ribs any more perfect than they already were.

We ran into Diane Fourton at a barbecue event about a month before we traveled to Dallas, and she told us that the length of the lines increases as each day goes by, so Thursday was the ideal day if you didn't want to wait quite as long. Despite our best efforts, we couldn't make it until a Saturday, when we joined an already-long line of customers a good 45 minutes before opening. That placed us solidly in the first third of diners, but it didn't guarantee us a bite to eat. Sure enough, when we worked our way to the head of the line, the beef ribs and all the sausages were gone, leaving brisket, pulled pork, and pork ribs for a three-meat combo tasting.

Those were no mean leftovers. The brisket was everything you want in great barbecue, only magnified. The meat was moist to the point of ridiculousness, without being too fatty, and it really seemed as if it would be possible for it to melt when you pressed your tongue to it. The crust was thick and dark, and it held together beautifully, although the cuts were about a half-inch thick. It was brisket heaven, to be sure, and well worth the wait. The two pork dishes showed Fourton's willingness to go against convention, and he succeeds brilliantly. The ribs were firm, with a thin skin seasoned with plenty of black pepper, not the sweet ribs common everywhere else, and every bite just made you want more. Pulled pork also abandoned the common sweet profile for a little spicy kick that was welcome indeed, especially when balanced with a touch of sweet sauce.

The coleslaw also bucks trends by including a welcome dash of cayenne pepper. Each of the side dishes has its partisans, with many in line swearing by the macaroni and cheese, which features green chiles stirred in and bacon sprinkled on top. But we would tell you not to overlook the bacon-laced collard greens or the fried okra either. Let's face it, you'll likely welcome most anything Pecan Lodge has to offer. Closed Monday, but dinner added to Friday and Saturday nights.

The Slow Bone

2234 Irving Blvd., Dallas, TX 75207; (214) 377-7727 **Founded:** 2013 **Pitmaster:** Jack Perkins **Wood:** Hickory

It seemed only fitting that Jack Perkins should open a barbecue joint after winning the brisket category in Dallas's 2012 Meat Fight fund-raiser. But the Slow Bone, located in the trendy Design District, is about more than barbecue. From the moment you enter, a hipster vibe mingles with a funky retro spin that makes the place appeal to millennials and baby boomers alike. You wind your way through the line where a series of friendly carvers are ready to take your order and maybe hand out a sample or two. Instead of using butcher paper or a Styrofoam plate, however, the staff loads your food on an authentic replica of an old-school cafeteria tray, complete with indented areas to hold your order, which could be barbecue or a vegetarian array of the tempting side dishes. Your pickles, onions, and sauce are available at a condiment bar that bears a slight resemblance to a jukebox. It's along a wall adorned with photos that command more than a moment's attention.

Once we sat down, however, all eyes were focused on the meat in front of us. Slabs of brisket with a bit of coffee in the rub were surrounded by a dense bark that helps keep the fatty cuts oh so moist at the center. Toothsome ribs had a thin outer coating, but the smoke color seemed to permeate the pork with an irresistible shade of pink. Those two vie with each other to be top sellers at the Slow Bone, Perkins says, and one, if not both, usually sells out before 2 p.m. Pork loin with a fennel sausage stuffing scored big. Jalapeño bratwurst won over the entire table, though the heat level could have been slightly higher, while the more traditional sausage packed a juicy wallop.

Something's Smoking in the Pit:
Barbecue, Music & Sex

You can't separate music from barbecue. For close to a century now, recordings about barbecue have been a part of our cultural heritage. Well, songs that mention barbecue, at least. What most of these musicians mean when they sing about barbecue is actually a euphemism for sex. Adam's rib apparently knows how to shake and bake.

A handful of standouts that combined melody and meat include:

"Struttin' with Some Barbecue": Louis Armstrong's wife, Lil Hardin, is billed as the composer of this classic from the late 1920s, and we can only imagine what the "barbecue" in the title refers to, though there are enough hot licks from the entire band to give you some idea—and it ain't food. Lyrics mentioning ribs didn't appear until the 1950s, but it didn't matter. By then "Struttin'" had claimed its rightful place in music history and has been covered by everyone from jazz great Pete Fountain to one of Texas's favorite musical sons, Willie Nelson.

"Barbecue Any Old Time": Brownie McGhee grew up in Tennessee, not Texas. And while the barbecue styles of the two states differ, the blues know no state lines. So, when broken-hearted McGhee asks the woman who left him who she gave his barbecue to, we all know he's not looking for a plate of brisket. This is the title track of a spicy compilation called *Barbecue Any Old Time: Blues from the Pit, 1927–1942*. In "Pepper Sauce Mama," Charlie Campbell and His Red Peppers sing about the woman who makes a man's meat red hot because she knows how to shake her pot around. The Four Southern Singers know "Ham Bone Am Sweet," while Georgia White's "Pigmeat Blues" showcases Les Paul in his first recording. Other highlights include Bessie Jackson's sassy "Barbecue Bess," Richard M. Jones's Jazz Wizards on "Smoked Meat Blues," and "Big Boy" Teddy Edwards's two-part "Who Did You Give My Barbecue To?"

"Bar-B-Q": ZZ Top formed in Houston back in 1969. Three years later they recorded "Bar-B-Q," and it seems like a spiritual if not musical descendant of these saucy songs. In the lyrics the singer begs his lady friend over and over again. What for? You probably have as good an idea as we do, until that last line when it is revealed that he has a hankering for her barbecue.

"Something Like That (BBQ Stain)": Tim McGraw's contribution to this list is only marginally about barbecue, but that stain on his white T-shirt is the singer's connection to his first kiss.

"Barbeque": Okay, so the songs mentioned so far have been as subtle as the name of the Dallas joint, the Slow Bone. But they've covered jazz, rock, blues, and country. Now we get to Texas singer-songwriter Robert Earl Keen, whose work covers a number of musical styles. His song "Barbeque" is actually about sliced beef, ribs, and sausage. Meat is his temptation, and he gladly gives in, knowing he's eventually headed for the devil's own charcoal pit.

The list goes on to include any number of pieces, including Clarence "Gatemouth" Brown's "Sheriff's Barbecue" and Rhett & Link's "The Barbeque Song," a twangy ditty that manages to cover most barbecue styles of the Deep South in five minutes. Pick your favorite musical style, from country to hip-hop, and you'll find evidence in which the smoke of the pit and some tender meat have inspired men and women alike to song.

We were equally taken with the eclectic array of seasonal sides, such as the Southern soul food specialties macaroni and cheese, collard greens, fried okra, buttery yellow squash, and, most especially, hush puppies. Our favorite, though, was the cheese-coated mixture of cauliflower and brussels sprouts, which may seem odd at first, but it makes complete sense when you taste it—and it goes well with the meats, especially the sausage. (Think of it as a low-carb version of mac and cheese.) If you visit the Slow Bone and your favorite side isn't available, it could be because of the time of year. "When the fresh vegetables get less local, we switch," Perkins says, explaining that his popular green bean casserole had to be taken off the menu when he could no longer find good green beans, but it will return when they're back in season.

Hush puppies loaded with corn flavor go so well with the meats that you'll wonder why you don't encounter more of them at barbecue joints.

The Slow Bone was only a few months old when we visited, and changes were being made to make it even better, which is always good to see, no matter how old a place is. "The quality continues to improve, and I think we're already good, but we can get better," says Perkins, adding that he even tweaks his pit processes almost daily. He doesn't like the word "pitmaster," however. "We call ourselves pit slaves," he says with a laugh. "As the person in charge of the pit, you are subject to the whims of the pit. You have to follow where she takes you."

Smoke

901 Fort Worth Ave., Dallas, TX 75208; (214) 393-4141; www .smokerestaurant.com **Founded:** 2009 **Pitmaster:** Tim Byres **Wood:** Hickory, Pecan, Oak, and more

Smoke is Dallas's foray into the small but growing world of upscale barbecue dining, a world where even a few of the cocktails are made with smoked ingredients. The menu is filled with the likes of Coffee Cured Beef Brisket with house-made bread and butter pickles; a smoked pork chop with apricot preserve and dumplings; and Cabrito & Masa, smoked goat stuffed into corn pockets and served with *cajeta,* green apple salsa verde, and goat cream. This is obviously not a place where you can get a three-meat plate with beans and slaw.

Chef, pitmaster, and owner Tim Byres earned his creds at another Texas culinary palace, Stephan Pyles Restaurant, before starting out on his own. He toured the South, drawing from barbecue styles wherever he went, to create a menu that pays homage to well-loved flavors while showcasing them in his own way. One of his most traditional dishes would be the pulled whole hog,

with its strands and chunks of various cuts of smoked meat, all loaded with rich pork juiciness as well as salt and a hefty handful of spices. The heaping mass is served with slaw on the side, but not just any old version: Byres's has blue cheese in it as well as plenty of celery seeds and a dash of green Tabasco sauce, all of which beg to be eaten together with the pork, though the two are served separately on the plate.

Our great surprise was how excellent the vegetables were. A plate of deep-fried pimento cheese croquettes arrived with what you might consider a garnish of grilled romaine. It's no garnish. The flavor has haunted us months after our visit. The same is true of the grilled broccoli rabe with its smoky vinaigrette.

Smoke is adjacent to the Belmont Hotel, which has been a fixture on the Dallas scene for decades. The patio bar there offers a great place to have a drink, such as the No. 901, which is made with maple-infused rye mixed with Cointreau, orange bitters, and maraschino cherries. You can also enjoy a spectacular view of downtown Dallas at night without having to face the traffic. And you can take a taste of Smoke home with you—and not just in a doggie bag. Byres's cookbook, *Smoke: New Firewood Cooking*, offers up many of his secrets, some of which are simple, such as the blue cheese coleslaw, while others go into all you need to prepare, say, a whole hog.

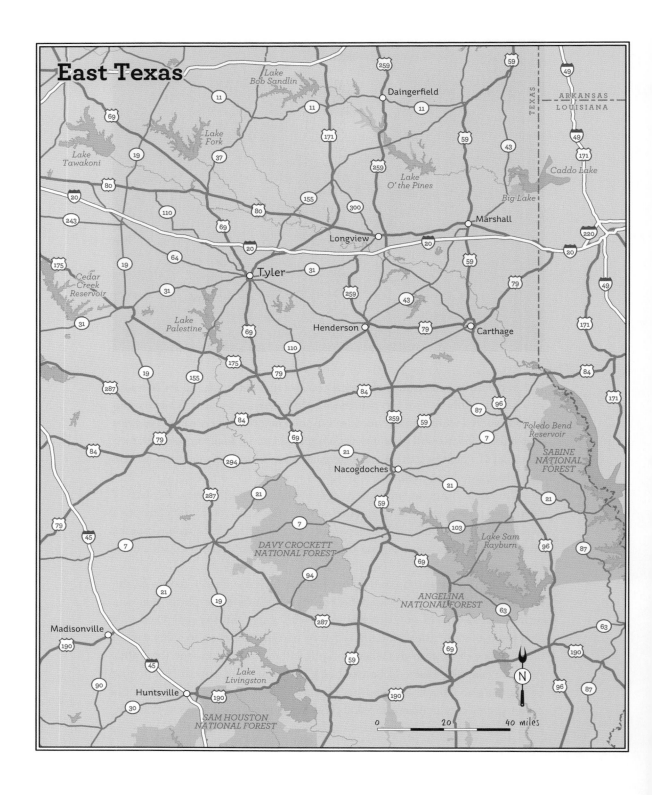

East Texas

East Texas

Your impression of East Texas, from the climate to the barbecue, is going to depend a great deal on what direction you're coming from.

Folks driving in from the west, from Lockhart, say, or even Midland, will notice a change in the air as they enter the world of the Piney Woods. The climate is more humid, thanks to the region's high annual rainfall and an increased number of rivers, including the Brazos and the Red River as well as the Neches, the Trinity, the Sabine, the Angelina, and the Sulphur. There's no mistaking it: This is, as a character in the movie *Bernie* tells us, "the beginning of the Deep South." Folks driving in from the east should be able to tell you the same. Its pioneers were from Georgia, Alabama, Mississippi, Arkansas, and Louisiana, and their traditions, especially when it comes to food, live on.

In terms of barbecue, that means meat larded with a Southern richness and a noticeable filigree of sweetness that carries over into the rubs, the sauces, and the side dishes. Perhaps that's why pork ribs rule here, and you can find some mighty good ones if you taste enough. Occasionally, you'll find pit bosses who'll admit to using the centuries-old technique of parboiling those ribs to soften them up before they're placed in the smoker. This is a Southern approach that lives on in nearby Louisiana, thereby blurring the barbecue border line.

So, what role does brisket play? It's still important, even if it doesn't go by the name of brisket on menus. That's right, if you want brisket, you'll have to look for what's merely called *beef* in these parts. And you order it sliced or chopped. Expect only the lean cut, unless you specifically ask for the moist end, and it'll arrive with a sweet, tomatoey sauce ladled over each bite—again, unless you ask for it otherwise. Hickory is the wood of choice in these parts, though some folks prefer oak or pecan, or a combination thereof.

The abundance of rivers and lakes in the region must have plenty of East Texas folks thinking of fish, because fried catfish is a fixture at a good number of barbecue joints. Or maybe, once again, it's that Southern heritage shining through. That is the reason why so many of the side dishes offer their own brand of Southern comfort. Sure, you'll find potato salad and coleslaw, but you'll also find yourself debating whether to get the fried okra, the collard greens, or candied yams—and in the Deep South side dishes are actually as important as the meat, even in the world of barbecue.

Pintos are on the menu—this is still Texas, after all. But don't expect ranch-style beans cooking away with some bacon fat, onion, and occasionally a jalapeño. These are going to be baked in brown sugar and a sweet tomato-based sauce. That's what people in these parts grew up with, that's what they want when they eat out, and that's what everyone knows how to make, as if by osmosis.

Expect to wash it all down with gallons of sweet tea and heaping helpings of Southern hospitality, because, like everywhere else in Texas, the people serving your food give you equal parts love and pride in what they do.

Bob's Bar-B-Que

1205 Pope St., Henderson, TX 75652; (903) 657-8301 **Founded:** 1980
Pitmaster: Bob Allen **Wood:** Hickory

Bob Allen has run his East Texas barbecue joint for 33 years now. But it's not just his show—it's a full family operation with his wife, Billie Jean, and their son helping with the workload. All of them exude a fine sense of Southern hospitality, and they make you feel right at home by talking with you about anything at all, from the high school football to their business. Just don't ask for any trade secrets, such as the recipe for the pecan cobbler. The Allens keep those close to their chests.

What isn't a secret is how good the sliced beef is in this joint. Since open-

ing in 1980, Bob Allen has earned a statewide reputation for turning hickory and brisket into a work of culinary art. It's earned him high praise from barbecue connoisseurs and customers alike. They love the tender beef whether they get the usual dry cut or they ask for the fattier end with its dense bark. (Thanks go out to *The Prophets of Smoked Meat* author Daniel Vaughn for prompting an order of the latter. He's insisted upon it in most every piece he's written about the place for *Texas Monthly*, his blogs, or his book.)

But Bob's appeal doesn't end there. Pork ribs, chicken, ham, and boudain will all feed what you're craving. Just pick up a moon of cheddar on the counter to go with your plate, and enjoy the addition of a little dairy fat along with your 'cue.

The biggest surprise is the fresh flavor of the chopped beef and sausage sandwiches, which are slathered with sauce. Sometimes, this is a sign of leftover meat being fobbed off on an unsuspecting public, often with the

Find out why cheddar cheese is such a great addition to your barbecue meal. Grab one of the rings at the counter and enjoy.

name Sloppy Joe attached. Not at Bob's. Allen wouldn't have any of that at his place. And you can rest assured that your sandwich is every bit as good as anything else on the menu.

Just don't leave without a cup of cobbler, either pecan or peach. Both are made in-house and they're as much a link to the Southern traditions on display at Bob's as the meat is. Closed on Sunday and Monday.

Carter's Bar-B-Que

519 S. Eastman Road, Longview, TX 75602; (903) 236-3271
Founded: 1994 **Pitmaster:** Curt Carter **Wood:** Hickory
Carter's is housed in a renovated gas station and convenience store. Nothing much has been done to cover up its origins, except for the stacks of hickory situated in front and on the side. And it doesn't really matter, because despite the presence of neat, well-kept community tables for dining, most customers in the morning seem to want their barbecue to go. It's been that way since the place opened as a Bodacious Bar-B-Que in 1986, eight years before Curt Carter changed its name to his. It's a shame, because when you sit back at one of the community tables while waiting for your meal, you can take a look at the collection of assorted paraphernalia that adorns the walls, from local notices to a poster for the Glen David Gold mystery, *Carter Beats the Devil*.

But your attention is soon diverted by the appearance of a plate that boasts solid sliced beef with a good level of hickory smoke. It's not chief among the

restaurant's crown jewels, however. That honor belongs to the pork ribs, especially if you're lucky enough to sink your teeth into one the moment it emerges from the smoker. The skin was crackling from the still-melting sugar in the rub as it mingled with bubbles of fat. The pink meat underneath scorched the corners of the mouth, urging faster and faster consumption until nothing was left but bone and cartilage. Get there when the doors open and try your luck at sharing the same experience. But be warned: Lines can form quickly and those ribs will fly out of those smokers faster than you might think possible.

Carter's joys don't stop there. If you're in the mood for a little spice, try the boudain. The spelling may seem odd, but that's the way the sausage makers in Beaumont spell it on their packages, so it's the spelling that Curt Carter uses, too. But the spelling doesn't matter as much as the infusion of hickory into that glorious mess of rice, ground pork, and spices. Closed on Sunday.

Daddy Sam's Bar-B-Q & Catfish

111 N. Maple St., Carthage, TX 75633; (903) 693-7400 **Founded:** 1983
Pitmasters: Dennis LaGrone, Brandon LaGrone, Natonya Hurd,
Chris Miller, Hubert Hatcher **Wood:** Hickory, Pecan
The movie *Bernie* takes place in Carthage and includes several scenes supposedly shot inside Daddy Sam's. But once you step inside, you'll realize that only

the exterior was used. That didn't stop people in the region from flocking there after the movie was released. What they found was good East Texas–style barbecue with ribs that you can't wait to sink your teeth into. Brisket smoked low and slow in hickory has a good bark and is moister than what you find in a lot of East Texas without specifically asking for it. Jalapeño-cheese sausage seems to burst out of its skin with flavor, while succulent ham, chicken, and turkey are also available. The big difference here is that you're served your meat without sauce on it. That can be found at every table.

But Daddy Sam's doesn't stop with barbecue. It is a true Southern-style restaurant in that it offers a little bit of everything to suit your palate, and the folks in the kitchen pay attention to how each dish comes out, whether it's mac and cheese, cabbage, fries, daily specials of smothered pork chops or chicken and dumplings, or the ever-popular deep-fried catfish, which has a following as devoted as the barbecue's. It could be something as major as the beans, which are loaded up with beef and sausage in the mix, or it could be as seemingly minor as offering pickled okra in between tubs of pickle spears and jalapeños. And if that weren't enough, "We also sell burgers," says Natonya Hurd, who's been at Daddy Sam's for 15 years now. She started on the cash register and has since moved up to evening shift manager.

The cakes and assorted desserts, as well as the coleslaw, are made inhouse by Altha Hatch, who's affectionately known as "Miss Bene" to the rest of the staff. A taste of her peach cobbler or pink cake will leave a smile on your face—that is, if you can figure out which dessert you want from the ample display.

Dennis LaGrone, who owns the restaurant with his wife, Rhonda, named Daddy Sam's after his grandfather. He liked Daddy Sam so much that he used the name for his other business, which you can learn about on the flip side of his business card, available at the cash register. It's Daddy Sam's Bail Bonds, and someone's available to help you 24 hours a day. Sometimes, we wish places like Daddy Sam's Bar-B-Q were open 24 hours a day, too. You know, in case of emergency. Closed Saturday and Sunday.

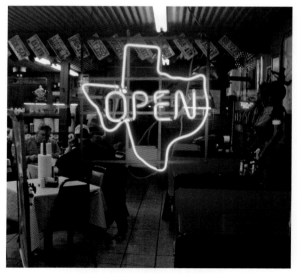

Smoke Screen

Hollywood loves its barbecue as much as anyone else. Here are several movies filmed in Texas in which the smoke from the pit permeates the on-screen action.

Giant (1956): A Texas-size barbecue is thrown for Virginia-born Leslie (Elizabeth Taylor) on her arrival in Texas. Director George Stevens allows his camera to linger over the pits and the food, including the unwrapping of a cow's head as part of the *barbacoa* that's the center-piece of the feast. Her husband, Bick (Rock Hudson), relates in great detail what's happening, but a combination of the heat and the sight of the head is enough to make the newcomer faint.

The Texas Chain Saw Massacre (1974): Tobe Hooper's groundbreaking slasher film still horrifies 40 years after its release. The use of the Cele Store in Manor as a location within the film adds to its creepiness. The next two films in this list also use images of the Cele Store, and the dilapidated building comes off differently in each.

A Perfect World (1993): Kevin Costner's character in this period drama is on the lam after breaking out of prison. He needs a place to hide, and what could be more perfect than a build-ing so old that it's practically invisible? And so the Cele Store becomes a haven where he and his hostage can take a break.

Secondhand Lions (2003): A young city boy is forced to live with two cantankerous old uncles (Michael Caine and Robert Duvall) in the hinterlands of Texas. Soon his eyes—and his imagination—open to the wonders of the world around him. In this film the Cele Store becomes a place of magic, the kind of ephemeral structure that exists only in children's minds and in the movies. The magic continues when a gang of teenagers pick a fight with Duvall and quickly find themselves out of their league.

Barbecue: A Texas Love Story (2004): Former Texas governor Ann Richards lends her distinctive voice to the narration of this documentary, which is, in essence, a video tour of the barbecue trail and the food that Texans love. Many of the places depicted, from Opie's in Spicewood to the Salt Lick in Driftwood, are still with us, but a lot has changed on the Texas barbecue scene in the past 10 years, making this a fascinating time capsule.

Planet Terror (2007): Robert Rodriguez's film was originally part of the exploitation dou-ble feature *Grindhouse,* but he beefed up the story for its solo DVD. In doing so, he fleshed out the storyline of a barbecue pit boss (Jeff Fahey) who'd rather die than part with his secret recipes.

Bernie (2012): The story is so farfetched that it has to be true: An assistant funeral director in Carthage murders a rich woman and stuffs her body in a freezer, but hardly anyone seems to care. The camera captures people from all corners of the East Texas town as they offer their opinions of what happened. Naturally, some of the scenes take place inside a barbecue joint. The exterior used is Carthage's own Daddy Sam's Bar-B-Q & Catfish, but the interior is actually Zimmerhanzel's Bar-B-Que in Smithville—the bright orange chairs are the giveaway.

Mike's Barbeque House

1622 South St., Nacogdoches, TX 75964; (936) 560-1676; www.mikes barbequehouse.net **Founded:** 1986 **Pitmaster:** Mike McClellan **Wood:** Oak

Here's a place that illustrates spelling doesn't matter so much as long as the folks in the smoke pit know what they're doing. Just what is the real name of the Nacogdoches favorite? On the sign out front, the place is advertised as "Mike's BarBQ House" (presumably hyphens cost extra in neon). On the front window, it's "Mike's Bar-B-Q." On the website, it's both "Mike's Barbecue House" and "Mike's Barbeque House." That last one is the winner. But, once again, the only people who care about such things as proper (or at least consistent) spelling are the barbecue writers and any retired schoolteachers driving through town. Mike's has been in business for close to 30 years, under the leadership of Mike McClellan, whose family goes back much further in the trade.

McClellan knows that his customers are more concerned with what they'll taste when they sink their teeth into the messy, flavorful Beef and Link Po'boy, with both meats drenched in plenty of tangy sauce, or their eyes are bulging over the Super Stuffed Potato, which features layers of butter, sour cream, Sloppy Joe mix, bacon, chives, and cheese all in a potato. It's small wonder these two treats are the restaurant's bestsellers. They feed the same primal urges that drive many a barbecue lover: The portion size is unapologetically gigantic. Eating either dish transgresses the bounds of etiquette, as you'll end up dripping in sauce of some sort, but the flavors are richly satisfying.

Both dishes also seem to exemplify East Texas barbecue with their Southern influences and their reliance on barbecue sauce as an essential part of the equation. If you'd rather stick to cuts of meat by the pound, your choices include the expected likes of beef, ribs, sausage, and hot links as well as turkey, pork loin, and ham, while chickens are available half or whole. Another East Texas favorite, fried catfish, has its own following.

Spud lovers, rejoice. The Super Stuffed Potato is an eyeful and a mouthful.

Side dishes are limited to barbecue beans (baked beans with a touch of tangy sauce cooked in for good measure), Cajun rice, coleslaw, and a kind of mashed potato salad. Far more interesting is the multiberry cobbler that sends its siren's call through the glass. Don't resist.

All this is served in what can best be called a well-used, old-fashioned Texas barbecue joint that favors rustic decor, with a saddle tossed over the side of one booth and a wooden Indian standing guard by the door. He doesn't care about the spelling either. Closed on Sunday.

New Zion Missionary Baptist Barbeque
2601 Montgomery Rd., Huntsville, TX 77340; (936) 294-0884
Founded: 1979 **Pitmaster:** The Reverend Clifton J. Edison
Wood: Oak, Hickory

In the mid-1970s Annie Mae Ward started making barbecue for a crew of workers who were repairing their hometown house of worship, the New Zion Missionary Baptist Church. But, as any true barbecue lover knows, the aroma of smoke mingled with good meat attracted more than just hungry workers. People off the street were soon asking Sister Ward if the barbecue was for sale. She decided that she'd sell a little extra as a fund-raiser for the church, but the response proved so great that, by the end of the decade, an official barbecue restaurant was up and running next door to the church. In no time, it seems, word got out about the small operation, and barbecue disciples from all over the world were making what amounted to a pilgrimage to Huntsville.

"We've had people from Australia in here, you name it," says the Reverend Clifton J. Edison, who now oversees the barbecue operation. "Someone from Germany even wrote a book about the place."

Edison's week is divided between barbecue and congregational duties, with a little time off for fishing. It's an arrangement that echoes St. Paul's work as both tentmaker and spreader of the gospel. The pastor sees it as his semiretirement plan, after a career working in Texas's correctional system.

Edison's menu is largely unchanged from Ward's day, and most of the recipes are hers, too. The meat is slow-cooked using oak and then flavored with hickory. Brisket, moist and fork tender, is placed in the smoker at 6 p.m. with a steady temperature of 225°F. It doesn't leave until 8 the following morning. You can have it by itself or in a sandwich, but why not try a few slices in a three-meat plate, partnering it with fine sausage and ribs that display just the right amount of give before leaving the bone? They're all covered in a medium, sweet-tangy sauce in the East Texas style.

Brisket is the big seller, Edison says, because people think they're getting more for their money when paying for their meat by the pound. Too much of

the pork rib's weight is given over to the bone. The usual sides are available, and the beans are the standout. If anything could be said to compete with the meats for attention, though, it would be the pies, with the buttermilk earning higher praise than the fine pecan and sweet potato. The pastor makes the pies, too, and the buttermilk is made to his recipe. His secret? There's no secret, he says. It's a ploy he learned from a television interview Sister Ward once gave. She told the reporter there was no secret to her recipes, she just didn't tell people what was in them. And that ended Edison's talk about buttermilk pie.

In the modest dining room, dominated by a lengthy community table, you're as likely to hear a barbecue lover raise a joyous "Hallelujah!" or an "Amen!" as you are to see families bow their heads for a word of grace before chowing down. It's a lively mix of races, cultures, and, most likely, creeds. The sight of them all breaking bread together offers great nourishment for the soul, while the barbecue feeds the body. Closed Sunday through Wednesday.

The buttermilk pie is almost worth the trip by itself.

Outlaw's Bar-B-Que

1404 Linda Dr., Daingerfield, TX 75638; (903) 645-3444
Founded: 1994 **Pitmaster:** Mark Brundige **Wood:** White Oak
Outlaw's is open until 8 p.m. most nights, but the staff of this barbecue joint knows that on an autumn Friday night, the unofficial closing time is whenever the game gets under way at the nearby high school. The *Friday Night Lights* way of life is as widespread as Texans' love of barbecue.

The Gospel and the Pit

The barbecue lover's devotion to finely smoked meats is so intense that you'll often hear a litany of religious terms used to describe a particularly transfiguring experience with a brisket that approaches perfection or ribs that induce glossolalia. Author and blogger Daniel Vaughn, self-described BBQ Snob, took this to a new plateau with his Full Custom Gospel BBQ blog and book, *The Prophets of Smoked Meat*.

But to many pitmasters in this Bible Belt state, faith—most commonly the Christian faith—is a vital part of the job. Stubb's in Austin hosts a weekly gospel barbecue brunch. Elsewhere, you'll find crosses, religious pictures, blessings, and words of assurance adorning walls of joints throughout Texas, no matter the race of the owner. But perhaps the strongest expression of this spiritual foundation can be found in the African-American community.

Adrian Miller, author of *Soul Food: The Surprising History of an American Cuisine One Plate at a Time*, says one reason for this is the historical link between barbecue and the African-American church. The pit-smoked meats were a regular feature at the family meal that followed Sunday meetings. Soon, barbecue plates became fund-raisers for many of these congregations, and the people in the pit occasionally found a path to their own business. In the case of New Zion Missionary Baptist Church in Huntsville, the church simply opened its own barbecue joint, which has been in operation for decades now—and it has kept the church financially stable in the process.

Chubb's BB-Q in El Paso grew out of a fund-raiser Curtis Vaughn held for his church, True Holiness. Response was so great that, within a few months, he was looking for a storefront. "I thank God," says Vaughn (no relation to Daniel). "I wouldn't be doing this if it weren't for him." You'll hear similar stories of blessings from people such as Ed and Waldean Ashford of Ed's Smok-N-Q in San Antonio and Kathy Burns of Burns BBQ in Houston. But don't expect a sermon as a side to your ribs or sausage. As Curtis Vaughn says, if you're just in for food, that's what he's going to serve you. Amen.

Best of NATURE

That means about the only customers you'll find at Outlaw's on a Friday night are people passing through town, such as traveling barbecue lovers who are more interested in ribs than in the Tigers' progress on the field. So, while one employee was mopping the floor, the other served up a heaping four-meat plate of sliced beef, ribs, pork loin, and sausage. The meat had a pleasant oak flavor that worked well no matter what animal it came from. Side dish options, arranged cafeteria style for easy service, were in great supply, which means that a vegetarian might be able to put together a satisfying meal, something ridiculed by many a barbecue fanatic but a reality even in Texas.

The cucumber salad is a refreshingly light counterbalance to the weight of the meat.

"Ain't nothing wrong with fresh vegetables," says manager Robert Hanna, adding that even a few carnivores come in for a multiple-vegetable plate on occasion.

Nothing, indeed. Except it begs the question: Why is it that the more choices you've got, in terms of both meat and side dishes, the more you want all of them? Closed on Sunday.

Porky's Smokehouse & Grill

504 E. Carolanne Blvd., Marshall, TX 75672; (903) 927-2144; www.porkysmokehouse.com **Founded:** 1996 **Pitmaster:** Donna Burns **Wood:** Pecan, Red Oak

When you step up to Porky's, you have to walk past a window painting of a happy mother pig feeding her litter. Surrounding this scene of maternal bliss is the slogan: "Porky's—Where you always get plenty t'eat!" It's a bit of small-town humor that seems to reflect the spirit of the whole place.

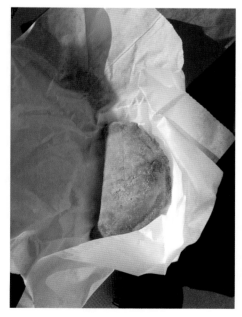

This isn't one of those serious temples of barbecue that you find in, say, Central Texas. In fact, the word "barbecue," no matter the spelling, appears on the menu only when referencing the sauce. The meats here are smoked with pecan and red oak, and they're available either on sandwiches or by the pound. Smoked chicken is a big seller among the meats, followed by beef and ribs, made with a dry rub on the outside. "We get asked a lot if we do dry or wet, and I have to educate my staff about that," owner Donna Burns says. "We do a dry rub." But the real meat star is the Porky Pig Sandwich, which is old-fashioned pulled pork.

There's a scene stealer on the menu that isn't even smoked. It's the fried catfish, which draws people from all over town and even the region who like the touch of spice in the batter, a reflection perhaps of Burns's Louisiana background. Salads, burgers, and loaded baked potatoes round out the varied menu, while side dishes include some crispy fried okra, fries, and onion rings in addition to the smoked beans, potato salad, and coleslaw.

What you cannot miss are the handmade fried pies served for dessert. This is a tradition that Burns carried over from the previous restaurant that had been in the same spot, Neely's. If all you've had in life is a fruit pie from a fast-food drive-thru or the counter at a filling station, then you're really in for a treat. The filling—your choice of cherry, chocolate, apple, apricot, or coconut—may seem somewhat familiar, with a touch

A cherry fried pie is your reward for eating all your barbecue.

of cornstarch as a thickener, but it's really the pastry that makes it memorable. One bite—when it's cool enough to bite into, that is—will make you want to return to Porky's. Closed on Sunday.

Rhea's Hot Links

204 S. Fannin Ave., Tyler, TX 75702; (903) 592-0781 **Founded:** 1945
Owner: David Rhea

It's time for a short detour. In East Texas you may find hot links mentioned on a handful of barbecue menus. These aren't the spicy hot links you'll find in the western part of the state, but they are a regional dish worth investigating, even when they're not smoked. That's what prompted a stop at Rhea's Hot Links in an old cinderblock building in downtown Tyler. The lunch crowd was in full swing, and there was only one open table in the place. A few folks had bowls of chili in front of them, but the rest were enjoying the only other item on the menu, the hot link.

These thumb-size sausages are made largely from the cow's head, as *barbacoa* is, with the meat being ground and then stuffed into a casing, says owner David Rhea, who is the third generation of the Rhea family to run the place. The meat is faintly glandular in nature, which makes it taste like dirty rice, only without the rice.

Rhea's version is baked, not smoked. After they're removed from the oven, the links are cut apart with a pair of scissors. Each little snip allows all of the grease built up inside to pool onto the plate. You can then scoop up the meat or the whole link onto a cracker or bread, and enjoy. That is, if you're not put off by the sight of that grease. Even Rhea admits that both the sight and the taste can be a bit polarizing: "You either love 'em or you hate 'em." But those who love them become devoted followers, which is why Rhea sells between 1,500 and 2,000 pounds of them every week.

The links are made fresh four days a week, and they find their biggest fan in their owner, who claims to eat them every day for breakfast. "Nobody eats more of them than I do," Rhea says, adding that he likes his on crackers with ketchup and a little hot sauce on top.

Rhea follows the same recipe his grandfather, Henry Rhea, used when he opened the place in the mid-1940s. His uncle, Joe Rhea, eventually took over and ran it until 1999. When Joe's daughters showed no interest in running Rhea's, David bought it. His daughters are showing interest in carrying the place into the fourth generation, he says. That's good news for those who don't want these handmade East Texas hot links to disappear from the scene. Closed on Sunday.

Stanley's Famous Pit Bar-B-Que

525 S. Beckham Ave., Tyler, TX 75702; (903) 593-0311; www.stanleys famous.com **Founded:** Mid-1950s **Pitmasters:** Nick Pencis, Jonathan Shaw, Jordan Jackson **Wood:** Pecan

A bumper sticker in the window of this joint says it all: "Support your local BBQ joint. Eat at Stanley's." The people of Tyler have taken that message to heart. Even on a weekday, a line will form long before the 11 a.m. lunchtime begins, and it'll trail right out the door. What is it they want? Beef ribs? Brisket? Pork ribs? All of the above, says Nick Pencis, who owns the place with his wife, Jen.

It wasn't always so simple, especially to a musician who had never smoked meat in his life. In fact, Pencis was a drummer out on the road with a group called Greyhounds. How does a drummer get into the barbecue business? "I've always been in the restaurant game," he says. "It was kind of my first job, and I was good at it. My dad was good at it.

"My idea was to combine them [music and the restaurant business]. So, I got off the road and I decided I'd go finish my degree in business. I didn't

want to be one of those people who think they can open a place but have no idea how to run it. So, that's what I was doing. I was taking classes and I was bartending at a country club. I was 28 years old, and I was in the second week of my second semester when the guy who owned this place asked me, 'Hey, can you come help me out?' He wanted to give somebody the opportunity to take over. Well, I had to ask myself if I wanted to jump in and take something that's been established. There was also the fact that it was a place people my age had never heard of."

J. D. Stanley opened his barbecue joint in the mid-1950s, providing the barbecue that people loved while crowning the building with an ornate neon sign that still stops traffic. The place had fallen on hard times when Pencis took over. Yet he saw potential in the project, so much so, in fact, that he dropped out of school to work on the place full time.

There was a drawback: Pencis had never smoked meat before. "I'm a Texan tried and true," he says, adding that he grew up in Austin and his family has ties to Lockhart, but he'd never minded a pit before. He didn't let that stop him, and he started at Stanley's in 2005. A year later he bought the place and spent some time just trying to keep it afloat. It wasn't wholly successful, however. So, he took a trip to Lockhart to see how the Barbecue Capital of Texas was doing things. "I got up early and went straight to Smitty's," he says. "I was just blown away. I knew we needed to reconnect with our roots . . . It was a life-changing trip."

It was also a menu-changing trip, because Pencis wanted to make his brisket as moist and tender as what he'd sampled. He knew he was on the right path when David Gelin stopped by to talk about barbecue for his book, *BBQ Joints: Stories and Secrets from the Barbecue Belt*. Then Stanley's made *Texas Monthly*'s Top 50 barbecue list in 2008. "It was validation, for sure," he says. "Is it the measure of all we do? No . . . But it is great to be recognized for being one of the best. And it pushed us even harder." Then, for two years in a row, the Stanley's team took top honors for their ribs at the Texas Monthly BBQ Fest.

Pencis has since added two pitmasters, Jonathan Shaw and Jordan Jackson, to help prepare the pecan-smoked meat that locals can't seem to get enough of. Word began to spread of brisket that would practically melt in your mouth and beef ribs loaded with meaty juices, not to mention sausage, hot links, pulled pork, and turkey. Sides include a mayonnaise-based red skin potato salad, made from a recipe that dates back to the original Stanley's.

What is perhaps most admirable is the way Stanley's handles the variety of customers it receives. Tyler is situated somewhere on the western edge of East Texas, the northern end of Central Texas, and the eastern end of the Dallas area, so it gets customers from all over the place, and each one arrives armed with a preconceived notion of what brisket should be. So, Stanley's has a sign at the cash register that asks people up front, "How do you like your brisket? Lean? Fatty? End cut? Extra bark? No bark?" You can have it any way you want, but you do have to specify when you order.

"We're trying to please a whole range of people here," Pencis says.

That holds true for Stanley's hours as well. Breakfast was added a couple of years ago, and it essentially offers customers the breakfast sandwiches that the staff would fix for themselves. The roster includes the Mother Clucker, a chicken sandwich topped with a fried egg, cheese, and, if you ask, candied bacon, or the Shrove with grilled ham, cheese, and chopped beef. (The Ex-wife, pulled pork and sliced brisket on a bun, was given its name by the customer who created the "Support your local BBQ joint" bumper sticker.)

Stanley's is also now open for dinner. To entice people in with more than just fine barbecue, Pencis has added a bandstand for local and regional music acts. Yes, he's been known to pick up his drumsticks on occasion and join in. A bar has been added, while expanded deck seating means more than 150 can hang around with friends after work and relax.

The increase in business has meant Pencis has had to triple his staff to keep up with his customers' needs. He's obviously proud of these "people who share your dream, your passion." He saves the most credit for his wife, Jen, who is the key to Stanley's current success. "She's been the nucleus of all," he says. "This was her first child . . . She made this happen." Closed on Sunday.

Texas Best Smokehouse

16243 US 271, Tyler, TX 75708; (903) 877-0800 **Founded:** 2007
Pitmaster: Amer Khalousi **Wood:** Hickory, Oak

Texas Best Smokehouse is a chain in the making, which you can tell from the appearance of the place. Think of a market attached to a gas station just off an interstate, much like a Buc-ee's or a Love's. In other words, it's a place that caters to tourists passing through, and it offers them barbecue to fill them up after they fill up their tanks.

First, though, you have to get past the jerky stand where you can get dried slivers of meats, ranging from beef and venison to bison and elk. There's a fine array of old-fashioned sodas, from Moxie to Lemmy, plus plenty of candies and snacks. And you can load up on all the Texas souvenirs you want. There's also a Sonic hamburger joint as well as a *kolache* stand for those who don't have an interest in barbecue.

The whole place sparkles with the comforts some people have come to expect from restaurants that feel like a chain. That means, if you pay attention to the reviews on Yelp or Urbanspoon, you'll love the restrooms, which patrons claim to be the cleanest around.

But we're here to talk about the barbecue at the two pits worth considering, which are at stops off the interstate in Tyler and Longview. Both are under the supervision of Amer Khalousi, who is one of the few—if not the only—Texas pitmasters in the state of Arabic descent. He offers all of the traditional cuts and styles you expect in East Texas: sliced and chopped beef, ribs, chicken, and turkey, all cooked in open fire pits using indirect heat. He even has the sausage made especially for Texas Best. "This is a travel stop, yes," he says, "but it has built a barbecue reputation that is not a secondary operation to

the store." And it's not just for tourists: Texas Best has its regular clients who want the meats for parties, games, or just Saturday dinner.

As fine as the meats are, the vast array of side dishes, served up cafeteria style, is even more impressive. These include the expected, such as both baked and ranch beans, potato salad, and coleslaw, but then you see fried okra, greens with pork cooked in, a broccoli salad, and, high on the list, macaroni and cheese. There are so many choices, you may just want to get a to-go order of sides to enjoy a little later on the road. "Nearly 90 percent of the sides are made from scratch," Khalousi promises.

One difference you'll find here from many barbecue joints in East Texas is that the meat is served without sauce. You can add that yourself at the sauce and condiment bar, which features as many pickles, onions, jalapeños, and the like as you'd want. Then sit back in one of the wooden rocking chairs on the front porch and enjoy your meal while the world races by.

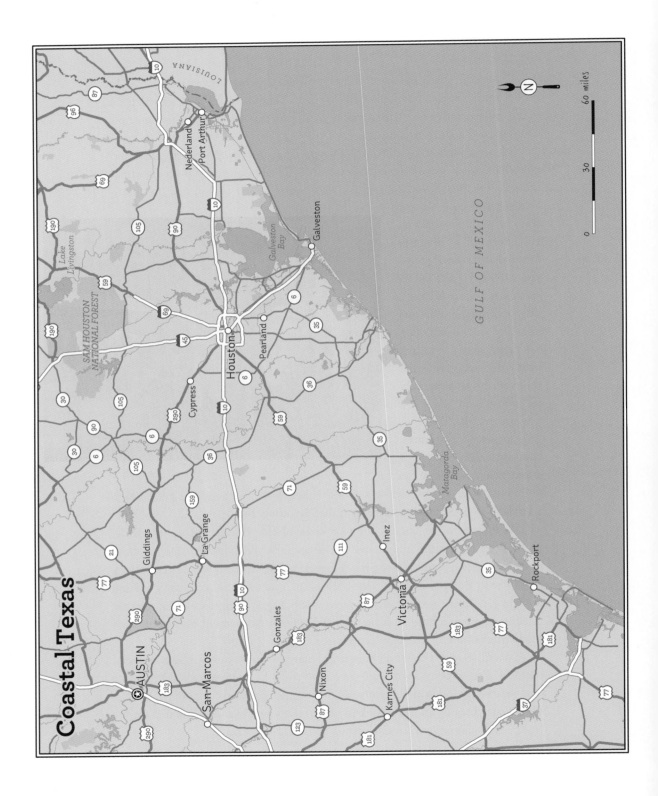

Coastal Texas

LOUISIANA

GULF OF MEXICO

Sam Houston National Forest

Lake Livingston

Galveston Bay

Matagorda Bay

AUSTIN
San Marcos
Giddings
La Grange
Gonzales
Nixon
Karnes City
Victoria
Inez
Houston
Cypress
Pearland
Galveston
Nederland
Port Arthur
Rockport

60 miles
30
0

Coastal Texas

Cross the state line from Louisiana into Texas near the Gulf Coast, and you won't find much has changed. The talk is often peppered with a Cajun dialect, while the languid air, dipped in the humidity of the nearby waters, makes it seem as if things were moving at a slightly slower pace—until you hit the highways, that is. The food is heavily seasoned, creating a heady mixture of treats that use every last scrap of whatever is edible. Its form could be dirty rice or boudain or barbecue.

The barbecue takes its style from several directions and sometimes all at once. You could find the Central Texas preference for oak smoking through thick slabs of brisket, served alongside an East Texas array of side dishes, such as tangy collard greens and buttery corn bread. Or you could bite into a sauce-covered rib spicy enough to set your tongue a'tingle for a moment.

Customers here don't seem to care how you serve their smoked meats or where you serve them, as long as they're good. You'll find barbecue coming from sit-down restaurants, through the window of a weathered shack, from a food truck, or even at a roadside pop-up. You'll even find one place with a smoked brownie to finish off your meal.

Since you're along the coast, it also makes sense that seafood of some sort has worked its way onto the menu. That's where the regional favorite, barbecue crabs, comes into the picture. These beauties are not smoked; they're dipped in barbecue seasoning and then deep-fried, which is where the name comes from. But why be picky about a name or a cooking method, when the end result is this good?

Back Porch Bar-B-Q

2871 Garcitas Creek Rd., Inez, TX 77968; (361) 782-0881
Founded: 2000 **Pitmaster:** Michael Sacky **Wood:** Mesquite, Oak
Back Porch Bar-B-Q is only open for a few hours during the week, but that's enough time for the brisket to run out. Still, sliced brisket is not the main reason to visit this tiny stop somewhere northeast of Victoria. The real star

of the show is the massive BBQ Frito pie. The recipe for this marvel hangs behind the counter. It promises "1 cup chopped beef, 1½ cups beans, 1 bag Frito's, 2 types of cheese, onions and sauce." But that only begins to describe how the crunch of the corn chips, the smoky meat, the sweet sauce, and the velvety strands of cheese somehow melt together as a whole. Have this with a big cup of sweet tea, our fun and sarcastic server, Betty Cowan, advised.

If you get there in time to snag some of the sliced brisket, you can pair it with your choice of pork loin, chicken breast, or sausage, all of which arrive

with the sauce poured over it. You can also get your choice of meats filling what the Back Porch calls "Texas-sized sandwiches." Drinks are included with most meals.

The dining area is pure Texana, with plenty of animal horns and a few stuffed critters fighting for wall space with old tools and some fading pieces of artwork. Or you can eat out on the front porch, which is also adorned with a great many interesting objects, including an array of old license plates framing one window. Christian music floats in the air—that is, if you can hear it over the din of traffic from nearby Highway 59. "You might put in there, we don't use roadkill," Cowan deadpanned. Open Tuesday through Friday.

Comeaux's Bar B Que Pit

1848 Bluebonnet Ave., Port Arthur, TX 77640; (409) 982-3262
Founded: 1986 **Pitmaster:** Emmett Comeaux **Wood:** Little bit of everything, but pecan is best.

The southeast corner of Texas is liberally seasoned with Cajun influences, and you can hear the lilting accent ring through the conversations of the customers of Comeaux's, an old-time shack that serves up some mighty aromatic barbecue. Thankfully, the flavor matches the intoxicating smells, whether you're trying the house-made beef sausage, a loose grind with plenty of spices added, or the "bones," which refers to the spine and neck of the pig. The meat on those bones ranges from a thin end that seems to be approaching jerky to moist

morsels by the bones themselves. Tender or chewy, the texture doesn't matter as much as the great pork flavor in each bite.

All of the meat arrives with a rich sauce on it that also suggests Cajun heritage, plus you can get it with mustard added. Squeezed straight from a store-bought container, the mustard adds a bracing touch of vinegar to mingle with the heat of the sauce. Your meat plate is just that, meat—and a couple slices of white bread. If you want sides, you can buy the potato salad or the rice dressing, also known as Cajun dirty rice, separately.

Don't expect to eat at Comeaux's. Sure, there's a single table with a couple of chairs in one corner, but those seem more for the people waiting to get their orders. Also, bring cash with you, as a handwritten sign over the order window reminds you. How long has that sign been tacked up there? Long enough for someone to come along and add underneath it, "Also, no smoking." The measure of a place is in the taste. One bite of Comeaux's meat will have you picking up the accent and exclaiming, "Ah, *cher*, that's just fine." Open Tuesday through Saturday.

Gonzales Food Market

311 St. Lawrence St., Gonzales, TX 78629; (830) 672-3156; www .gonzalesfoodmarket.net **Founded:** 1959 **Pitmaster:** Jose Ramirez **Wood:** Oak, Mesquite

This family-run business started in 1959 when Richard Lopez's grandfather and father opened the market on St. Lawrence, a short walk from the town square in this historic Texas town. If you drive to Gonzales, plan to spend some time walking around the square and get a feel of the local history.

Lopez's dad and granddad dedicated 40 years to the grocery and barbecue market. Lopez himself worked in the corporate food business, too, but finally stepped in to take over the market with family partners and wife, Diane. The restaurant owners, in addition to Richard Lopez, include Ray Lopez and Rene Garza.

To this day, the house-made sausage is still the top-seller, made with the same recipe that Lopez's grandfather and father obtained from a family friend. The lamb ribs have also become another popular item along the way, and you don't want to miss these—they're not available in every barbecue joint you go to. Plus, the Gonzales version is good, boasting a dark, chewy crust over a warm layer of melting fat that bastes and soaks into the pink meat on the bones.

The barbecue is pit-smoked with indirect heat, fueled by a mixture of oak and mesquite. The chicken and sausage get a different but effective treatment, cooked by direct heat, or grilled over coals. A cafeteria-style line forms at the steam tables, where you order and pick up your barbecue and sides. But the massive and well-used butcher-block table is where the meat-cutting happens well within your view.

While much about Gonzales Food Market is steeped in history, there is little remaining of the original grocery—just a meat counter that Lopez says might even be taken out before too long. "We just stock some cheese, bologna, cold cuts. If someone comes in and asks for six rib-eye steaks, we send them over to the store."

"Our sausage and our barbecue speak for themselves. If you like it, you will come back," Lopez says. As with many other barbecue purveyors we spoke with, he said it's the consistency of the food as well as its flavor that brings customers back.

According to Lopez, "If you're good at noon, you should be good at 7 p.m. And the owner has to be here in order for the business to succeed." Closed on Sunday.

KB's BBQ and Catering

Victoria, TX; (361) 649-8049 **Founded:** 2001 **Pitmaster:** Kevin Broll
Wood: Mesquite

Kevin Broll used to run KB's BBQ out of a brick-and-mortar establishment. In fact, he had two restaurants. But now he operates out of a food truck that can be found most every day somewhere in the Victoria area. "Call for location and time," his card says. You might need a direction or two before you find him, but hopefully you'll be less directionally challenged than we were. Still, even after calling KB's three times during Broll's busy lunch rush, he never lost patience with us. And we were glad we persisted in tracking the truck down.

Plenty of customers were waiting on orders when we arrived, but it didn't take too long for us to figure out what we wanted to sample from the fairly extensive board. But first we had to get past the shock of not seeing brisket on the menu. It was there, you just had to tell Broll how you wanted it: sliced, in a sandwich, or in a taco with a spiky *pico de gallo* on top.

Pit-cooked *barbacoa*, also available on a plate or in a taco, drew our attention, as did a combination of pork sausage and country ribs, which satisfied in no small part because of the excellent sides: smashed new potatoes with

plenty of pepper, and baked beans with *pico* swirled in. A loaded baked potato and chicken in a number of ways (Buffalo, Cajun, or barbecued) show that Broll is not hindered at all by the size of his mobile kitchen, complete with pit.

Broll swears by mesquite, which isn't the easiest wood to find in an area that prefers oak. "We have to drive all the way to Luling to get our wood," he says.

When we caught up with KB's, Broll said he had plans to open a second barbecue truck, which was likely to happen by the time this book was published. Hopefully, you'll have no trouble finding either one the next time you're visiting Victoria for barbecue.

Killen's Barbecue

3613 E. Broadway, Pearland, TX 77581; (281) 485-0844 **Founded:** 2013 **Pitmaster:** Ronnie Killen **Wood:** Peach, Pecan, Oak, Hickory, among others

To most folks in Pearland, the abandoned building at 3613 E. Broadway was nothing but an eyesore that should have been torn down long ago. To Ronnie Killen, it was a treasure waiting to be restored. The restaurateur, whose Killen's Steakhouse is revered by carnivores throughout the region, remembered going into the building daily when it served as the cafeteria for the schools nearby. And he thought it would be the perfect home for a new barbecue restaurant.

The pecan pie may seem a bit steep at $4.50 a slice, but it is worth every cent. What is it that makes this pie head and shoulders above most every other pecan pie in Texas? More nuts? Sugar instead of corn syrup? You ask Ronnie Killen and see if you can get the secret out of him.

Before work began, however, Killen used the grounds around it as the setting for a weekend pop-up barbecue joint. Within minutes, or so it seemed, word got out across the state that Killen's Barbecue, with only a few picnic tables, a large canopy, and a makeshift carving area, was producing some of the finest barbecue in the state.

That's why several dozen people could be found hanging out long before the 11 a.m. opening time. "I think it's better to get here an hour early than come at 11 and wait an hour and 45 minutes," one barbecue lover said. Besides, Killen hauled out a tap and offered cups of free beer to folks waiting in line, which only endeared him further to anyone waiting to buy his beef ribs, which are so tender and moist that you'd swear you never had one before. The well-marbled brisket will also make you shake your head in wonder. (If you want lean brisket,

be prepared to pay an extra $2 per pound.) And if that's not enough, a slight dip of either in the coffee-flavored barbecue sauce just makes the beef even more riotously good.

There's no secret, Killen swears; his rub is simply kosher salt and three peppers. And while he uses different woods, including oak to finish off the meat, they're not what keeps everything so juicy. It's all in the cooking—and it holds true for all 1,600 pounds of meat that Killen's team carves up each weekend. By the way, closing time is posted as 2 p.m., but the meats are usually gone by 12:30 p.m.

Sausage links, pork ribs, and chicken fill out the meat menu, while the sides are limited to beans, an eggy potato salad, and coleslaw made with ramen noodles. (It was a pop-up, after all, and there was limited space. All that may have changed when the building was refurbished and Killen's barbecue became available Tuesday through Sunday.)

The pop-up was staffed by Killen's employees from the steak house, and a few brought their kids to help out. It added to the family feeling of the low-key event. Killen himself pulled up with the smoking pit hitched to the back of his truck. Everyone kept tabs on that smoker, because it had previously gone missing for two weeks. After massive media coverage in the area, the smoker suddenly surfaced practically intact and was restored to its owner.

The outdoor pit at the new restaurant won't slip away so easily, Killen says, "unless you have a crane." It will be one of two pits in use. The other is what the chef and pitmaster calls "a reverse-flow fire brick pit" that will be indoors. How is that possible? The building's interior features ceramic brick walls, which means it is a kiln and can safely house an open pit. Those walls are the reason Killen saw the potential in an old building everyone else had dismissed.

If all this sounds a bit too gussied up for barbecue, remember that Killen is a combination of Texas native and Cordon Bleu–trained chef; his first restaurant was Killen's Kountry BBQ, but he's also cooked several times at the prestigious James Beard House in New York City. For his Art of Smoke dinner there in early 2013, he left diners amazed at the versatility of smoke by using everything from coastal hay to sassafras. He capped off the meal with a deconstructed Black Forest cake that contained a surprise for the guests: When each one cut into the cake, a puff of cherrywood smoke was released. You won't find that on the menu of the new Killen's Barbecue, but who really needs it when the beef ribs are available? Open Tuesday through Sunday.

Leon's World's Finest In & Out Barbeque

5427 Broadway St., Galveston, TX 77551; (409) 744-0070; www.leons bbq.com **Founded:** 1987 **Pitmaster:** Leon O'Neal **Wood:** Oak

The menu at Leon's World's Finest is bound to give you a chuckle. Instead of chicken, you can get either a half or a whole "yard bird." The sliced sausage is billed as the "link du jour," and the ribs aren't just any rib, they are "young & tender spare ribs." Of course, extra-lean brisket costs $7 extra per pound, which is the way barbecue lovers tell you it should be.

You might also chuckle in slight disbelief at the sight of your meal when it's being served to you. Leon O'Neal, also known as Dr. Bar-B-Q, is generous with his portions. That three-meat plate of ribs, brisket, and house-made beef links is so expansive that there's no room for the sides, which are served in bowls alongside your plate. The brisket is fatty and delicious without your having to ask for it cut that way. The ribs are sliced across the bone, so you can gnaw away at plenty of meat, which is largely tender and all of it intensely porky. The home-made links are loosely stuffed in the style you find in many African-American barbecue joints. In other words, they're juicy without being greasy.

Sweet corn bread brushed with butter will come as a relief to anyone who's grown tired of all the white bread that's been piled high on your plate even without your asking for it. But you better get your order in for that early, because the kitchen often runs out. Side dishes include a tangy mess of turnip greens with just the right amount of bacon and onion in the pot liquor, spicy rice, and brightly seasoned barbecue beans.

Leon's is a full family affair, with everyone pitching in, from making the sauce to the buttermilk pie. But it is Leon O'Neal who dominates the place, even when he's not there. His presence can be found in the many newspaper and magazine articles that have chronicled his 'cue through the years. "He taught me everything" about barbecue, says Lawrence Roberson, who's been working at Leon's for 23 years now, "how to cook, how much time it takes, how to cut it, how it should be served."

Back in 2008, Hurricane Ike did its best to shut down Leon's, but the storm was seemingly no match for O'Neal and his family,

Hot corn bread with butter. What else do you need to be told? It's that good.

who resurrected the business and restored it to its current state of barbecue excellence. "It's a simple operation," Roberson says modestly but with a sure grasp of why people love Leon's: "We stay consistent with it. We know what works."

Mumphord's Place

1202 E. Juan Linn, Victoria, TX 77901; (361) 485-1112; www .mumphordsplacebbq.com **Founded:** 2000 **Pitmasters:** Ricky Mumphord, Keith Mumphord **Wood:** Oak, Mesquite

If you arrive at Mumphord's Place before the doors open, you may notice clouds of smoke billowing from the pit in back. Also coming from the pit could be a snatch of old-time blues sung by one of the pit crew, Rickey Thomas, whose bass voice resonates throughout the spacious parking lot.

We suggest you arrive at Mumphord's as early as you can, not just for the music, but because lines form quickly, even on weekdays. And the custom-

ers are hungry for what they can get. On most days it might be the moist brisket, ribs that cling to the bone, or chicken with a crackly skin over tender meat, all served by the pound or in sandwiches, but on Thursdays, Fridays, and Saturdays, sliced pork loin and turkey are added.

The restaurant grew out of a combination Juneteenth celebration and family reunion, says Ricky Mumphord, who runs the place with his brother, Keith.

And it has maintained that family sense in the genial nature of the staff, who do their best to accommodate customers. The brothers developed the recipes—family secrets, of course—drawing on tradition and tastes of the area, Ricky says. As you sit at your table, with the red-and-white-checked tablecloths protected under plastic, you can enjoy that homemade sausage by itself or in a barbecue sauce that's thick and sticky, almost like an Asian sweet-and-sour sauce in texture but with enough seasoning to match the smoked flavor of the meat. The pinto beans have a definite layer of cumin added, and the coleslaw is sweet in a style you'll find throughout the South.

If you've got a sweet tooth, don't pass by the table laden with handmade brittle (pecan or peanut) from one of the local churches and sold, no doubt, as a fund-raiser. It's one of the many touches in the dining room that let you know Mumphord's has more than a little Victoria in its history. As the sign over the door says when you leave, "Mumphord's Place—Giving Back to the Community." Closed on Sunday and Monday.

That's a Brisket Melody

Texas barbecue has even made it to the stage. *Das Barbecü* is a musical romp that retells Wagner's 20-hour *Der Ring des Nibelungen* in a scant 2 hours but with a great many more laughs. The epic's location has been transported to Texas ranchland, where the Rangers are on the lookout for the River Maidens' stolen gold. Songs like "Hog-Tie Your Man" and "Makin' Guacamole" fill out the score, though the showstopper is "Barbecue for Two," a duet for a pair of brokenhearted divas. In their musical banquet of laments, they serve up plenty of ham, smoked and otherwise. (An original cast recording released on Verèse Sarabande is out of print, but used copies can be hunted down on the Internet.)

Pioneer BBQ

213 S. Nixon Ave., Nixon, TX 78140; (512) 626-8001; Food truck at
corner of TX 119 and TX 80, Gillett; www.pioneer-bbq.com
Founded: 2012 **Pitmasters:** David Walbert, Jacob Walbert
Wood: Oak, some Pecan

The father-and-son team of David and Jacob Walbert operate two Pioneer
BBQ locations. The Nixon location is a sit-down restaurant, while Gillett is the
town where they operate their food truck. Either location is worth seeking out
for some exceptional oak-smoked meats.

"Our family used to own a ranch in Prairie," Jacob Walbert says. "So, you
see, our everyday meal was barbecue."

And they learned their lessons well. The brisket, smoked 16 hours, is
moist with a dark bark; the ribs have a good give that'll have you gnawing

every last bite down to the bone; and
the sweet, saucy pulled pork is a perfect use for two slices of white bread.
Pecan-smoked sausage, chicken, and
chopped beef–stuffed potatoes fill out
the menu.

Side dishes include sweet barbecue beans and a mayo-based potato
salad, as well as coleslaw made with
apples and cabbage cooked with bacon.
A fan favorite is Firecracker Corn made
with jalapeños and cream cheese.

You eat all of this in a brightly lit
dining area, where patrons have begun
to cover the walls with their comments:
"Best BBQ ever tasted . . ." "Best barbecue in Texas!" "Most excellent!" One
commenter singled out the best foot-
long (sausage, not hot dog), which is a
Pioneer specialty and was designed for
when the truck is at a local event. Take

a smoked foot-long and smoked chopped beef, then boil both in Shiner Bock.
Slap the boiled meats on a bun and add jalapeños, pickles, onions, cheese, and
Pioneer's own Scorpion Sauce, which has a touch of habanero in it.

The desserts are made in-house. But, to be more specific, they're made in
the pit. That's right, you can get pit-smoked peach cobbler and brownies. This

was inspired by one of those fortuitous accidents in life. Jacob Walbert had a girlfriend from Luling, whose grandmother made a pecan pie that wasn't up to her standards. She set it aside in the smoke pit, so no one would see it. When they found it later, Walbert had a taste and a new line of smoked goods began. On special occasions a Dutch apple pie is featured, and it's Walbert's favorite. Call him a day or two in advance so he can make some. And have it with a scoop of another Texas favorite, Blue Bell vanilla ice cream. "The smoky flavor throws you a little, when you first taste it," Walbert says. But the ice cream brings everything together.

Sartin's Seafood

3520 Nederland Ave., Nederland, TX 77627; (409) 721-9420; www .sartinsseafood.com **Founded:** 1997

There is no pitmaster at Sartin's Seafood. No wood is used here. But there is a type of barbecue on the menu that you will find only in Texas—or to be more specific, only in the southeast corner of Texas. The item in question is barbecue crabs.

We first learned of these beauties in Robb Walsh's 2012 *Texas Eats* cookbook, where he provides a detailed history of the dish as well as recipes on how to make them. It seems you take a live blue crab, rip the carapace right off, dredge it in barbecue spices, and drop it in the deep fryer. It's a great regional creation, and we're glad Walsh documented its preparation, but we'll leave the cooking up to the professionals. If you want to attempt it yourself, Bolner's Fiesta Spices out of San Antonio markets the spice blend under the name Bar-B-Que Crab Seasoning.

The original Sartin's was in Sabine Pass and it was a legendary place that could, at its zenith, seat up to 500 people, almost all of them picking their way through piles of the succulent crabs. Charles Sartin opened that restaurant, using a recipe he'd developed while working for the Texaco refinery. The story goes that he made dozens of attempts before he was satisfied with the recipe that is still in use today.

Charles Sartin and the original Sartin's are both gone now. In their wake have come several restaurants in the area that offer the dish. The Sartin trademark, however, belongs to Kim Sartin Tucker, Charles Sartin's ex-daughter-in-law and owner of the Nederland restaurant, Sartin's Seafood. She started working at the original Sartin's in 1985 and opened her own spot in 1997. When we were doing our research for this book, we discovered that die-hard barbecue crab fans crowned her spot as being the best, so we knew just where to go to try this specialty.

After a gluttonous day filled with brisket, beef ribs, and more, it may have seemed excessive to order up a plate, which comes with six whole crabs and two sides. Far from it. Every last crab on the plate was picked clean before the waiter was allowed to clear away the mound of broken shells. They're that good. They're also different from boiled crabs in that the frying in vegetable oil causes the meat to stick a little more to the shell. But those barbecue spices with a generous touch of cayenne complement the delicate sweetness of the crabmeat without overwhelming it.

Your crabs come with a choice of sides. Pickled green tomatoes offer a nice acidic touch that cuts through the richness of the crabmeat.

If you can't take the heat, you get the crabs dipped in cornmeal before frying or you can order one of the grilled seafood options. But why would you do that if it's barbecue you're after? These treasures are as unique as the smoked meats in the official barbecue joints that dot the Texas trails, and you owe it to yourself to include at least one stop at Sartin's Seafood for a whole new barbecue experience.

Houston

When we told people that we were headed to Houston for some barbecue, their response was not positive. "Houston has good barbecue?" they asked, incredulously. We heard the same from several pitmasters when we arrived in town. But the answer is yes, you can find good barbecue in Texas's largest city. Part of the reason, we discovered is that there's a new generation of pit bosses on the scene and they have exciting ideas of how their barbecue should look and taste—and they're executing those ideas in ways that'll make you happy. That, in turn, seems to be rejuvenating the old masters, who are practicing their craft according to the same tried-and-true methods they've used for years, only now with a dash more excitement.

All of the attention that has been focused on barbecue, from the media and carnivores alike, has sent people to their cars in search of great new flavors that they can compare with old favorites. So, they're traveling from one end of the city to the other—and across the barbecue lover's favorite street name, Post Oak Boulevard. They're even heading out to the hinterlands of Cypress and The Woodlands because word has spread that the food trucks up north are turning out some of the finest barbecue in the region.

While the benchmark has been raised in the past few years, it's still true that Houston lacks a dominant style of barbecue. Influences from the Deep South, including a love of sweet sauces and baked beans, could be tasted at one place. At another, however, you could encounter the Central Texas reverence for oak with savory pintos on the side. Both are equally valid and help keep Houston's barbecue scene a lively place of diversity, with something for everyone.

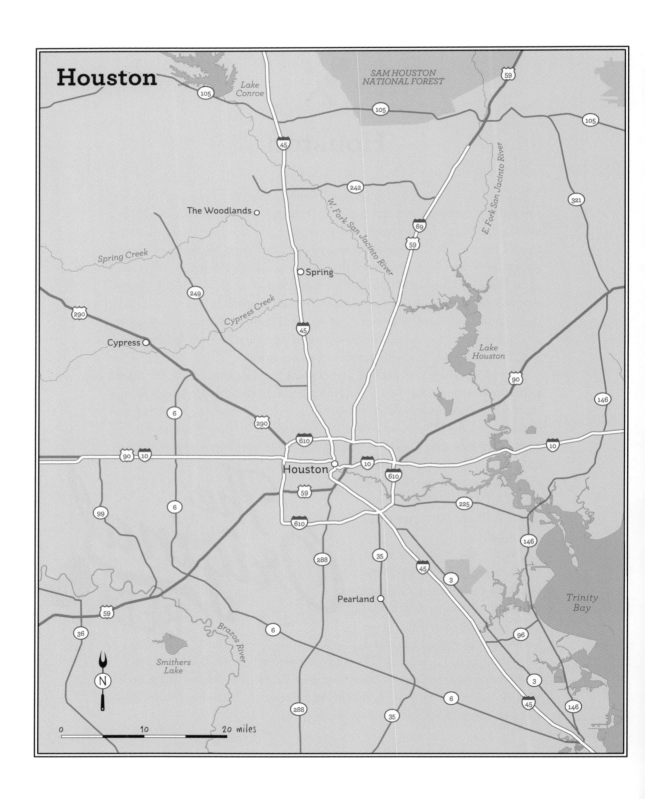

Houston

SAM HOUSTON
NATIONAL FOREST

Lake
Conroe

The Woodlands

Spring Creek

Cypress Creek

W. Fork San Jacinto River

E. Fork San Jacinto River

Spring

Cypress

Lake
Houston

Houston

Smithers
Lake

Brazos River

Pearland

Trinity
Bay

N

0   10   20 miles

The Brisket House

2775 Woodway, Houston, TX 77057, (281) 888-0031; 3217 Center St., Deer Park, TX 77536, (281) 884-8058; thebriskethouse.com **Founded:** 2010 **Pitmasters:** Wayne Kammerl, Jorge Castenoda **Wood:** 60% Oak, 40% Pecan

If the name on the sign says "The Brisket House," that's a pretty firm statement about what the best item on the menu should be.

The owner, Wayne Kammerl, has two restaurants bearing this name, and the brisket is every bit as good as it should be. It's cooked low and slow in a Southern Pride smoker, and the beef comes out juicy, tender, and as smoke-kissed as is expected. That big stainless-steel smoker does have a gas line

leading to it, but the gas is used only to stoke the fire when it runs low. The wood Kammerl uses is a blend of 60 percent oak and 40 percent pecan.

Kammerl might be one of the friendliest guys you'll ever meet, a valuable trait to have for someone who wants to succeed in a hospitality industry—that, along with the ability to work very hard. He's an Aggie who got an engineering degree and worked at Tom's Barbecue & Steakhouse in Bryan. The engineering degree went by the wayside when Kammerl decided he was more suited to the restaurant industry. His career includes a long stint of managing Hard Rock Cafes in a number of cities, including Denver and San Antonio.

"Since I worked at Tom's, I always wanted to do my own barbecue," says Kammerl. "This place came up for lease and I had a best friend who always told me if I wanted to get my own business, he'd help. That was three and a half years ago, and things have been great ever since."

Kammerl was the original pitmaster as well, but has now trained a crew, including Jorge Casteneda, a chef who has a full-time day job at the restaurant next door.

"They say they're better than I am now," Kammerl says, joking. One of his dictums is that his employees consider all the meat they cook a potential competition entry. Would it be good enough to win? Considering that they are cooking pricy Certified Angus Beef, Kammerl is wise to be sure it's treated well.

The pork ribs are tender but not overly so—the meat pulls away from the bone with a little tug, and the top has a good bark, or crust. He uses the St. Louis cut, a shorter rib that he predicts we'll be seeing more of than baby backs, because they produce a more consistent product.

We asked Kammerl about pulled pork's growing popularity. He said that as beef gets more expensive, offering items such as pulled pork, made from the less expensive pork butt (also called shoulder), is a way to recoup some of that cost.

The Brisket House's side dishes are freshly made and include a super-creamy creamed corn and mashed sweet potatoes, as well as loaded baked potatoes and potatoes stuffed with cheese, butter, sour cream, and chives. Salads, slabs of cheddar cheese, whole pickles, and pie by the slice round out a good brisket house menu.

Brooks' Place

18020 FM 529, Cypress, TX 77433; (832) 893-1682; www.brooksplace bbq.com **Founded:** 2009 **Pitmaster:** Trent Brooks **Wood:** Oak, Pecan

"Houston is not known for barbecue," Trent Brooks says bluntly. And the city is not known for being hospitable to food trucks either.

So, what's a pitmaster who wants to sell his barbecue from a food truck supposed to do? Move to where food trucks are more welcome, of course, and proceed to smoke some meats so memorable that people start lining up for them before the 11 a.m. opening.

That's what has happened to Brooks, who parks his truck in front of the Ace Hardware store at a busy intersection in Cypress, a community northwest of Houston. "My customers like the smoky flavor and the tenderness of the meats," he says. That holds true of his brisket, with its black crust and succulent layer of fat; his toothsome ribs; and his chicken, which has an elaborate rub that includes

chicken seasoning and a touch of sugar. The choices are all so popular that his customers often go back and forth on their favorites. Sometimes it's the brisket; other times it could be the ribs or pulled pork.

It wasn't always that way. Brooks struggled to find an audience for his pulled pork. He almost took it off the menu because it just wasn't selling. "Then the *Houston Chronicle* wrote me up," he says. "They put me up against any pulled pork anywhere." That brought a whole new wave of customers, those with a hankering for Southern-style barbecue with plenty of sauce.

In a world with countless baked bean recipes, Brooks's is unique. He loads his with chopped brisket, which is fresh since there are never any leftovers, and he doctors them with a little mustard, crushed red peppers, oregano, and cinnamon as well as his barbecue sauce. He also offers garlic potatoes, a side dish you'll not likely find anywhere—until someone borrows the idea, that is. (He'll also fry or smoke turkeys to order for the holidays. He sets up his eight fryers near the truck and prepares as many as needed.)

Getting into the barbecue business came as something of a surprise to Brooks. "This is not something I planned to do," he says. But when his wife, Norma, wasn't able to work, he decided to try his hand at selling barbecue on the weekends to earn a little extra money. He'd learned the skill from his father, who's a barbecue caterer in the region. A little extra money wasn't the half of it. Soon Brooks was making more in two days from his smoked meats than he was from his weekday job. That was a good thing, because Brooks eventually lost his 9-to-5 job. "I've been fired off every job I ever had," he says with candor. Losing the last one made him realize that he had to make barbecue work.

He eventually bought out a partner he'd had at the beginning and began transforming Brooks' Place into a destination spot for barbecue lovers. Part of the experimentation has been in equipping the truck properly. The cramped quarters have forced him to become creative. His smoker will accommodate up to 25 briskets at one time, but that also means "there is less than 100 square feet of space," he says. Things become challenging when three people, including Norma on occasion, are working there at the same time. Brooks has had to store his wood back at home, which now covers half of his backyard. Only half, he explains, because that's all the space his wife will give him.

All of his efforts are paying off. In 2013 *Houstonia* magazine included Brooks' Place among the best barbecue joints in the city.

"It's a lot of work," Brooks says. "It's harder than anything I've ever done." But it's also the most rewarding work he's ever done, and the freedom that has come with being his own boss suits him.

"I'm in it to make money, sure, but if I don't like the way a brisket looks, I'm not going to sell it for the sake of the money," Brooks says. "We are 100 percent about quality. We don't focus on the numbers. If you're into quality, the numbers will follow."

Burns BBQ

7117 N. Shepherd Dr., Houston, TX 77091; (715) 692-2800
Founded: 2010 **Pitmaster:** Kathy Braden **Wood:** Post Oak

Talk with Kathy Braden about the history of Burns BBQ, and you'll discover that she sees it as the same place that her mother and father, Willie and Roy Burns Sr., started back in 1976. After all, her dad taught her the business. "He showed me everything," she says. "How to make the wood breathe, how to

know when the meat's done . . ." She swears the recipes haven't changed a bit since her parents died more than five years ago. That extends from the meats to the potato salad and baked beans and on to the buttery peach cobbler.

It's the meats, of course, that people keep returning to Burns BBQ for, especially the ribs, which have a good play of tender meat gently attached to the bone. The style of barbecue here is Southern, which means you can expect the meat to arrive covered with a sweet sauce. Houston has made this a legend throughout the city and not just in the black community in which the restaurant is located. You can find jars of it on the shelves of H-E-B and specialty stores in the area. The sauce is a prominent feature of the sandwiches that Braden offers. Her lineup includes the Nikki Special, with chopped meat, a hot link, onions, and peppers, as well as a popular rib sandwich. (Ask about the "Regulars," which are irregular cuts of meat, if you want the burnt ends.) And check out the daily desserts, which could include lemon cake or Southern tea cakes as well as cobbler.

Even though "Mr. Burns," as Braden refers to her father whenever she's talking about the restaurant's background, took her under his wing, he couldn't make the path of being a pitmaster any easier. "It's hard work. Seriously," she says, adding that it's a reason why there are so few women pitmasters in the Houston area. She knows of only one other than herself. But she's willing to teach other women how to smoke ribs that are as sought after as hers. That's the focus of a reality show on BET called *Burns BBQ*, which features Braden teaching the four women who work with her how to do the job.

The days are long, often starting "at 4:30 or 5 in the morning and going on until 9 or 10 at night," Braden says. "Sundays I go to church and I sleep all day after that." Open Sunday for prepaid orders only and closed on Monday.

Corkscrew BBQ

24930 Budde Rd., The Woodlands, TX 77380; (832) 592-1184; www.corkscrewbbq.com **Founded:** 2009 **Pitmaster:** Will Buckman **Wood:** Red Oak

"We sell out daily," Corkscrew BBQ's website says.

"We sell out every day! Please, no whining," reads a sign tacked to the side of the food truck.

"We sell out every day," owners Nichole and Will Buckman say several times a day most every day to customers who have had to wait for who knows how long in line.

So, the lesson you should learn before you head out to the Houston north known as either The Woodlands or Spring, depend-
ing on your map, is one that locals have come to grasp the hard way: Get to Corkscrew as close to the 11 a.m. opening as possible, espe-cially on Saturday, if you want to try a certain item on the menu. Otherwise, you could end up in line watching the list on the "Sold Out" board grow. And "big, big orders," as Nichole Buckman calls them, generally come in for Saturday pickup.

Brisket is a must, and pitmaster Will Buckman tries to make enough of it so it sells

out last. Sometimes he's not successful at doing that. What results is a perfect illustration of how essential beef is to Texas barbecue. When it's announced that the brisket is gone, most of the people in line leave, too. It's that simple. One taste and you'll know exact why this is. One sight, actually, could cause the same epiphany. That's because this meat arrives in a juicy thick cut with a bark on it that is as black as opal and crackly.

You can have the brisket three different ways: cut, in a sandwich, or in a taco. The sandwich is not served up Southern style, Nichole says. She can't bring herself to coat it in sauce, so she'll place it on the side and let the customers doctor theirs to suit their individual tastes. The taco should not be missed, even if you're ordering the brisket cut as well. That's because there's something irresistible about the addition of corn tortillas, *pico de gallo*, cabbage, and Corkscrew's outrageously good green chile ranch dressing. (You can also get the tacos made with pulled pork, turkey, or sausage, if there's any left. See the recipe for Corkscrew BBQ-Style Tacos on p. 225.)

What else is good at Corkscrew? Listen to the people in line and you'll find partisans for every other item on the menu, from the chicken and ribs to the macaroni and cheese and the spinach salad. That's right, you can get your barbecue on top of a bed of spinach with tomatoes, carrots, cabbage, and the like. Or you can get a purely vegetarian salad, which may seem odd for a barbecue joint, even one on wheels. But Nichole insists it has its fan base and, yes, it sells out along with the rest of the menu. "I eat healthy," she says, "and I told [Will] that we were definitely having a spinach salad. We get a lot of trainers, CrossFitters—they all eat salads."

The couple got their start in the catering business before turning to a barbecue food truck. Will had worked for a barbecue joint when he was in high school, but his work for Corkscrew is largely self-taught, he says. Their effort became successful so quickly that they outgrew their first truck and are now ensconced in a second that's just about permanently parked on what had been a vacant greenway by a shopping plaza. A canopy covers a good section of the

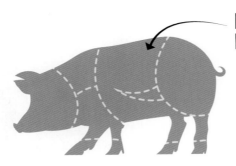

FRESH
BEST IN TOWN!

waiting line as well as two rows of picnic tables. The smokehouse, with red oak ready for burning, is on the opposite side of the lot from the truck. Will says he prefers the wood because of its "middle of the road" flavor. It supports the meat without overwhelming it.

The Buckmans haven't let their fame go to their heads, even though the *Houston Chronicle* has dubbed them the city's answer to Aaron and Stacy Franklin of Austin's lauded Franklin Barbecue. They also don't plan on moving into a brick-and-mortar location despite the acclaim their barbecue has received and the long lines. But they do have plans. "We want to expand on what we have here," Nichole says. That includes getting a beer and wine license (there's a BYOB policy in effect until then) and adding more customer conveniences—all of which will likely make Corkscrew BBQ even more popular. Closed on Sunday.

Gatlin's BBQ & Catering

1221 W. 19th St., Houston, TX 77008; (713) 869-4227; www.gatlinsbbq .com **Founded:** 2010 **Pitmaster:** Greg Gatlin **Wood:** Hickory

We took a few wrong turns finding our way to this small but highly touted establishment in the Heights area of Houston. But the road finally led us to the right place for sampling some excellent barbecue that has gathered a faithful following and awards since it opened in 2010.

Once inside the single dining/ordering room, a tall, friendly fellow greeted us, indicated that yes, he was one of the owners and pitmaster, Greg

Gatlin. He then saw to our orders. He also came outside to sit with us at a picnic table and talk as we dug into what was a very good late lunch. Had we come sooner, we were told, we'd have run into a crowd.

Gatlin cooks with hickory, and his excellent brisket gets a simple salt-and-pepper rub, something that, he says, "lets the beef itself be more prevalent in taste." Salt and pepper, by the way, is the choice of

Wood Smoke: The Primary Seasoning in Texas Barbecue

If you ask Texas pitmasters what their favorite wood is, you'll get different answers from different parts of the state. And sometimes the answers differ in towns relatively close to one another.

Usually, the preferred wood is the one that the pitmaster—and customers—like the best, the one that gives the best results. Just as important is logistics—what wood they can source most efficiently from the trees that grow in their area.

Barbecue experts from Texas A&M University's BBQ Genius Counter addressed the issue at the 2013 Texas Monthly BBQ Festival in Austin. Dr. Jeff Savell of the Meat Science Section of the Department of Animal Science verified what we'd heard from pitmasters across the state: Most pitmasters, if not all, "use the wood that is close at hand." Shipping in loads of oak from Central Texas to a barbecue joint surrounded by acres of mesquite obviously makes no economic sense.

Wood that is close and easy to get, though, isn't always the best choice, Savell says. Soft, sappy woods—conifers such as pine, spruce, fir, or cedar—will give an off flavor to the meat and are not recommended for that reason. Some wood is thought to produce a heavier flavor, though oversmoking with any wood doesn't yield good barbecue.

Texas A&M University's Texas Barbecue website (http://bbq.tamu.edu/bbq-science) has this to say about the woods that smoke foods best:

"Generally, fruit and nut trees make great wood for smoking foods. Specifically, we cook with hardwoods that have low sap/resin content . . . As a rule of thumb, mild-flavored woods like alder and fruit woods are best for foods light on seasoning and sauce. Whereas strongly flavored woods like hickory, mesquite, oak, pecan, and walnut are more suited for foods with a lot of spices/sauce.

"You also shouldn't use green wood that hasn't been cured (dried) or wood that is moldy or lumber scraps (paint, treated, etc.)."

At the San Antonio Stock Show & Rodeo Bar-B-Que Cook-Off & Festival we found contestants running two pits: one for chicken, another for ribs and brisket. The chicken, cooking over direct heat, was fired up with fruitwood—peach and cherry, for instance—while the beef pit was smoking mixtures of mesquite and oak or pure hickory.

The pitmaster might mix and match wood, using one because it will start a fire quick and hot—this is something mesquite is good for—then another, such as oak, for the low and slow cooking process. Even then, they might toss in another wood, such as pecan (or pecan shells), for another level of flavor—using wood as one might mix spices.

Milder-flavored woods like alder and fruitwoods won't overwhelm lightly seasoned chicken or quail or even fish. Woods with stronger flavors—the oak, red oak, hickory, and mesquite, along with the somewhat lighter pecan—are sought out for smoking red meats, adding sublime, smoky perfume and taste that works well with a signature rub, or just salt and lots of pepper, which is the seasoning used by many of the state's top pitmasters.

some of the top barbecuers in the state for the same reason.

The pork ribs had a well-balanced dry rub and were tender and lightly clinging to bone—be sure to add these to your plate. Try both kinds. He makes baby back ribs and the popular St. Louis cut, which has more meat and comes on flatter, rather than curved, bones. Sausage choices are spicy, deer, and smoked.

Gatlin's mom is a key player in this barbecue business, and her recipes for side dishes include the Louisiana-style dirty rice, something not often seen in a typical 'cue joint, as well as smoked corn on the cob. The rice is now firmly lodged in our food-loving databanks, its wonderfulness challenged only by her made-from-scratch banana pudding. The menu includes a list of Texas-size potatoes stuffed with a choice of beef, pork, sausage, turkey, or chicken. Or, throw caution to the wind and try the "loaded" french fries.

We picked up cookies, managed to avert our eyes from the Lemon Butter Pound Cake, but couldn't say no to banana pudding. Not that we dislike vanilla wafers in our banana pudding—they're part of the classic recipe—we just really appreciated the homemade white cake that was sliced and laid in layers between a creamy custard with freshly sliced bananas. We took another to go to have with coffee in the morning. As we finished our meal and licked the top that came off the plastic container of banana pudding, Gatlin laughed and said, "I always do that, too."

Gatlin's is homey and hospitable and serves up some excellent barbecue—don't miss it. Closed on Sunday and Monday.

Pizzitola's Bar-B-Que

1703 Shepherd Dr., Houston, TX 77077; (713) 227-2283; www .pizzitolas.com **Founded:** 1935 and 1983 **Owner:** M. J. Pizzitola **Pitmasters:** Carlton Gould, David Reynosa

Quite a few things about Pizzitola's are out of the ordinary. Part of that is because it's been open for such a long time that there is even a "historical" marker on the front wall. Though the sign declares that the building was not in existence on March 2, 1836, when Texas declared its independence, the barbecue joint has been around long enough to qualify as a landmark on its own. It is approaching its 80th anniversary.

The owner for the past 30 years, M. J. "Jerry" Pizzitola, is at his store every day it's open, tending his staff, greeting customers, and hanging out with

pitmasters Carlton Gould and David Reynosa, who have been with him since he took over the lease on the property.

No one needed to ask them if they loved their jobs. It shows in their faces and in the easy way they react with each other. But these are no ordinary pitmasters. They tend the only brick open-pit barbecue in Houston. (The health department now prohibits this style of cooking, but Pizzitola's was able to have its permit grandfathered in.)

The way the pit works is the meat is laid right over the charcoal on grills. The meats are seared over direct heat, then moved to an area off the fire but close to the smoke, where they pick up plenty of hickory flavor before they're through cooking.

The dining room is draped in team flags and memorabilia, and many of the items were donated by regulars. They add color, but there's only one that means anything to Pizzitola: the maroon and white flag of Texas A&M. He's an Aggie to the core, and he played football during his four years of school there, 1961–64.

He has hired a staff of waitresses who are genuinely friendly as they take you to your table, hand you menus, bring you water, and take your order for barbecue. There's no standing in line, no apprehensive glancing toward a blackboard to see what is coming up sold out. There is always enough food, says Pizzitola, who sat with us at our booth to tell us stories about the build-ing, the people who started the business, and the restaurant's history as we dug into plates of brisket and ribs, plump and savory; crackly sausages made in Cistern by two Czech brothers; and a bowl of simple, tender, and peppery pinto beans—what Pizzitola calls "beans and rice" beans.

There's metal flatware at your table to eat with, and the meat arrives on china. The real cloth napkins at the table are a treat, only to be outdone by the warm, wet linens that come to the table with the food, a welcome touch for those who ordered the ribs.

"Why the linens?" we ask.

"I'm crazy," he responds.

Whenever you're at a barbecue joint, you have to check out any historical photos on the wall. At Pizzitola's, images of the original owner, John Davis, hang near the front door. And if Pizzitola is around, have him share a story or two about his out-of-the-ordinary African-American predecessor, who opened the business during Franklin Roosevelt's administration. In those segregated days, blacks were often forced to go to the back door to conduct any business or even pay a social visit. Davis reversed that practice. In his establishment, blacks could enter his front door to buy barbecue, but whites had to line up out back. The barbecue was so good, nobody seemed to mind where they had to stand in order to buy it. Closed on Sunday.

Virgie's Bar-B-Que

5535 Gessner Dr., Houston, TX 77041; (713) 466-6525; www.virgies bbq.com **Founded:** 2005 **Pitmaster:** Adrian Handsborough **Wood:** Oak

In what once was rural farm area, Adrian Handsborough's parents, Jessie and Virgie Handsborough, opened a burger joint for teens. Since that time the location has been a grocery store and, at one point, a hair salon with a barbe-cue business on the other side. One day, that wall would come down and the business would be devoted to what they did best—barbecue.

Adrian Handsborough grew up cooking at his mom's side, learning the art of smoked meat.

"My mom [Virgie] and me cooked here for [customers] to take home from the store. We'd season the meat in the back of the store and get some wood—I didn't know I was cooking barbecue then. The guy next door sold us the wood, and he had an old barrel pit," Handsborough says. To this day, he cooks with oak—no gas, no electricity. He just burns wood.

A fine pitmaster and conscientious businessman, Handsborough appears to run a tight ship—one visit to the tidy restaurant told us that. Customers line up to buy the pit-smoked brisket, baby backs, beef sausage links, and chicken, and it's all good.

Our favorite, though, was the pork ribs, and these are purely things of beauty. We visited on a Wednesday and a sign on the counter mentioned that day's special of ribs, and we were glad we heeded its call. The blackened crust over the naturally sweet, tender meat came away from the bones with just enough resistance to make our barbecue-loving hearts more than happy. The potato salad and coleslaw were delicious, and if you go for the first time and just order these three things, you'll be happy, too. But you won't go wrong with anything else on the menu.

It hasn't been easy for the Handsboroughs. A fire in 2011 (caused by electrical wiring, not pit issues) set them back a good three months. But when they reopened, the loyal customers came right back.

"It's been a blessing—every quarter since then, we've seen an increase," he says. "I have never looked to market or pump up the product . . . I did do fliers for a couple of weeks. But whenever we need a boost, something happens."

A serious-minded man, Handsborough respects anyone who tackles a pit and makes a living of it. "All barbecuers, all pitmasters, I have much respect for. I know what they endure." Closed on Sunday and Monday.

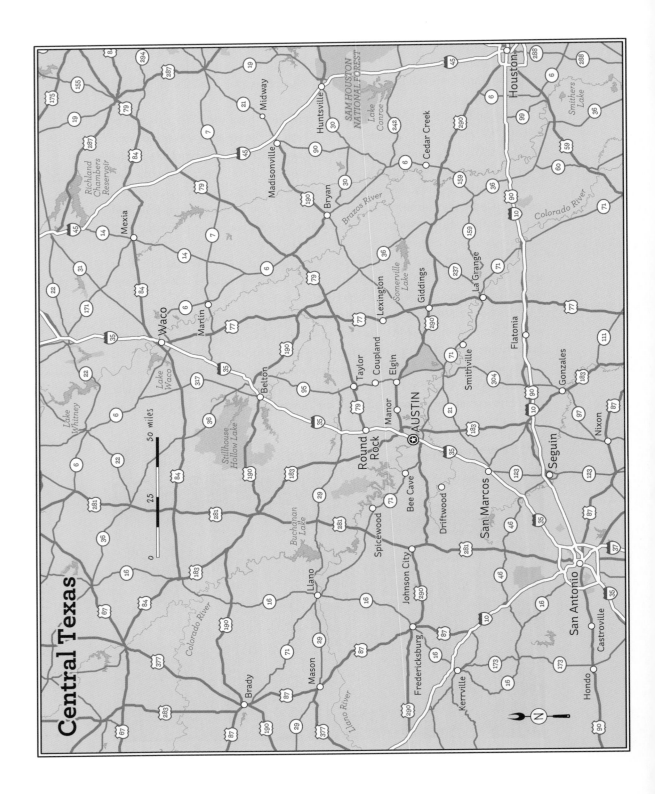

Central Texas

Central Texas

Take your time exploring barbecue in Texas's central region. It covers a vast stretch of land, from Kerrville in the west up to Waco in the north and over to the land this side of the Piney Woods in the east. This is the area that post oak transformed into a barbecue magnet, attracting carnivores from all over the world. And because of that, this is the home of what many people think of as being Texas-style barbecue. As the rest of this book illustrates, however, the matter is not that one-dimensional. Yet, there's also no use denying the appeal of Central Texas barbecue, with its bold flavors infusing every bite of marbled brisket or handmade sausage ring.

The famed barbecue centers Austin, Lockhart, and Luling are all part of Central Texas, though we deal with them in separate chapters. That leaves barbecue joints in plenty of tiny towns such as Marlin, Spicewood, and Midway, places that don't always show up on Texas maps. Yet these people are as serious about the barbecue they produce as many of those with far greater acclaim. The places could be as famous as Louie Mueller Barbecue in Taylor or Snow's BBQ in Lexington, or they could be rising stars, such as Fargo's Pit BBQ in Bryan or Miller's Smokehouse in Belton. At any of these, you can expect to be treated right.

Enjoy the drive. The Texas Hill Country is rolling in wineries and welcoming towns that wear their German and Czech heritage like a charm. In the spring, you won't even mind getting a little lost, just as long as you're on the wildflower trail rambling past open acres filled with carpets of bluebonnets, evening primroses, Indian blankets, and asters.

You won't be able to cover all of Central Texas in a weekend or even a month, so choose your spots carefully and find out exactly when you need to be at a certain place before they run out. In other words, if you want to taste the best of the City Meat Market in Giddings or Snow's, you have to be there bright and early on a Saturday morning. So, you might want to stay in the area overnight. One option would be the Old Coupland Inn and Dancehall, which will fill you up with barbecue and then let you dance it off to some live music before turning in, all in the same place.

Benny's Texas Bar-B-Que

1688 TX 71, Cedar Creek, TX 78612; (512) 332-2812; www.bennys
texasbar-b-que.com **Founded:** 2006 **Pitmaster:** Benny Ochoa
Wood: Post Oak

Benny's Texas Bar-B-Que has your barbecue basics covered. The trio of main meats—brisket, pork ribs, and sausage—as well as the three expected sides are all available. But owner Benny Ochoa doesn't stop there. He's open for break-

fast every day but Monday, with tacos stuffed with whatever egg combination you'd like, from beans to bacon. There are even brisket and egg tacos to get your barbecue trip off to a great start. But you don't want to overlook the Big Ben, an over-size burrito-like treat in which a couple of tortillas are stuffed with eggs, potato, beans, slices of sausage, and a thick cut of bacon all covered in *pico de gallo*.

The smoked meats come out at lunch, which is when you'll find Ochoa's juicy beef ribs with the full bone. But you'd better hurry: They sell out early. If you're lucky to get a serving, make sure you get them with green beans boast-ing the tang of vinegar and onion, and smashed new pota-toes—that is, if they're offered

that day. Just grab one of the picnic tables in front of the wooden shack and relax while the traffic whizzes by on Highway 71.

The brisket is thinly cut, with a good smoke ring and a generous amount of post oak smoke filtering through each bite. It may appear to be on the dry side, but there's actually a good amount of juice in it. It is served with a sweet tomato sauce on it, unless you ask for it otherwise. The chopped beef sandwiches, with the brisket and sauce married to good effect, have a strong local following. The chicken also has its partisans because it's moist while the smoke offers good support to the natural meat flavor without overwhelming it.

You should also enjoy the hospitality of Debra Ochoa, Benny's wife, who handles the orders and makes you feel right at home. That's as important to enjoying your visit to a barbecue joint as the banana pudding. And Benny's delivers on both. Closed on Monday.

Bill's Bar-B-Que

1909 Junction Hwy., Kerrville, TX 78028; (830) 895-5733; www.bills bbq.net **Founded:** 1982 **Pitmaster:** Joe Marino Jr. **Wood:** Live Oak
The delicious smell of smoke and meat is the barbecue trail's most irresistible charm, and you'll be wrapped in it before you pull into the parking lot at Bill's Bar-B-Que. This homey-looking restaurant in Kerrville has been in the family for the past three decades, and it's chock-full of mementos, from photos to beer signs and animal heads on the walls, that help tell the story.

Joe Marino Jr. and his wife, Jane, own Bill's. Friendly and talkative, Marino will tell you those stories himself if he can take time off from manning the big outdoor pits, where all of the meat that's served at Bill's gets a good dose of live oak smoke. During this everyday task, Marino is careful about consistency as well as quantities. "I'd rather run out than serve leftovers," he says.

Marino says the meaty beef and pork sausages, firm in snap and texture, are sourced from Fredericksburg's specialty meats house, Dutchman's Market Inc. They are good enough to be his top-selling item.

The ribs are good, too—don't miss them. The smoky heat works its magic on the crust, blackening it and protecting the delectable meat. Justly touted as one of the top items, they're cooked fresh every day.

Marino seems to have a special touch with pork, though, as the pork rump roast is another not-to-miss meat. It's served in manageable chunks, not shreds, and sports more of that blackened bark that might be the only thing holding the meat together. It's that tender.

The decor at Bill's Bar-B-Que leans to Texana, and the mounted heads on the walls add to the local color. One trophy, however, is said to be a head of the terrible chupacabra. (You won't have much trouble picking it out.) Most folks consider this a mythical beast, yet sightings are reported now and then, generally during television sweeps months. It's Texas's version of the yeti. How did that fearsome head get on the wall? Ask Joe Marino Jr.—or one of the staff.

The brisket, both lean and fatty, has the required smoke ring and dark crust that accompany well-smoked tender beef. Marino uses a beer and vinegar sop and does some foil wrapping to help ensure consistency. The brisket receives a good 11 hours of smoke, he says. Turkey breast, in addition to the smoke, sports a robust black pepper seasoning, and the meaty slices are as moist as any turkey we found on the Texas barbecue trail.

The side dishes are made according to recipes from Marino's mom, Sharon. We liked the bright taste of pimiento in the creamy-textured potato salad, as well as the sweetness to the coleslaw that provided a good balance to the vinegary edge in the potato salad. Whether for his restaurant customers or busy catering service, Bill's does the basics right—and then some. Closed on Sunday and Monday.

Buzzie's Bar-B-Q

213 Schreiner St., Kerrville, TX 78028; (830) 257-4540; www.buzzies bbq.com **Founded:** 1997 **Pitmaster:** Harold E. Hughes **Wood:** Mesquite, Oak

Buzzie's Bar-B-Q sits off Kerrville's main streets and the entrance is even removed a bit from the road it's on, but that certainly hasn't stopped any Texas barbecue hounds from finding it. The qualities of this place, run by Harold E. "Buzzie" and Brenda Hughes, seem to mount quickly from the moment you step inside the door. First, you'll notice how immaculate the spacious interior appears under the bright lights and how family-friendly it seems.

Leftover Barbecue: Treat It Right and Eat It!

Leftover barbecue can be good in anything from chopped meat sandwiches to stir-fry. It's just a matter of careful refrigeration and even more careful reheating. Treat it with the care that you or the pitmaster originally did. Rather than microwaving it, wrap it in foil and place it in a low oven, letting it warm up slowly without overheating. We've added a little water to sliced pork that was thoroughly cooked to help with the moisture content when it's reheated.

Reheats: Sliced brisket will taste fine, just the way you had it the first time—slowly reheated and served with leftover beans and coleslaw and a slice or two of white bread. The same goes for the rest of the meats, as long as they were good to begin with. Watch that you don't overcook sliced sausage, though, as those juicy, tender slices toughen up fast.

Sandwiches: If you kept some of the barbecue sauce from the restaurant and have some sliced raw onion and dill pickles, make sandwiches. Pulled pork, brisket, rib meat, barbecued chicken—it will all work on sliced bread or a hamburger bun, if it's chopped, dressed with the sauce, and warmed up. You can also use this chopped meat on top of a baked potato with sour cream, chives, and cheese added to the mix.

Tacos: Our intro to the brisket taco was more than 20 years ago at a long-gone San Antonio barbecue restaurant. They used good, smoky fresh brisket, not leftover, wrapped in tortillas that were hot off the grill. Since that time we've used nearly every kind of leftover barbecue in tacos. Add cabbage or coleslaw, barbecue sauce, or even *pico de gallo* (a raw, chopped salsa made with hot green chiles, tomato, onion, and cilantro) to your taco.

Breakfast: Barbecue for breakfast is never out of the question. Barbecued sausage and scrambled eggs are good, and shredded brisket and eggs, with salsa stirred in, are fine, too.

Stir-fry: This suggestion came from owner and pitmaster Joe Marino Jr. at Bill's Bar-B-Que in Kerrville. Leftover barbecued chicken is stir-fried with vegetables, and his clientele goes for it. Chicken (meat off the bone), pork, and beef can probably even take a dousing or two of soy sauce. Be bold.

When you get to the meat counter, you'll encounter a sign warning you that "extra lean brisket" costs an extra $3 per pound, a move that never fails to raise a chuckle from those of us who want our brisket moist and marbled. And that's the best way to describe Buzzie's version, with its generous smoke flavor mingled with the natural beef richness and a welcome red ring under a coating of black bark.

Good beans are always worth singling out, and Buzzie's beans score, thanks to a thick broth and a good peppery kick.

The pork ribs are old-fashioned in the best way: You will have to hold the bone in one hand and just let your mouth rip every tasty morsel of meat from it. (You may want to scope out Buzzie's for a Wednesday visit, when it's all-you-can-eat rib day.) Pork loin, turkey, and ham, along with chicken and sausage, are also available, either sliced or in sandwiches. Sides included the expected coleslaw, potato salad, and some fine, peppery beans, while your dessert choices are cobbler three ways: peach, cherry, or blackberry.

There's a help-yourself bar in one corner of the main dining area where you can get your sauce, while the other is taken up by a rarity in Texas barbecue joints: a soup and salad bar. We didn't try it, but it was as well-tended as the rest of the restaurant and looked like a refreshing alternative on those days when you just don't want 'cue. When those days are, we don't know.

By the way, if the name Buzzie's rings a bell, perhaps it's because Buzzie himself appeared on the TV show *BBQ Pitmasters* and came out a winner in the brisket and cowboy steak competition. Closed on Monday.

Cele Store

18726 Cameron Rd., Manor, TX 78653; (512) 869-9340; www.celestore .com **Founded:** 1951

The menu at the Cele Store changes depending on the day you visit. On Thursday evenings, you can have your choice of sausage wraps or baby back ribs. On Fridays and Saturdays, brisket, sausage, and ribs are offered. All of the above are worth trying, especially since the rub boasts a simple but effective blend of salt and pepper to season, not overwhelm, the meat. It's all

smoked in the old-fashioned brick pit that's been a fixture at the general store for decades.

Just be aware, when you visit this roadside attraction, that the building itself is as famous as any meats served here. That's because the exterior of the building, which dates back to the 1890s, has been featured in a number of movies. Key scenes in both *Secondhand Lions* and *A Perfect World* were filmed there, as well as the first three installments of the Texas Chainsaw Massacre movies.

But the Cele Store is no museum. It's a vital part of the Manor community, thanks to both the barbecue and the live music, which brings people together for a chance to relax or dance the night away. Open Thursday through Saturday.

City Meat Market

101 W. Austin St., Giddings, TX 78942; (979) 542-2740 **Founded:** Early 1940s **Pitmaster:** Gerald Birkelbach **Wood:** Post Oak

The traffic zooming past the intersection of Main and Austin Streets (aka US 290 and US 77) in Giddings seems hell-bent on getting out of town as quickly as possible. It's too bad more of those racers don't take the time to check out the once-thriving downtown area. Tough times may have affected the area's fortunes somewhat, but the City Meat Market is still going strong after more than 75 years in business.

The business day begins at 7:30 a.m., and barbecue lovers know to get there early if they want the full array of meats offered, which includes brisket, sausage, pork ribs, and chicken, and if they want to avoid really long lines. On Saturday the first smoked meats are ready as soon as the doors open, owner Gerald Birkelbach says; during the week the barbecue's ready about an hour later.

Every item sells out every day, but no one knows the order in which they'll disappear. Ribs were gone by the time we dropped by, so we dried our tears

with some mighty, moist brisket, including end cuts encrusted with plenty of salt and black pepper. Sausage is equally praised here, and the recipe used dates back to the market's opening in the early 1940s. It's a loosely ground beef-pork blend that shrinks a little within its skin during smoking, but that doesn't bother the flavor any, which gets a boost once again from a good dose of black pepper. Birkelbach has been making the sausage since he bought the market in 1982, and he admits he's had to tweak the recipe slightly in recent years because a growing number of customers have asked for a leaner, drier link than before. Chicken is the unsung hero, not overly smoky but tender, with enough natural juices to keep it from drying out.

There is a meat market, which you pass through if you use the Austin Street entrance. Then you hit the dining room, which appears to be covered with its own layer of smoke, which is just right for a barbecue joint. On the walls you'll find photos of some of City Meat Market's more famous customers, including Lyle Lovett, Willie Nelson, and George Straight. The final stretch of this lengthy building is the pit area, which is about 3 feet behind the counter where you order your meal. Your carver simply reaches into the pit, grabs a brisket or a chicken, and starts cutting away to your likes before heaping the meat on butcher paper and weighing it out.

As soon as an item runs out, Birkelbach will step out and announce that to the line. The news rarely makes a difference to the out-of-towners who have driven miles to get a taste of the most lauded barbecue in Giddings. The only

Busy Days on the Barbecue Calendar

You can probably guess the busiest days in a Texas barbecue joint's year: Christmas Eve, New Year's Day, game days on TV. But would you have put the day after Thanksgiving high on your list? That's right, Black Friday, as retailers call it, is a time when pits across the state are strained to the max. The reason is easy to explain, says Gerald Birkelbach, owner and pitmaster of City Meat Market in Giddings: "After one day of turkey, people have had enough of that. They want barbecue."

people who leave before everything is gone are the locals. "Sometimes, they'll take a look at the line and say, 'Oh, no. I'm not waiting. I'll come back Monday,'" he says. And they do.

There's plenty of history within these walls, including the story that the City Meat Market is the place where Tootsie Tomanetz of Snow's in Lexington first learned how to tend an oak-fired pit. She still buys her sausage from City Meat Market, and so can you, giving you the chance to have your own taste of Giddings when you get back home. Closed on Sunday.

Cooper's Old Time Pit Bar-B-Que
604 W. Young St., Llano, TX 78643; (325) 247-5213; www.coopersbbq llano.com **Founded:** 1962 **Pitmaster:** Louis Garcia **Wood:** Mesquite
While there are three Cooper's Old Time Pit Bar-B-Que restaurants in Texas (and one planned for Austin in the fall of 2014), the one in Llano is the original,

owned by Jason Wootan. Its name and motto, Home of the Big Chop, have spread beyond the state lines. Even on the cold day we were there, there was a line ahead of us awaiting turns at a warming pit where all the meat is laid out, fragrant with the mesquite used for the direct-heat cooking and speckled with a delicious-looking seasoning—the same seasoning used on all the meats.

First rule: Do get their specialty, big pork chops. They are about a pound each, juicy and beautiful as they beckon from the grill. But there are plenty of other choices; ask for a slice or two of brisket—it's good. Your carver will show you exactly where he'll slice and how much, cut off a section of pork ribs or slice of prime rib, still pink in the center. And there's more—chicken with a seasoned gleam, rib eye steak (after 5 p.m.), an assortment of sausages (we liked the jalapeño cheese), beef ribs—the list goes on.

From there on it's pretty much the regular barbecue-joint drill: The meat is weighed and wrapped in butcher paper, you pick up side dishes and head to one of the long tables in the big dining room, or across a breezeway to an overflow room. The long tables are set with condiments and rolls of paper towels, a loaf of white bread, and a gallon jar of pickles.

Even if you're not a sauce user, give Cooper's a try. It's a thin, vinegary style that we like better than sweeter versions found elsewhere. It's especially good for dipping in chunks of pork chops, a taste that haunts our memory and calls us to head up to the Hill Country for more.

For side dishes, we recommend the peel-on red potato salad with just a bit of minced pimiento. And don't miss the blackberry cobbler. It's served warm with plenty of the crusty topping.

Talking with several of the employees we'd seen out working in the pit area, including one of the pitmasters, Louis Garcia, we found that these men train many of the cooks that go on to the restaurant's other locations in New Braunfels and Fort Worth. They also pointed out that the original Cooper's has an edge on atmosphere as well—it has just "more of a rustic, back-home country atmosphere," Garcia said.

As we sat down to eat, another group of diners nearby were finishing up, admonishing one of the older men who didn't show the same inclination to hurry and pack it up.

"Don't eat too much—you'll get burnt out," one said.

His mild response was, "Well, I don't see how you can get burnt out on this."

Our thoughts exactly.

Cooper's Pit Bar-B-Que

502 San Antonio St., Mason, TX 76856; (325) 347-6897 **Founded:** 1955
Pitmaster: Duard Dockel **Wood:** Mesquite

The legendary pitmaster George Cooper opened his first restaurant here in the mid-1950s. He's not with us anymore, but his restaurant is—and it's still being operated in keeping with his standards. Making sure of that is Duard Dockel, who bought the place in 1983 after working with Cooper for 10 years. He still makes everything according to the original recipes.

Not too many places in Texas offer cabrito sausage, and Cooper's version is the best we've sampled.

This place—not to be confused with the unrelated Cooper's Old Time Pit Bar-B-Que in nearby Llano or the Cooper's in Junction—has come to be known as one of the best barbecue joints for that most traditional of West Texas meats: *cabrito.* Yes, you can get a shoulder of goat, the backstrap, or, better still, house-made goat sausage, as well as enormous beef ribs, pork chops, and, on weekends, pork loin in addition to the best-selling brisket, pork ribs, chicken, and regular sausage.

This Cooper's operates like a meat market. You stand by the pit, looking over the extensive selection, and pick out what you want, which will be served to you on butcher paper. You pay by the pound, and the sides you want are extra. In other words, there are no two-meat plates or sandwiches. But you can get small amounts of four meats to try, if you want, and if you are hungry for a sandwich, then just make one up. The bread, the sauce, the pickles, the onions, and even the jalapeños are all available in the dining room, so you can fix everything just the way you like it. And if you have any leftovers, you simply wrap them in the butcher paper it was sold to you in and you're set to go. There are no frills, nothing really to detract from the reason you're at Cooper's in the first place: to get some good meat.

If you want to bring the taste of Cooper's home to your own pit, you can even buy the mop, or basting sauce, as it's called here, plus the red sauce.

Cranky Frank's Barbeque Company

6079 US 87 South, Fredericksburg, TX 78624; (803) 997-2353; www
.crankyfranksbbq.com **Founded:** 2003 **Pitmasters:** Dan Martin,
Glenn Wilke **Wood:** Mesquite

The sign of good barbecue at Cranky Frank's Barbeque Company wasn't the
bold, printed one at the entrance of the highway. The scent of smoke is a clue,
but the real giveaway is people—barbecue lovers hitting the line before 11 a.m.
to get some of Cranky Frank's brisket or to make a late breakfast out of a sausage plate or super-stuffed potato. Or to grab some meat by the pound to take
home.

The building has been a barbecue joint for the past 30 years, and the
interior, while vintage, is bright with red walls, neon beer signs, wood-grain
composition tables, business cards pasted to the counter area, pick-up publications, and free bumper stickers. Side dishes are self-serve, from chafing
dishes set up just past the ordering counter.

The Martins moved in 10 years ago and brought with them little in the way
of experience in the barbecue restaurant business.

"We learned as we went," Kala Martin said. "It was expensive. It took a
while to learn—and really, any education is expensive."

They named the restaurant after their son, now 11, whose middle name
is Frank. He was a cranky baby, but he's not so much anymore, his mom says.

The Martins learned the right way, judging by the good results. Dan Martin uses indirect heat in a wood-fired brick oven, starting in the wee hours of
the morning. He makes enough for a day's serving, and they close when it's
gone.

At the counter you'll be asked "marbled or lean," and the cutting is done
in plain sight, the best way for customers to really see
what they're getting, ask for particulars, or maybe
change their minds.

The brisket boasts the benefit of long, slow cooking in smoke from well-aged mesquite (the only wood
they use). Brisket is the big seller, but the loaded
stuffed potato as well as the Boatload, with Fritos,
beans, chopped beef, and cheese, sell fast as well.
For kids, the most popular item is the chopped beef
barbecue sandwich—it's easy for them to hold and
tasty with plenty of sauce. Closed every Monday
and the first Sunday of each month.

Curly's Carolina, TX

112 E. Main St., Round Rock, TX 78664; (512) 537-9227; www.curlys carolinatx.com **Opened:** 2013 **Pitmasters:** Jay Yates, John Brotherton **Wood:** Oak, Pecan, Hickory

When we tried to find Curly's, our smartphone searches sent us first to a couple of vacant lots. But we persevered and finally discovered the joint nestled in Round Rock's charming Main Street. Once inside the door, we found ourselves standing behind a woman and her very young son, who were placing their order.

Mom: So, what would you like to eat?

Son: I want pig.

That was our reaction, too, when we saw the menu, with its variety of pulled pork sandwiches topped with the likes of smoked cheese, mustard sauce, and, of course, coleslaw. This place is a dream come true for every Carolina native

who hungers for a taste of barbecue like they have back home, and the folks we've sent since our visit have come back singing its praises for that very reason.

Though Curly's had only been open a short while when we dropped in, the owners proved they were up on their history by offering a Sam Bass Shootout sandwich, which features chopped brisket, smoked sausage, smoked bacon, and smoked Gouda, all in honor of a shootout that occurred on this very block of Main Street back in 1878.

We settled in with a satisfying Wolfpack sandwich (pulled pork, bacon, smoked Gouda, and Carolina sauce) and a three-meat plate of brisket, pork ribs, and sausage. We would have included beef ribs in that, but they had sold out by the time we arrived, which was only about 90 minutes after they'd opened for the day. If the meat we had was an indication, those beef ribs must be wonderful. The brisket had the right amount of black crust, a robust smoke ring, and moisture throughout each succulent slice, while the pork ribs had an appealingly sweet rub over tender meat that filled your mouth with all the pig flavor you want.

As we were finishing up, one of the owners, Jay Yates, came around to talk to us. He mentioned that the sausage, good as it was, would likely be better on our next visit because Curly's was expanding. And the new space would include an area where sausage could be made and cheeses, including Gouda and cheddar, could be smoked.

It seems that Yates and his business partner, John Brotherton, who also joined us, both had food trucks in the area specializing in barbecue, one of which had parked at various times in both of those vacant lots. They joined forces on a sit-down restaurant that capitalizes on their twin successes of pulled pork and beef. They have also brought the Deep South and bit of Asian fusion with them by way of a variety of side dishes, including a wasabi cole-slaw in addition to a regular version, as well as a cucumber salad in rice wine vinegar, hush puppies, house-made potato chips, and a buttery pan-fried corn bread. The desserts are worthy variations on two 'cue classics: There's banana pudding with an airy, whipped texture as well as plenty of fruit, and a pecan pie loaded with caramelized bacon.

When they developed the name for their place, Brotherton and Yates decided to merge the Carolina roots of their pulled pork with the Texas emphasis on beef and brisket in particular. It turns out that there actually was once a Carolina, Texas, which was incorporated in the 1850s. It was a community founded by immigrants from the Carolinas. "We got lucky on that one," Yates says.

And we got lucky finding Curly's. Open Thursday through Sunday.

Davila's Bar-B-Que

418 W. Kingsbury St., Seguin, TX 78155; (830) 379-5566 **Founded:** 1959 **Pitmaster:** Daniel Ramirez **Wood:** Mesquite

The Davila family has a long history in Texas. The old-time photos on the wall are family, including grandfathers and great-grandfathers. Sit down with Adrian Davila, and he'll share with you a printed genealogical record that starts back in the late 1780s and includes a professional trick roper, Alexander "Tex" McLeod, who achieved a measure of fame working in silent films.

The family opened a meat market in the early 1950s, then moved to Lockhart in 1957, where they began the business of barbecue. In 1959 the Davilas headed to Seguin, where the barbecue restaurant and the family have been ever since. The current address is the sole location now, as the Davilas recently closed the store on N. Highway 123 Bypass. "We were operating two restaurants and a food truck, and killing ourselves," Davila says.

Now, along with pitmaster Daniel Ramirez, Adrian Davila and his dad, Edward Davila, are concentrating on putting out mesquite pit-smoked lamb ribs, brisket, and pork ribs, along with some homespun dishes such as nachos, burgers, po'boy sandwiches, smoked turkey drumsticks, and fried shrimp and catfish. There's no alcohol, but a bottle of A&W Root Beer and iced tea were fine for us during a mid-afternoon visit.

Tender lamb ribs and pork ribs are two of the items not to miss. The meat pulls off the bone easily, but not too easily. The pork is brushed with just a touch of sweet-tangy sauce. The sausage is peppery and made well, in terms of both the assertive flavor and the firm texture of smoky, medium-grind meat in well-stuffed casings. Two barbecue sauces, one mild and one spicy, are your choices, and we recommend you go with the spicy, especially with the sausage, which it seems to have been made to match.

It's traditional barbecue with a few new touches. Davila says he's considering adding pulled pork, a rising star on the Texas barbecue scene, to the

menu in the near future. "We gotta keep up with the times," he says. "It's a balancing act—doing what we do and doing it well."

Fargo's Pit BBQ

720 N. Texas Ave., Bryan, TX 77803; (979) 778-3662 **Founded:** 2000 **Pitmaster:** Alan Caldwell **Wood:** It's a secret.

Don't ask Alan Caldwell what wood he uses to smoke his delicious barbecue. He won't answer you. And he won't show you his pit either. It's not that he's surly or mean about it, but it is his secret—and he plans to keep it that way. So, when a posse of barbecue travelers tried to peek through the covered chain-link fence he'd built around the pit, he was forced to enclose the pit area within high cinderblock walls. If that doesn't kill your curiosity, then maybe you'll have to rent a helicopter and fly low overhead.

But why concentrate on what happens out back when you could be filling up on well-marbled brisket with a smoke ring that you know wasn't faked with an injection? (Lean brisket is available, but you should opt for the good stuff when you're asked.) Ribs, chicken, and sausage all have their fans, so any and all of the meats are worth piling up into a multiple meat combination meal.

Caldwell's partner in Fargo's is Belender Wells, who manages the counter service and makes sure the customers feel right at home. Both of them learned the business from family. "I got mine working with my father and Alan with his family," Wells says. So, they both consider themselves to be the second generation of barbecue masters, and they're passing on their knowledge and gifts to the third generation, including Wells's son, Maurice Wells, and Caldwell's niece, Fenecia Caldwell. "We're cooking through family experience," Wells says.

For 12 years Fargo's operated out of a take-out-only stand, which a Swedish magazine called a "kiosk." But in 2013 they moved into a larger place with a dining area. It was a good move, because they needed the extra space when they landed on *Texas Monthly*'s widely read Top 50 list. It brought in many newcomers who were treated to some fine barbecue and a heavy dose of Texas A&M memorabilia. And why not? The school is in nearby College Station.

Newcomers will discover that Wells, who had 35 years of food service experience before opening Fargo's with Caldwell, won't settle for the usual side dishes of beans, potato salad, and coleslaw. "We just try to incorporate something different," she says. So she mixes her lineup with choices that could include Cajun-style red beans or a seafood salad with shrimp and Krab in it. Plus, you can get the sides in the size you like, from 4 ounces for those who prefer to concentrate on the meat to 16 ounces for those who want to share with their family.

Everything you try at Fargo's is infused with "one big pot of life experiences," Wells says. And no small amount of smoke, though what type of smoke it is remains Fargo's big secret. Closed on Sunday and Monday.

Hays Co. Bar-B-Que & Catering

1612 S. I-35, San Marcos, TX 78666; (512) 932-6000; www.hayscobbq .com; @Hayscobbq **Founded:** 2007 (previously Woody's BBQ) **Pitmasters:** Michael Aaron Hernandez, Omar Serna **Wood:** Post Oak We visited Hays Co. Bar-B-Que before they moved into their new location at the address above. We have to say, the previous location we visited did house one of the nicest areas for pit smokers we'd seen on the barbecue trail.

In a huge, screened-in room were several monstrous pits, post oak fires crackling while fall breezes tossed the still-leafy branches of surrounding trees. While the cool October temperatures outside blew in some natural air-conditioning, the two pit bosses showing us around, Michael Aaron Hernandez and Omar Serna, said midwinter finds them huddling between the two fires at adjacent pits. Midsummer in the open-air pit room brings its own challenges, of course.

The two may be a decade or more apart in age, but their passion for pit-smoked meat was obviously shared. Serna had been a house painter before the dangers of that business began to worry him (scaffolding was a particular danger he mentioned). He'd worked in barbecue before and was very grateful for the opportunity to return to it at Hays Co. Hernandez, at the age of 20, has caught the bug, too.

"It's great, I'm not thinking about anything else I want to do. I'm in it until I retire," Hernandez says. He feels pride in the fact that he's reportedly the youngest pitmaster in the state of Texas. He admits that it won't be long before the "youngest" distinction changes, if for nothing but the passage of years. He may be the youngest, but having started at the age of 14, he's no neophyte.

Hernandez's step-father, co-owner Michael Hernandez, was his teacher. "He was taught a little about pits by the former owner and mastered it by himself—then taught it to us," says the younger Hernandez. His mother, Asenette Hernandez, is the other owner.

Seated in a spacious dining room later, we appreciated the tender brisket, with its melting layer of fat and ample crust of simple salt and pepper, smoked to a thick, dark bark. Certified Angus Beef is what Hays Co. uses—and treats with care.

Quality is important, but equally vital is consistency. "One of the biggest killers in the business is lack of consistency," says Hernandez, words we'd heard from far older and more seasoned pitmasters.

The sausage, made in-house, was one of our favorite styles: a firm texture within shiny, tight casings and well-balanced seasoning—just the right amount of salt. It was good with one of the two sauces Hays Co. makes, especially a lighter-colored sauce with a sweetly fruity flavor.

A robust crust on the pork ribs covered a generous portion of pink meat just right to the tooth. As we headed out, Hernandez cut us a sliver of pork chop off the bone. That was dessert. We took this snack on the road with us. It was juicy and had the same good salt-and-pepper crust. What really came through, in addition to the smoke, was the real, honest porky flavor polished with a little crackling fat.

We think Hays Co. Bar-B-Que & Catering is a place to watch—they have the passion. Serna puts it well: "I always liked cooking barbecue. It's a hot, dirty job, but I wouldn't have it any other way. I like getting here early in the morning, starting the fire—and playing with knives."

The new location, where Hays Co. was preparing to move when we visited, is supposed to have a pit even more "gi-normous" than the one we saw. Also, there will be live music, beer sales, and a play area for the kids. "It'll be more family-oriented," Hernandez says. Closed on Sunday.

Jasper's Bar-B-Que

105 Clifton St., Waco, TX 76704; (254) 732-0899; www.jaspers barbecue.com; @jaspersbbq **Founded:** 1919 **Pitmaster:** J. D. Bost **Wood:** Pecan

The history of Jasper's Bar-B-Que is as well-seasoned as its meat. Jasper DeMaria began the business back in 1919 at what was the last stop of the Interurban Railroad before people moved on to Dallas. It was the first year after the end of World War I, and Waco was facing great changes. The Elite Cafe, which would be the first place in town to use refrigeration, opened. So did a Baptist hospital, now known as Hillcrest Baptist Medical Center. On the minus side, the city lost its Texas League baseball team, the Waco Navigators. None of that must have mattered to the commuters who simply wanted a butcher paper–wrapped package of beef or sausage and a Coke as cold as it could be to wash it down.

Jasper's has changed hands over the years, but the place has retained some of its original appeal, even if the neighborhood it's in has faced a downturn in fortunes. Today, you still get your food on butcher paper, but the lineup has grown to include ribs (available every day), chicken, and bologna, all of which can be purchased by the pound, by the serving, or in a sandwich. You can even mix a few items in options such as the Big Creek (chopped brisket and two ribs) or the Big-Tex Sandwich (two meats and three slices of bread). Whatever you try, make sure you get the ribs—and maybe even some more ribs after that. They are tender but not so overcooked that they fall off the bone. As Goldilocks would say, they're just right.

Instead of barbecue sauce, Jasper's offers what it calls gravy, made from DeMaria's original recipe. It's one of those love-it-or-hate-it items that must be tried at least once. It's made with meat juices and spices and who knows what all. If you love it, just dip a corner of your sandwich in and let the bread sop up its meaty goodness.

Get to Jasper's early. The "sold out" sign gets posted on a regular basis, most often by 1:30 p.m., one of the employees, Stan Haugh, says. Closed on Sunday.

Joel's Bar-B-Q

I-10 West and FM 609 (exit 661), Flatonia, TX 78941; (361) 865-2454; www.joelsbarbq.com **Founded:** 1978–79 **Founder:** Joycelyn Kubesch **Pitmaster:** Chris Kubesch **Wood:** Mesquite

Over the years, many a highway traveler has stopped at Joel's Bar-B-Q. The shack-like structure on the north side of the interstate might not catch everyone's eye—there are far shinier, newer pit stops along that stretch between San Antonio and Houston—but it's been one of our traditional stops for the past 25 years.

The rustic structure itself is one-of-a-kind, a mix of building materials (logs and mortar, stone) with large mesh screens that cover the window openings. No glass. The big butcher case just inside the door is an attention-grabber, too, with homemade pickles, sausage, peppered bacon, and other offerings that are fun to look at, even if you're just dropping by for a sandwich or a brisket plate.

In addition to mesquite-fired pit-smoked brisket, handmade sausage, and sliced pork sandwiches on traditional white bread, we also recommend Joel's really good potato salad.

Joel's started off as a smoker parked wherever the owners, Joycelyn Kubesch and her husband at the time, Joel Kubesch, could find space and pull in some clientele. That was in 1978. A year later they decided they needed

a more permanent home and built what is now the kitchen area on the site where Joel's still stands.

The indoor picnic tables rest next to those rough-hewn walls, and the blackboard menu next to the ordering stand is carefully hand-printed in colored chalk. There are fliers on the wall and door, and the traffic roars a few hundred feet away. Folks who reside in the area swing up to the door in their big trucks and are usually good for a smile.

The fact that the restaurant is so close to an interstate freeway also draws in some interesting characters. A favorite memory we have is sitting at our picnic table eating our sandwiches one summer afternoon when a big pink-and-white RV pulled into the gas station next door. A dazzling creature with platinum-white hair falling down past her knees, wearing short-shorts and glittery platform shoes, and as pleasant as could be, left the vehicle and walked on over. Exotic dancers love good barbecue as much as the rest of us. Closed on Sunday.

Johnson Bar-B-Que

12148 TX 21 East, Midway, TX 75852; (936) 349-0067 **Founded:** 2011
Pitmaster: Wiley W. Johnson Jr. **Wood:** Post Oak, White Oak, Pecan, Hickory

Midway is one of those tiny towns (population 227) that most of us would only stumble upon while passing through from one place to the next. In this scenario, the way would be southwest out of Nacogdoches on what's known as

the Old San Antonio Road, or Highway 21.

Wiley W. Johnson Jr. left Midway several decades ago to join the service. He returned home a few years ago and opened a barbecue joint in an old gas station. The sign out front promises "Soul Food, BBQ and Car Wash," in case your vehicle needs a cleaning while you enjoy your food.

Though Midway is on the edge of East Texas, Johnson wouldn't describe his food as being traditional to the area. His place is "on the other side of the river," he says, referring to the Trinity. It's out of the Piney Woods area, just barely, which serves as the line of demarcation separating the Deep South traditions and foods of East Texas from the rest of the state.

So, instead of a strict reliance on hickory to smoke his meats, Johnson uses that in combination with oak and pecan, burning what he feels is necessary to bring out the best in his meat. He produces a good brisket with the requisite smoke ring and a touch more moisture than you'll find among his more eastern counterparts. But the real star of the show is his touch with ribs, which have a robust porky flavor that will have you gnawing each to the bone.

Sides are simple, just like the rest of Johnson's approach, but the beans and the potato salad are both satisfying. He gets his desserts from his minister's wife, who certainly knows her way around the kitchen. A carrot cake is moist and dense under the silky cream cheese frosting. You can find chocolate cake and pound cake, too, and there was a promise of that Southern staple, tea cakes, but none were to be had the day we stumbled across Johnson's path.

Though Midway barely registers on a map, Johnson's Bar-B-Que has become a hit with barbecue lovers, including the Texas BBQ Posse out of Dallas. It's a great surprise in what many have considered the middle of nowhere. Closed on Sunday.

Kirby's Barbeque

4592 TX 14 North, Mexia, TX 76667; (254) 562-5076 **Founded:** 1991 **Pitmaster:** Kirby Hyden **Wood:** Green Post Oak, Hickory

If you can get your mind wrapped around something besides meat (or at least in addition to it) while you're on the barbecue trail, make sure you get the buttermilk pie at Kirby's Barbeque. That is, if you can find the place. Don't rely on your smartphone to get you there. Do stop and ask for directions. Everyone in the small town of Mexia (pronounced ma-HAY-ya) should know the place. At some point in time, they, too, can be found in line waiting for their share of smoked meats from Kirby Hyden, a third-generation Texas pitmaster who has been plying his craft since 1980.

"Brisket is my No. 1 product," Hyden says. And just the sight of it is enough to kick your hunger into overdrive. The black crust, the rosy smoke ring, the burnt red of the sauce, and the visible moisture of the perfectly cooked meat will almost taunt you until you get that first taste in your mouth, and then

Stumping for Something Smoked

Barbecue has been a part of the country's political scene since George Washington's day.

The 36th US president, Lyndon Baines Johnson, came from Texas barbecue country, and he never forgot it. On more than one occasion, LBJ used barbecues to entertain everyone from heads of state to the press corps. He's also said to have been the first to introduce Texas-style ribs to a White House barbecue. His caterer, Walter Jetton, billed himself as the "King of Barbecue" and became a celebrity in his own right. Jetton's BBQ of Fort Worth is still celebrated on a Facebook page (www.facebook.com/Jetton.bbq) filled with historic photos that ably illustrate his showmanship and his mastery of the open pit.

President George H. W. Bush held a barbecue for Congress each year on the South Lawn, and his son, George W. Bush, continued the tradition during his tenure. A barbecue had been set for September 12, 2001, but the terrorist attacks of the previous day forced the cancellation of that event, Buffalo Gap restaurateur Tom Perini of the renowned Perini Ranch Steakhouse once told us. All of the meat that was to have been served went to feed the rescue workers who had come to help out at the Pentagon. The younger Bush has sampled his share of Texas barbecue and is known for being fond of many places, including Cooper's Old Time Pit Bar-B-Que in Llano and Kirby's Barbeque in Mexia.

They won't be the last to see the political potential of the mighty brisket.

you realize that the flavors are even more impressive. (Make sure you ask for your sauce on the side, if you don't want it added automatically.) The ribs, available only on Fridays and Saturdays, boast a dry rub that creates a fine bark, giving your taste buds a salty-sweet note. The meat lightly clings to the bone and has a fine porky flavor. Turkey, ham, pulled pork, and, of course, sausage are also available.

The sauce and the dry rubs are both made according to the recipes created by Hyden's maternal grandfather, W. C. Holloway, who opened his own place in 1959. Kirby's unforgettable buttermilk pie is made from a recipe passed down from Hyden's grandmother, Dessie Faye Holloway. Both are signs of Hyden's belief in following tradition, but he's not a slave to it. His smoking approach has evolved over the years to where he now uses green post oak with just a touch of hickory for added depth of flavor.

The barbecue and that buttermilk pie aren't the only reasons that'll make your visit to Kirby's memorable. Hyden and his staff go out of their way to make you feel right at home, and that kind of Texas hospitality can't be beat. Open Wednesday through Saturday.

Legal Tender Saloon's Brisket & Brew

3932 US 77, La Grange, TX 78945; (979) 242-2458 **Founded:** 2012
Pitmaster: Robert O'Reilly **Wood:** Oak

Legal Tender may be on what's called a highway, but it's really just sort of a road out in the middle of nowhere that connects La Grange and Giddings. Funny, but in Texas, that just doesn't seem to prevent people from finding out where really good brisket is. And so traffic to this spacious joint with a robust red paint job has increased steadily, thanks in large part to good word of mouth. "We've been busy," says Rose O'Reilly, whose son, Robert O'Reilly, serves as owner and pitmaster. "We've been real blessed."

The family's barbecue background includes the Legal Tender catering company in nearby Warrenton, but O'Reilly is quick to point out that this place is the work of her son. His brisket is moist, with a fine smoke ring and a good layer of marbling that supports the beef flavor. A touch of the sweet and tangy tomato-based sauce, made according to Granny's recipe, adds a

welcome richness, even though some might argue that it's not even needed. (Legal Tender's sauce may not be commercially bottled yet, but you can get jars to go.)

Brisket in every form is so popular that there's none left by the end of the day, O'Reilly says. Two-meat plates with brisket and sausage that has plenty of welcome snap to the skin seem to be exceptionally popular—and why not? They go together so well. But every meat on the menu has its share of supporters. "Ribs, chicken, sausage—all across the board, they're buying everything," she says.

While you're waiting for your meat to be carved, you can grab any cold handmade sides you want from the iced-down, self-serve areas near the counter. Don't miss the cucumber salad, if it's available. When Legal Tender first opened, savory pintos were offered, but so many customers asked for sweet baked beans that the recipe was changed to accommodate them.

As the full name of the place suggests, there's something on Robert O'Reilly's menu that goes even better with brisket than a link of sausage, if such a thing is possible: an ice-cold beer. That way, you can relax with friends and sip away at a longneck while you enjoy your barbecue for as long as you like.

Louie Mueller Barbecue

206 W. Second St., Taylor, TX 76574; (512) 352-6206; www.louie muellerbarbecue.com; @LouieMuellerBBQ **Founded:** 1949
Pitmaster: Wayne Mueller **Wood:** Post Oak

For those uninitiated to Texas barbecue, Louie Mueller in Taylor is often one of the top suggestions for a place to start on the barbecue trail. The warm aroma of post oak smoke embraces the old building before you get inside. Once you're in, the scene is classic Texas barbecue joint: the wooden floors and furnishings, high ceilings, original beer signs, the old sausage-maker (named Cranky), neon, an old red Coke machine, and a wall devoted to customers' business cards.

A display near the counter sells the famous Louie Mueller rub—and there's no secret about it: It's nine parts pepper and one part salt—and you'll taste its spicy glory on the thick, black crust that adorns the beef ribs and brisket.

The restaurant is spacious and old, but also inviting. Families and locals are always welcomed, though the restaurant's public recognition has boosted the tourist trade. No matter—on our recent visit we enjoyed watching a father and his two young daughters take a table, briefly bow their heads while Dad said grace, and then dig into their lunch.

Current owner Wayne Mueller says that his idea of the classic Texas barbecue plate features a meaty beef rib, brisket, and an all-beef sausage. Being the third generation of Muellers to put out a storied product gives him the authority to say things like this.

Wayne's grandfather, Louis Mueller, opened the barbecue business at another location in 1949. He'd moved to Taylor in 1936 to open and manage the town's first Safeway grocery store. The barbecue business moved to the present location in 1959. Louie Mueller's son, Bobby Mueller, took over the business in 1974, and during this time, until his death at 69 in 2008, the awards and recognition began to flow. After his death, all three of his children, Wayne, LeAnn, and John, moved into the barbecue business. Wayne took over the Taylor restaurant; both John and LeAnn have their own barbecue businesses in Austin (pages 144 and 146, respectively).

Going into the art and craft of pit-smoking meat wasn't Wayne Mueller's intention for his future. "I ran from it," he says. "I didn't always know that I'd be the one to take the business over. I left for college and swore I'd never come back. And my father never pushed me on this."

Mueller studied architecture and engineering, then moved on to business and finance and got his MBA, with a focus on sports marketing. He worked for the Houston Astros and eventually started his own consulting firm.

In 2013 Louie Mueller Barbecue came in among the top four barbecue restaurants in the state in a list compiled by *Texas Monthly*. Later on that year the restaurant was once again honored by the James Beard Foundation in their article "Our Favorite Dishes (and Drinks!) of 2013" (www.jamesbeard.org/blog). The latter came about due to a meal Mueller had prepared at the 17th Street BBQ MBA in Murphysboro, Illinois. Mitchell Davis, executive vice president of the James Beard Foundation, was there, loved the brisket, and added it to the organization's best-of list.

Mentioning the Beard Foundation reminded Wayne Mueller of the day in 2006 when his dad bought a tuxedo before heading off to New York to accept the James Beard Foundation's America's Classics Award. Bobby Mueller had brought Wayne back to Taylor to tend shop in his absence. A few years later, family troubles led to Bobby asking his eldest son to return to help sort things out.

Now, after a few years back at the business, Wayne Mueller says, "I'm really a student of barbecue. I know I will learn something new every day."

You'll learn something, too, if you take his advice on ordering brisket (and beef ribs and sausage) here. The beef ribs are weighty treasures; the ebony crust of pepper and salt give your fingers a good handle with which to rip strands of silky meat off the bone. Mueller's sausages have a good reputation, and their snap and seasoning will tell you why.

We suggest picking up some of the creamy (not drippy) potato salad and a slab of cheddar cheese, which is an old meat-market tradition. Then, have some peach cobbler with Blue Bell ice cream. It all adds up to an authentic taste of the Texas-style barbecue experience.

Finally, if the boss is in, stop and say hello. Along the barbecue trail we found many friendly folks who were happy to talk if they're not swamped during the noon rush. We've enjoyed the tales they told. Wayne Mueller is continuing the legacy of friendliness and customer service that two generations of Muellers before him built. Closed on Sunday.

Meyer's Elgin Smokehouse

188 US 290, Elgin, TX 78621; (512) 281-3331; www.cuetopiatexas.com
Founded: 1998 **Pitmasters:** Gregg Meyer, Silviano Hernandez
Wood: Oak

The Meyer family has been in the sausage-making business since the 1930s, but this old-world craft goes further back into their history, says Becky Meyer, who manages Meyer's Elgin Smokehouse. The restaurant was founded in 1998 when the family decided that while their renowned Meyer's Elgin Sausage Company was thriving on Main Street, there wasn't a restaurant for visitors to sit down, relax, and sample the smoked sausages.

"People were getting turned away. So, basically the restaurant was a natural extension for the family," said Meyer. The family, including Becky's husband, Gary Meyer, and his brother, Gregg, representing the fourth generation of the family in Elgin, had been looking around at property with a restaurant in mind when the Biggers Barbecue restaurant site on Highway 290 became available.

As Becky Meyer tells it, they moved in on February 13, 1998—a fortunate move for the family and fans of their sausage. The previous owner, James Biggers, left a big pit smoker built by friends of his, which the Meyer family still uses. It can hold about 800 to 1,000 pounds of brisket. They've since added two gas-fired rotisseries: one that smokes up to 1,600 pounds of brisket at a time; the other, 800 pounds. Another piece of equipment, a vacuum tumbler, marinates and seasons  hundreds of pounds of brisket at a time, something that helps with consistency as well as moistness for their brisket.

The restaurant, obviously, has grown in the past 16 years. "We've been remodeling since we bought the place," Meyer says as she walks us around on a tour of the facility.

What that remodeling means for customers is having a large, pleasant area to dine in with plenty of tables and a genial, hospitable atmosphere. On the drizzly and cold day we visited, the best table in the house was the one by the fireplace, for its warmth as well as cozy ambience. Thanksgiving was just days away, and turkey with dressing dinners were on the menu in addition to the regular menu of smoked meat.

It's pretty much a given that you'll want to order Meyer's pork and/or beef links at the cafeteria-style counter, but pile some of the brisket on the plate, too, as it is slow-smoked, moist, and tender. Or, have a baked potato stuffed with chopped brisket. The pork ribs, beef ribs, potato salad, and mac and cheese are all good, too. The peppery lime-marinated chicken was so good, we were inspired to try to re-create it at home. The meat is available to go, by the pound. The restaurant caters and also ships its product.

Miller's Smokehouse

208 N. Penelope St., Belton, TX 76513; (254) 939-5500; www.wild millers.com **Founded:** 2008 **Pitmasters:** Dirk Miller, Robert Reid **Wood:** Oak

Owning a barbecue restaurant has "always been a dream of mine," Dirk Miller says with a broad smile that suggests he still somehow doesn't believe that the dream has become a reality. Perhaps it's because he started out working with his dad, before branching off to set up Miller's Deer Processing and Taxidermy shop. The business wasn't initially a success, but Miller stuck with it, skinning and butchering whatever the local hunters would bring in. The process involved making deer sausage with part of the meat. It was hard work, and it's only recently begun to pay off—so much so, in fact, that the plant, managed by one of Miller's sons, is now processing more than 1,100 deer during a single season.

While taking care of the deer, Miller piddled around, as he calls it, with the notion of opening that barbecue joint. In 2008 he finally bit the bullet and started a small barbecue area within the taxidermy shop. Back then he only had a few tables and all he served was a beef and pork sausage as well as pulled pork cooked in a Crock-Pot. Soon Miller had enough business that he and fellow pitmaster Robert Reid had a number of pits in place. They began turning out brisket

so moist and yet with such a rich black bark encasing it that barbecue writers took notice. Word of mouth began to build.

Then, in 2013, Miller's made *Texas Monthly*'s Top 50 list, and business practically tripled overnight. "People were coming in from out of state—and out of the country even," Reid says. Even better, people from Belton started coming in. "They had no idea we were even here," Miller says. "We're downtown, you see, and we got a lot of people who just never drive past the Walmart." Since then, Miller's Smokehouse has been profiled in *Southern Living* magazine and was featured on HLN in a story that ran in rotation for seven days.

How does Miller get his brisket so moist? His secret, he says, is to keep the temperature constant through the cooking process. He prefers a higher heat than many, he says, without giving away the exact temperature, but he adds that the even heat provides a good sear on the outside that seals in the meat's natural juices. Plus, it gives the meat a burnished opal blackness that gleams in the light.

The rub is a secret blend of spices that Miller created for the deer sausage. It has become so ubiquitous in the smokehouse that you'll find it in the beans, a pleasant surprise because they had a nice level of heat without being too hot to eat.

The ribs have their own following, and they are served only on weekends. So, if you land on a weekday, comfort yourself with some fine chicken, which Reid calls underrated, simply because it's chicken in what is really a beef lover's world. Miller's also sells jerky, but you'll be lucky to find any—it sells almost the moment it's dry.

With so much activity down at the pits and behind the counters, Miller's wife, Lisa, was able to quit her day job and work at the smokehouse full time. When we visited, the couple was putting the finishing touches on a baking area in the building next door where she would be able to make her pies, cookies, and seasonal treats, such as a mouthwatering pumpkin crisp in the fall.

Plans for the new building included a sausage-making kitchen as well as a private dining area for large parties. It sits next to the area where Miller has set up his four pit smokers as well as the stand smokers, which he uses for chickens.

You get a feeling that even though the couple's children are grown, Dirk Miller is far from being too settled in his success. Is it the web address, www.wildmillers.com, that gives it away? Perhaps it's the slogan, "Smoking the good stuff." Whatever the reason, that untamed spirit seems to be driving Miller to reach for more, and that can only be good news for fans of his smokehouse and his barbecue. Closed on Monday.

The Old Coupland Inn and Dancehall

101 Hoxie St., Coupland, TX 78615; (512) 856-2777; www.coupland dancehall.com **Founded:** 1993 **Pitmaster:** Tim Worthy **Wood:** Mesquite

In the 1970s the Old Coupland Inn was famous for its barbecue. But the place fell on hard times and had been closed for about five years when Barbara and Tim Worthy bought it in 1989. They first got the inn up on its feet again and then focused on cleaning up the dancehall that's next door, which was in even worse shape.

Not content to stop there, they set up a restaurant in the 100-year-old inn, where they offer barbecue once more, only this time on Friday and Saturday evenings. The massive pit in the kitchen out back is the place where briskets cook for 16 hours, slowly and steadily while a fine char crust builds up and seals in the meat's natural juices. Ribs, chicken, pulled pork, and a fairly loose sausage all add to the barbecue lover's options. Get the four-meat plate and just eat your way through most of what Worthy has to offer. Don't forget to try the thick, warm sauce, served in a pitcher on the side; it's made using the recipe that former owner Jack Sutton developed.

One thing wood aficionados might notice early on is that these meats are not prepared with oak, the choice of so many pitmasters in Central Texas. That had been Worthy's choice when he started. But one night, he had something to attend to, so he told his assistant, a man known for drinking a little too much, to load up the smoker with enough wood and meat. The next day Worthy tasted the meat and it was completely different. "What did you do?" he asked. Through his morning-after haze, the assistant couldn't remember, but he retraced his steps, showing Worthy everything he'd done, which was to grab wood from a pile of seasoned mesquite instead of oak. Everybody liked the end result so much better that seasoned mesquite has been the wood of choice to this day.

Tall tale from the barbecue trail? You decide. Just take the following words of Worthy's into account: "The best thing about barbecue is that you load up the smoker with good wood and you use the best meat you can. Then you go drink yourself a beer. You leave the fire alone and you get an even temperature. That's all there is to barbecue.

The beery borracho beans arrive in their own cast-iron pot, which keeps them warm throughout the meal.

"There are no secrets to barbecue. It's almost too simple. But it is outdoor cooking at its finest."

There may not be secrets, but there are always some fun twists to discover at each place. At the Old Coupland Inn, you'll find salmon and steaks both cooked directly over mesquite coals. Worthy mops the steaks thoroughly while they're on the grill, because his recipe for a really juicy steak is to keep the meat moist the entire time it cooks.

He also offers an appetizer that's unique in these parts: chicken-fried jalapeño poppers filled with smoked brisket. An order of four may not be enough.

Coupland is practically a stone's throw from Taylor, Elgin, and other Central Texas towns that have been highly touted for their barbecue, so Worthy knows his smoked meats have to measure up. In the past 20 years, he has gone from offering just barbecue to a menu that also includes fried catfish, chicken-fried steak, burgers, and even a veggie plate. Why the additions? "Well, you may get 300 people in here who eat barbecue and they eat you out of everything you have," he says. "Then another hundred people come in. What are you going to serve them? You can't speed up the meat."

The menu at the Old Coupland Inn also conjures up a sense of the Deep South by offering a raft of side dishes that includes sweet potato fries; cowboy potatoes; "real mashed potatoes," as the menu calls them; sautéed mushrooms; baked beans and borracho beans; fried okra; potato salad; and a New Orleans–style coleslaw with raisins sweetening the mix.

It's all part of the Worthys' efforts to make everyone feel at home when they drop by for dinner followed by some two-stepping next door. Open Friday and Saturday.

Opie's BBQ

9504 TX 71 East, Spicewood, TX 78669; (830) 693-8660; www.opies barbecue.com **Founded:** 1999 **Pitmaster:** Mark Oglesby **Wood:** Mesquite

Opie's doesn't look its 15 years of age. It has a bright, well-kept sheen that has a nontraditional appeal—traditional being the classic remodeled filling station or old country store look that Texans approve of in a barbecue joint. Part of the allure might be the long, polished pine tables and chairs, plenty of windows, and energetic staff.

But don't let all this perkiness fool you—it isn't false charm. The food speaks of well-worn tradition, mesquite wood-firing pits where the meat is ably done by pitmaster Marco Oglesby. Add to that some very good, as well as unusual, side dishes.

Just for starters, along with traditional coleslaw, there's also a sweet craisin-almond slaw billed as a healthy version. The hot Tater Tot casserole,

topped with crunchy fried onions, and a bubbling hot and creamy spicy corn should both be taken to your table as well.

This place gets busy, but when we stopped in at about 3 p.m., we found a dining room that was still plenty lively, though the line for choosing meat from the warming rack was fairly short. Across the spacious dining room, Austin musician Jeff Inman was playing the devil out of a guitar. Live blues will always get our vote for the best-possible music with barbecue. It inspired a couple of county sheriff's deputies to break out in dance steps as they came up the sidewalk leading to a side entrance.

On our (butcher paper) plate we first dug into a big beef rib that pulled easily away from the wide bone, weighty in our hands and giving up beefy good flavor. As others have observed, there's just no reason to tackle this thing with a fork and knife. Pulling the meat away from the wide, heavy bone with fingers—or teeth—is the best, most satisfying way to do it. The brisket had plenty of dark crust; hot and cheesy jalapeño sausages were spicy-hot as well. We also recommend the sweet and spicy baby back ribs, with a glaze that didn't overdo the sweet—and didn't hold back on the spicy.

We headed to the front of the house to talk to Kristin Ashmore, who founded the restaurant with her husband, Todd. She'd just handled a birthday party and had a talk with staff in the kitchen, but she took the time to sit and chat for a few minutes. Among other things, we wondered how the restaurant got its name. She said that when the restaurant was being built, the workers had some difficulty with the couple's dog, Opie, stealing their tools. They started calling the as-yet-unnamed restaurant "Opie's" and it stuck.

Opie, the pup, is no longer around, but Opie's BBQ is showing plenty of staying power, and is an excellent reason to drive out to Spicewood.

Prause Meat Market

253 W. Travis St., La Grange, TX 78945; (979) 968-3259
Founded: 1903 **Pitmaster:** Mark Prause **Wood:** Oak

Multigenerational sagas on the Texas barbecue scene can become as convoluted as a telenovela. But that's seemingly not the case with the Prause family. "If this business is going to work, we all have to work together," says Gary Prause, a member of the fourth generation of the family that has run the meat market and barbecue pits on La Grange's town square for the past century. The actual site may have changed a couple of times from one storefront to another, but the business has always stayed at the heart of the town.

Prause Meat Market moved to its current location in 1953. That was long before the fourth generation came on the scene, so it has always been the only meat market that the four cousins who run it today—Gary, Brian, Kathy, and

Mark—have ever known. "There's been a total of 22 Prauses who have worked here," says Gary, who acts as family spokesman when customers ask about the history of the place. He even keeps a box of family photos on hand, in an antique freezer that's been converted into a makeshift file cabinet, to show the evolution of Prause Meat Market from the days of their great-grandfather, Arnold; down through Grandfather Glen; and on to Glen Jr., Steve, and Jimmy.

In the older photos, you can see the tools of the trade that were put to use to butcher sides of beef and pork into the cuts that people wanted or into the meats that would go into the smoker out back. The same types of knives are still in use today, though an electric saw certainly adds speed as you watch a stack of steaks get cut in seconds.

Another old-fashioned touch to the setting is the use of sawdust and wood shavings to cover the floor, which Gary Prause says helps keep the place cleaner and safer, because any scraps that fall to the floor generally land on the wood chips, thereby preventing a greasy spot that someone could slip on. The cover is also easier to walk on and provides a cushion that the cement floor does not. Your back notices that after a long day.

Tradition fills Prause Meat Market, from a vibrant mural of cowboy life to the display of deer heads and fish on the walls. One change that Gary has noticed over the years is the rise of brisket as the meat of choice for barbecue lovers. "In the 1960s barbecue brisket was unheard of," he says. "When we started cooking it, we kept the bone in." They still do, which adds plenty of flavor to the meat.

If you want some of that barbecue, you may want to get to Prause fairly early in the day, because it sells out quickly. Mark Prause keeps his pit filled with everything from brisket to pork roll, a kind of porchetta. The ribs are still mopped with a pungent mixture of lard, vinegar, and water, which keeps them moist through the smoking process. But it's the from-scratch sausages simply wrapped in a slice of white bread that are as good as it gets, with plenty of juice bursting through the skin in each bite.

Mark took over barbecue duties in recent years when Prause's longtime pitmaster, Monroe Schubert, retired after more than 40 years of service. It's one sign of change in the business. Another is that the last surviving member of the third generation, Gary's father, Glen Jr., died in 2012. Will the fifth generation take over the operation in the future? The answer remains to be seen, but Gary admits there are not enough hands now to do all the work that Prause could do, so they've had to scale back on some operations. "In olden days, we used to do hams, we used to make jerky," he says, adding that the market once employed 10, as opposed to the 4 now running the store.

The next time you're in Prause Meat Market, you could find yourself being dished up a savory bit of history along with your barbecue. It could be a story of how in the days before segregation, white customers ate on one side of the building while blacks ate on another; in the mid-1960s, that line disappeared for good. Or perhaps you'll hear Gary relate a story about the day, back in the early 1930s, when his grandfather went fishing. A Model T pulled up alongside the water, and the couple inside the car engaged him in some small talk while they took a break from driving. It was the first time Glen Sr. had ever seen a woman smoke a cigar. He knew it was the infamous Bonnie Parker, who had Clyde Barrow at her side.

Or maybe you'll hear tell of how the Prauses have gone out of their way to help people when they needed it the most. At his father's funeral, Gary heard the story of how someone at Prause used to make deliveries to a woman in town who didn't drive, even if her order was only 12 cents worth of meat. He didn't know the story, but it wasn't a surprise to him. That's how folks in La Grange are, and that's what members of the Prause family have worked hard for more than 100 years to maintain in their community. Closed on Sunday.

Ronnie's Pit BBQ

211 US 281, Johnson City, TX 78636; (830) 868-7553 **Founded:** Early 1980s **Pitmaster:** Ronnie Weiershausen **Wood:** Oak

Ronnie Weiershausen didn't set out to be a pitmaster with a devoted following in the Johnson City area and beyond. He'd bought a convenience store in the late 1970s, but apparently so did a great many other people in the area. Suddenly the town was overrun with convenience stores and not enough business for all of them to survive.

So, Weiershausen got to thinking barbecue would be the way for him to go. He'd smoked meats for a long time with his father, and he was good at it. He'd even developed a technique that he would put to good use. He starts by turning oak into burning charcoal. In his opinion, this burns away any oil or creosote that might be in the wood. "It eliminates all your bitter flavor," he says. "At least, in my opinion, it does." The coals are then placed directly under the meat so they can cook. It's a method that lets him prepare his barbecue either slow or fast. His brisket still takes about 12 hours, and it emerges from the pit with a healthy black crust around it. As he cuts thin slices from it, you can see the juices push forth as your own hankering for a slice grows.

We've been stopping at Ronnie's for years now because Weiershausen has some of the best ribs we've ever tasted, especially when they are just seconds

from coming up from the pit and the fat is still sizzling on the surface. They may appear to be too hot to touch, but somehow you can't stop yourself from biting into them, first with a little tear of that scorching-hot meat, then with full force.

Is it any wonder that Ronnie's sells out of everything on Saturdays and even most weekdays? And they go for it all, Weiershausen's wife, Cindy, says. The turkey is especially popular with those in search of white meat, but there's also chicken, pork, and two types of sausage. You can try all of them on a sampler plate that is overwhelming, but in the best way imaginable.

Ronnie's also offers a healthy variety of side dishes that go beyond the usual suspects to include a sweet-tangy sauerkraut salad that fits right in with the area's German heritage, as well as one of the best cucumber-tomato salads going. There's pea salad, corn salad, and more. The more they put on the menu, the more it seems customers want, Cindy says, adding

Try the jalapeño poppers with plenty of cheese melting into a wrapping of crisp bacon.

that folks have asked for french fries and pasta salad, too. They don't have any more counter room to add more, not to mention time to prepare it. But apparently, if Ronnie Weiershausen likes a recipe, he'll add it to the menu.

When Weiershausen made the shift to barbecue, he started with only one table in his place. But his barbecue was so good, he almost immediately landed a catering gig more than an hour away in San Antonio. It called for him to feed several hundred people. At the event, "somebody asked me how could I, with only one table, get a job like that," he remembers. "I said I knew what I was doing." And he proved it.

Weiershausen has expanded the dining area into a vast room with red-checked tablecloths, where you'll find many Johnson City regulars meeting on a Saturday morning. It's a far cry from the vacant convenience store days, and Weiershausen knows it. "Hey, I'm making money now," he says. Closed on Sunday.

The Salt Lick

18300 FM 1826, Driftwood, TX 78619; (512) 858-4959; www.saltlick
bbq.com; @SaltLickBBQ; second location at 3350 E. Palm Valley
Blvd., Round Rock, TX 78665; (512) 386-1044 (see website for hours
and menu) **Founded:** 1967 **Pitmaster:** Scott Roberts **Wood:** Live Oak
The Salt Lick has been a favorite among Texans and travelers for more than 45
years. It's about a 40-minute drive from Austin, an hour and 20 minutes from
San Antonio. Don't let the drive daunt you, though, no matter which area of the
state you're coming from, as you'll be seeing some still-rural parts of the Texas

Hill Country's rolling terrain, oak
forest, and colorful wildflowers in
the spring. And you'll have a good
meal to look forward to.

The history of the family that
owns the Salt Lick goes back further than the 1967 opening of the
restaurant. Read the opening page
on the website, which paints a vivid
picture of the family's origins, how
they got to Driftwood, and what
inspired the opening of a place
that has become a well-loved and
famous barbecue location.

When you park your car in the
spacious parking lot, you'll be parking in what was once part of the
family property devoted to cotton
fields, says owner Scott Roberts.
The restaurant proper has grown over the years, and now has two big dining
areas as well as a wine-tasting structure, owned by Roberts's daughter, where
wine with the Salt Lick label is sold. Plans are in the works to add even more
to what has become a major destination in this part of the state, along with the
wineries that cluster in the area.

Walk inside the main serving area where you can pick up a T-shirt, or just
continue on to the place where you give your name to the host. All the while,
feast your eyes on a massive pit where meats are displayed to great, appetizing effect. Shiny sausages hang from racks above the big, circular grate in the
stone pit. Closer to the coals are racks of pork ribs with a deep red glaze and
blackened briskets seasoned with a rub of salt, black pepper, and cayenne. Both

Five Tips for Matching Wines and Texas Barbecue

BY CECIL FLENTGE

Texas barbecue may be one of the greatest foods on earth, but you don't want the greatest wine to go with it. That delicious, crisp, tangy, and bone-dry Chablis you love may have gotten a 90-plus rating and cost $45, but it doesn't go with barbecue.

However, a Moscato from Italy has a little sweetness, just like most of the barbecue sauces in Texas, and may work very well. Even some of the dry rubs that season the meat have brown sugar, and it is a rare barbecue sauce that escapes honey, sugar, molasses, agave nectar, or a fruit infused with sugar.

That sweetness is the key. The first and most important of all tips for pairing wine and food is that the wine must be as sweet as the food—or sweeter. Otherwise the wine tastes sour and the fruit flavors are subdued. Try it for yourself: Have a grape; it is tasty. Eat a pecan praline; it is nutty, toasty, and sweet. Have another grape and try not to make a face as the tart aspects hit you.

The second tip is to always drink what you like. But while we have our favorites, cull through the list to find something that is more barbecue-friendly. Maybe the fruity depth in a Spanish Garnacha calls to you, or you like the spiciness of an Australian Shiraz. If you want something homegrown, try the Duchman Dolcetto from Driftwood, Texas; like the Italian wines made from the same grape or from Barbera, it has a rich fruity taste that can blend in with a dry-rub brisket.

Do not ignore white wines. This is another way to enjoy the synergy between wine and food plus keep cool on a sunny day as you work on some ribs. An inexpensive Chardonnay with a touch of residual sugar, like Kendall-Jackson or one of the Aussie bottles with a cute animal on the label, can match with honey- or orange juice-laced sauces. Rieslings from Texas to Germany to Alsace, France, will actually help you taste more components of both the wine and the sauce.

Fourth, bubbles are beautiful. Sparkling wines like a Prosecco Dry or Extra Dry are great with that luscious smoked turkey. But for the rich, sticky-sweet, thick mopped-on sauces, try a sparkling Brachetto. It is red, it is sweet, it is cherry-cranberry fruity, and Brachetto wines from Italy are readily available.

Last, wine is for sharing, and so is Texas barbecue. Whether you dine at one of the places listed in these pages, take it home for a picnic, or smoke your own, there is an almost prehistoric calling to gather and share the bounty of great barbecue.

Cecil Flentge, a native Texan, is a former restaurateur and wine bar owner who teaches wine appreciation for novices and professionals.

are sauced once during the smoking process. Big, heavy beef ribs are kept warmed until they're hoisted up on the slicing block.

Turkey is brined for 24 hours in water, sugar, and salt before it's smoked. The beef ribs are from back ribs, rather than the increasingly popular short ribs cut. Roberts says he uses what is called a "Hollywood cut," where each rib has a thick portion of meat on either side, meaning that from a rack of seven bones, four bones will be discarded during the preparation.

Sauce at the Salt Lick was developed over the years and refined by Roberts's mother. And while each generation at the place has added its own touches, Roberts says he hasn't done much tweaking. "I don't think it's broke, so I'm not going to fix it," he says. "Bobby Flay said the beef ribs were the best he'd ever tasted, with the spicy sauce on them."

Be sure to get a taste of these ribs, brisket, sausage, and other items from the pit—they are all good. The sides are different: The potato salad and coleslaw aren't made with mayonnaise, since earlier owners didn't have the refrigeration to keep the foods from spoiling. But we've appreciated the dishes for their singular flavors.

We asked Roberts what is responsible for the long run of success and obvious growth of the business, including another location in Round Rock. He says that the business was founded on "Hill Country friendly and doing the best quality." Its success over the years, however, is due to his loyal, hardworking staff.

Snow's BBQ

516 Main St., Lexington, TX 78947; (979) 773-4640; www.snowsbbq .com **Founded:** 2003 **Pitmaster:** Tootsie Tomanetz **Wood:** Post Oak
Certainly the top female pitmaster in Texas, Tootsie Tomanetz was tending pits long before a 2008 *Texas Monthly* article on Snow's BBQ in Lexington put her in the international barbecue spotlight. She got her start in the mid-1960s, when her husband, Edward, was asked to find out if she would mind assisting the pitmaster at the City Meat Market in Giddings, where he worked.

"I don't know barbecue, but I'll do my best," was her reply.

She certainly did. She learned how to use post oak to bring out the best in pork ribs, chicken, sausage, and any type of beef you could think of. Well, any type but brisket, that is. "Brisket? People didn't start asking for that until the 1980s," she says.

She's been at a barbecue pit ever since, almost 50 years now. Through the years, the couple opened their own meat market, which they lost, but she continued to work for the new owners. In 1996 her husband had a stroke, but that hasn't prevented him from joining his wife at the pits on Saturday mornings. One day a Lexingtonian named Kerry Bexley approached her to see if she would work for him at a place he wanted to open. "I told him I'd made a commitment to work here, but I'd let him know if I changed my mind," Tomanetz says. "He'd stop by on some Saturday mornings, and finally I told him I thought I was ready to go work for him. I said, 'Let's sit down and talk.'"

Bexley asked her what kind of pit she wanted to use and set about making three pits to suit her specifications—one for sausage, two for the other meats. When everything was set to go, they opened Snow's in 2003. Five years later the *Texas Monthly* article declaring Snow's the best barbecue in the state appeared and landed Tomanetz in the international spotlight. People from all

over the world came to the tiny town of Lexington to line up for her mouthwatering brisket at 8 on Saturday mornings.

They still do, rain or shine, cold or Texas hot. And they find out for themselves why her beef, with its simple rub of salt and pepper, makes converts of people. She may not have started smoking brisket until the 1980s, but her mastery of bringing out the best in that cut of meat is largely unequaled. Or maybe they'll fall for the cuts of pork steak that practically melt in your mouth. Chicken, jalapeño sausage, and the pork ribs all have their admirers, too. Each one requires its own attention in the smoker. Tomanetz uses direct heat for the pork steak, ribs, chicken, and sausage, shoveling the coals under the meats and occasionally mopping all but the sausage until they're ready. The briskets, however, are cooked in indirect pits until the bark fairly glistens and seals in the natural meat juices.

Side dishes are limited to the three expected choices. All are made by hand and all have an honest simplicity about them that matches the meat. The coleslaw is vinegar-based, and the potato salad is creamy. But it's the beans, served from an all-you-can-eat pot, that had people in Snow's talking—and not just because they could help themselves to seconds. There's no secret recipe, Tomanetz says. She simply cooks them with salt, chile, and bacon fat until they produce a thick broth that coats the beans in plenty of flavor.

The response to the 2008 *Texas Monthly* article was so tremendous that Tomanetz got her son, Hershel, involved soon thereafter. "I told my son about all the people on the porch and lined up down the street," she says. "He came over just to see the crowd." Hershel was gradually pulled into the business. "I was doing everything [including putting briskets on the smoker at 2 a.m.]. So, I'd say, 'Hershy, put me some wood in the firebox,' things like that. Kerry finally asked him if he was interested in helping him, and Hershy said yes. So, now when Kerry is out working, Hershel will start."

Hershy's favorite day of working there was the day that Robert Duvall stopped by to sample Tomanetz's finest. He couldn't place the actor at first, but when the star of *Lonesome Dove* and *The Godfather* started to sign the guest book, Hershy blurted out, "You're Robert Duvall!"

Snow's is only open one day a week, the day that the cattle auction also takes place in Lexington. So, all three have day jobs that keep them busy during the week: Hershel works for a plastic molding company, Bexley for a mining company, and Tootsie Tomanetz does maintenance and grounds-keeping for the Giddings Independent School District.

Asked about all the hard work, Tomanetz says, "I was raised on a farm, I like the outdoors."

It's obvious she doesn't shy from hard work, but as far as encouraging other women to learn the pitmaster trade, she has to think a moment: "It's a hard job. In the summer it's a hot job, in the winter it's a cold job. You have to have a determination and an incentive to want to make a success of it. When I started in 1966, I had no idea that I'd keep on and come to this stature." Open Saturdays.

Southside Market & Barbecue

1212 US 290, Elgin, TX 78621; (512) 281-4650; www.southside
market.com; @southsideBBQ **Founded:** 1886 (William J. Moon), 1968
(Bracewell family) **Pitmaster:** Bryan Bracewell **Wood:** Post Oak

Southside Market & Barbecue is one of the two large sausage-making con-
cerns in Elgin. Its history goes back to 1886 when a butcher, William J. Moon,
opened up Southside Market on Center Street to sell his products.

"Also, in the true German tradition, he would grind his beef trimmings,
add salt and spices and the Original

Elgin Sausage was born," according
to Southside Market's folksy website,
which offers a time line of the company
history.

In 1968 Ernest and Rene Bracewell
moved their family from Austin to Elgin,
and started what has been three generations of Bracewells at Southside Market.
Bryan Bracewell is now at the helm of
this historic market and barbecue.

The restaurant is spacious, with a
tidy country atmosphere and a cafeteria-style ordering counter where you can
watch the ribs and brisket and many other menu items cut to order. While
these barbecue items are good, you don't want to miss the historic Elgin "hot
guts"—the spicy, beefy links that helped Elgin attain its status as sausage capital of Texas. For dessert, a scoop of Blue Bell ice cream will help end your visit
here on a sweet note.

Taylor Cafe

101 N. Main St., Taylor, TX 76574; (512) 352-8475 **Founded:** 1948
Pitmasters: Vencil Mares, Scott Morales **Wood:** Oak

The trains come so close to this vintage Texas barbecue joint that the whistles
seem to rattle the rafters and window frames. Sometimes, you'll hear the sound
of brakes, too, as the iron horse, as the Indians once called it, comes to a full
stop right there next to Taylor Cafe. It's there just long enough for someone to
run into the restaurant, say hi to owner Vencil Mares, then grab a couple big
bags of barbecue and hustle back to the train.

Mares, who celebrated his 90th birthday in 2013, opened the cafe in 1948.
He's changed just a few things about it since then. It will suffice to say that
both the interior and exterior are more old than rustic, but they have an honest

veneer that speaks of long, hard use. It's been the setting for Mares to build his reputation as barbecuer, and for people to check in with him, whether they've been there only once before or have come in several times during the week. Mares is quiet, yet he has a kindly charm befitting a Texas institution.

While he lets pitmaster Scott Morales do the heavy pit work, Mares is at the restaurant every day and has little intention of ever doing otherwise.

You'll find him seated down at the end of a long counter, usually signing copies of the *Taylor Daily Press* where a front page story about the "Texas BBQ Trail" features a photo of him on the cover. He hands these out to customers by way of souvenirs and has a few words with them. If they're new to the cafe, he motions for them to take a look at the glass-covered frame that holds his military medals. Mares was in the Army during WWII, having joined at the age of 16 with the blessing of his parents. He was a medic in the 102nd Evacuation Unit after the invasion of Normandy in 1944.

His customers walk in from locales throughout the world, Mares says, naming off a list of countries, including Russia. Through the doors at the back of the cafe, he is usually seated in his office ready to greet customers. Above his chair is a painting of him in his trademark red apron. There's just enough room there for a desk and a chair; the walls bristle with photos and mementos.

He uses a walker now to get back to the pit room, where Morales works. It's low, slow cooking, says Mares, and that makes the difference.

Taylor Cafe once had a wall separating two sides of the long building that segregated the customers. In its place is a full bar, where plenty of the customers come in for drinks—with barbecue on the side.

Check out the menu on the wall and ask one of the friendly helpers for suggestions. We wouldn't pass up the turkey and beef sausages, made in-house, that Mares is known for. They'll come with a little of the restaurant's thin, vinegary sauce. The brisket is another meat to get on your plate—it's won awards over the years and goes just right with a helping of potato salad. It's a cash-only kind of place, so don't rely on your credit cards.

As we departed, we did a gentle fist-tap with Mares. He'd given us a tour of the premises himself and had sat back down before we ventured a question (actually one we'd asked on previous visits). Would he ever consider retiring? After a little shake of the head, he gave the best reason a man could have: "I see my friends here."

Whup's Boomerang Bar-B-Q

1203 Bennett St., Marlin, TX 76661; (254) 883-5770 **Founded:** 2000
Pitmaster: Bennie Washington **Wood:** Post Oak, Mesquite

To someone who doesn't live in Marlin, finding Whup's Boomerang Bar-B-Q is a matter of following your GPS as far as it takes you and then going on faith for a block or two. Yes, it is that far off the beaten path—and the path looks as though it's been beaten fairly thoroughly. We headed out to Whup's on a rainy afternoon in which potholes of indeterminate depth made up more of the road than solid pavement or gravel, and we kept going further than our directions told us to—that is, until we came across a hand-painted sign pointing to a large green shack. It was so removed from the center of tiny Marlin that it seemed too residential for a business. Yet its location doesn't matter, especially not to those customers who were waiting in the cold ahead of us.

What mattered was Bennie Washington's fine barbecue, which we sampled by way of a three-meat plate filled with some brisket that boasted the right beefiness and moisture, sausage packed into a sturdy casing, and, best of all, pork ribs that had the right amount of give without any need for the tangy sauce served on the side. The meats didn't bear much sign of heavy rubs, which was fine because it meant you were tasting natural meat flavor with a judicious amount of smoke. Washington won't reveal any of his pit secrets, except to say that he uses a combination of post oak and mesquite on his meats, sometimes together and sometimes separately depending on what he has on hand. Both the potato salad and the coleslaw seemed to know their place as the supporting cast to the stellar meats.

There's little room to sit down and eat, which means an in-car picnic may be in order if you want to eat your barbecue while it's warm. You'll be glad you did. You can then find your way back to town on a full stomach. This is Washington's second barbecue joint. His first was largely a weekend-only place he had in the early 1990s while he was working for Pepsi-Cola. Handling both jobs got to be too much, so he had to shut the pit down. Once he retired, however, the time seemed right to open Whup's. Word of mouth quickly spread about the place and his largely local customer base has consistently grown, keeping his family and him busy for each of the three days they're open.

Washington named the place Whup's in remembrance of his father, Charlie Washington, who went by that nickname while a young Bennie and his brothers were known as Little Whups. The Boomerang was added because Washington hopes his barbecue is good enough to bring you back again. It will, as his track record has shown. But Washington's modest about the praise he has received, from customers and barbecue writers alike. "We just roll up our sleeves and try to produce the best food possible," he says.

By the way, bring cash or a check with you. There's not an ATM—or much of anything else—nearby, and Whup's doesn't take credit cards. Open Thursday through Saturday.

Zimmerhanzel's Bar-B-Que

307 Royston St., Smithville, TX 78957; (512) 237-4244; www .zimmerhanzelsbarbeque.com **Founded:** 1980 **Pitmaster:** Bert Bunte **Wood:** Oak

The folks at Zimmerhanzel's will tell you when they open on Saturday (it's 8:30 a.m.), but they don't set a closing time. They're just open until they sell out. Since that happens early most every week, you'd better get in line and be pre-

pared to stand for a while. The staff behind the counter works with assembly-line precision on getting your plate to you as quickly as possible, but slicing all that good meat takes time, even for the most seasoned carver, who is cutting each piece of meat to order almost as soon as it's brought in from the pit.

So, while you're waiting, take a good look around the place. If the dining room seems familiar, it's because it was used in the film *Bernie*, bright orange chairs and all (even if the exterior shots made the setting out to be Daddy Sam's in Carthage). You can even make out some of the staff, who essentially played themselves in the scenes. Or perhaps you saw the joint in Willie Nelson's music video for "Just Breathe." The location might not have been as prominent, but DeeDee Bunte, who owns Zimmerhanzel's with her husband, Bert, still gets excited about her chance to meet the legendary singer. "Willie Nelson was really cool," she says.

Encircling the dining room near the ceiling is a series of deer heads that emphasizes how important deer hunting is in people's lives here. There's also a stuffed wildcat who seems ready to strike out for your brisket if you're not careful.

Spend your time talking with the folks around you, too. You'll find a few meat lovers who are blazing their own barbecue trails, but you'll also find a great many locals who don't want a week to go by without some of the Buntes' barbecue. Brisket is obviously the star here, and it's what Bert Bunte smokes the most of each week. The fatty end is not too fat, but as soon as you watch it being cut, you can see it drip with juices that had been seared in during its time in the pit. The vast majority of Zimmerhanzel's customers, 70 to 80 percent, in DeeDee Bunte's estimation, prefer the lean cut anyway, which they keep moist with sauce. The house-made sausage is equally impressive, with a good snap from the casing and the inescapable lure of hot fat mingled with spices when you bite into it. (Zimmerhanzel is DeeDee's maiden name, and it has deep roots in the community. It should also clue you in on the sausage's German provenance.)

Grab the ribs while you can, because they've been known to sell out quickly. "I hope I get some of those ribs," a local woman in front of us said. "I've never been able to get those." She was in luck that day, and so were we.

We've rarely said no to pie, and the buttermilk pie here merits close inspection by fork and mouth.

We bit into the pink flesh and the flavor of black pepper seemed to explode into the natural pork sweetness, offering added texture and dimension. The standard sides plus macaroni salad do their duty, but the homemade desserts, from buttermilk pie to banana pudding, beg close investigation.

After you make your way through the line, you may want to sit at one of the community tables. Sure, the talk will be about the barbecue or whatever people are eating at the time, but you might also hear some tales of life in Smithville and why this town, with a population under 4,000, sees itself as the "Heart of the Megalopolis."

In the past, the Buntes had discussed the idea of moving closer to I-10, which might have meant more business, but DeeDee didn't want to. "I'm happy just to stay small and do our own thing," she says.

Bring your cash. No credit cards are accepted here. Closed on Sunday.

Lockhart & Luling

Lockhart is the Barbecue Capital of Texas. That's no empty boast. It earned those bragging rights back in 2003, when the state legislature passed a proclamation in the city's honor. But barbecue lovers knew about Lockhart's meaty charms long before the politicians did.

Through the years, word-of-mouth spread about the brisket or shoulder clod, German-style sausage links hand-tied into rings, crackling pork ribs, and massive pork chops you could find there. So, even though Lockhart has a population of only slightly more than 12,000, its reputation as the place to eat barbecue has grown to the point where it plays host to an average of 5,000 barbecue lovers a week, according to the city's website. And only a few miles down the road is Luling, which has two renowned barbecue joints. For many following the Texas barbecue trail, a visit to one town is not complete without a stop in the other.

First, let's look at Lockhart, which offers barbecue lovers four places to choose from: Black's Barbecue, Chisholm Trail Bar-B.Q. & Hot Sausage, Kreuz Market, and Smitty's Market, alphabetically speaking. Each has devotees that will swear by their favorite.

Those who know the history of Lockhart aren't surprised by the rich barbecue heritage that has developed. In the post–Civil War days, when Lockhart was still a part of Gonzales County, it was a stop along the famous Chisholm Trail. Cowboys initially drove their cattle to market through the city, but the area, with its rich grasslands, soon attracted its own ranches, so many of the heads of cattle originated there.

It was in this scene that the original Kreuz (pronounced Krites) Market opened on Commerce Street in 1900. It first operated as strictly a meat market but eventually added barbecue to its offerings. In an era before refrigeration, smoking was one way of preserving meat for at least a little while. Drying it into jerky was another. In 1948 the Kreuz family sold out to the

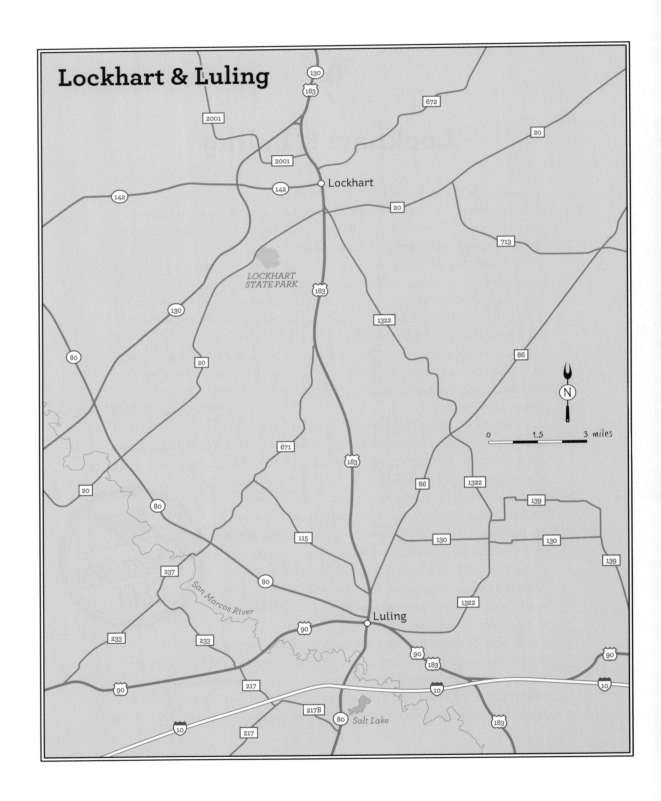

Lockhart & Luling

Schmidts, who kept alive the original name and the traditional approaches to both barbecue and butchering.

By the time of the Great Depression, the market for cattle had become as devastated as the rest of the economy. Driving cattle up the Chisholm Trail was no longer profitable, leaving ranchers with few options. One rancher talked Edgar Black Sr. into opening Lockhart's second meat market as a means of handling cattle that might otherwise have gone to waste. Black's opened in 1932, at the lowest point of the nation's economic misery. The family soon got into the barbecue business as well.

Time passed, and new generations of barbecue families have come into play. The Black family has continued to operate in the same location and under the same family lineage, which it brags about in no uncertain terms:

"Texas' oldest and best major barbecue restaurant continuously owned by the same family," reads a sign on the wall.

Floyd Wilhelm, who had worked at Black's for 18 years, left to open his own place, Chisholm Trail, in 1978. Then a Schmidt family squabble occurred in the late 1990s. The result was that Kreuz Market moved to a new location, while the family member who had inherited the building gave the barbecue place a new name, Smitty's, and set up shop in the original Commerce Street storefront. The rift was front page news at the time, and it has remained the subject of conjecture, rumor, and wonderment ever since. In fact, it has added to the mystique of the small-town aura that envelopes Lockhart like a fine ring of post oak smoke.

Luling, only 15 miles or so down the road, is less than half the size of Lockhart. It's the home of the Watermelon Thump, a summer festival that draws thousands of people from far and wide, but it's equally known for its barbecue. In olden days the town was known for being quite rambunctious, earning it the reputation of "toughest town in Texas." Nowadays the biggest question is which barbecue joint will you eat at first, City Market or Luling Bar-B-Q?

Black's Barbecue

208 N. Main St., Lockhart, TX 78644; (512) 398-2712 **Founded:** 1932
Pitmaster: Kent Black **Wood:** Post Oak

Edgar Black Jr. was 6 years old when his parents opened Black's in Lockhart back in 1932. From an early age, he worked in the family meat market and then the barbecue joint they opened. It was the Blacks' livelihood, and he took the importance of that to heart. After he married Norma, the couple worked the place day in and day out for decades thereafter.

The prime rib on weekends, with a touch of horseradish sauce, is a winning combination of smoky, creamy, and beefy richness.

"I don't know how my parents did it every day for 60 years," their son, Kent Black, says today with obvious pride.

They established a Lockhart tradition that thrives today, thanks to a firm acknowledgment of what worked in the past and a healthy interest in what today's customers want. So, when you walk in the front door, you're almost immediately greeted with a line that winds its way past an extensive cafeteria display of side dishes, ranging from black-eyed peas with green beans, macaroni and cheese, and candied sweet potatoes with marshmallows on top to creamed corn, pickled cauliflower, and pecan cobbler.

On the cutting board, you'll find the expected array of Certified Angus brisket, with black bark lining each moist, smoke-ringed slice, as well as ribs that glisten as they're being chopped from the steaming rack and hand-stuffed sausage rings that come in three flavors: jalapeño-cheddar, garlic, and regular. But you'll also find massive beef ribs, turkey breast that maintains its moisture, and, on weekends, succulent prime rib.

Kent Black is also trying his hand at a seasonal sausage, such as the green chile blend that appears in the fall. He's so sure people will like it, his staff hands out samples.

All of the meats are smoked with post oak using indirect heat, but Black does not stop there. He ages the wood six months to one year before using it. That way, the meat picks up a clean smoke flavor without any bitterness, he says. The sauces on the table come in several heat levels, and you can buy some to take home with you as a souvenir of your visit. The kitchen goes to the trouble of baking its own bread, so you aren't stuck with the usual spongy slices of white or wheat out of the bag. You can also get crackers, if you choose, which is a Lockhart tradition that reaches into the untraceable past.

With such a spread, it's little wonder that everyone, famous and unknown alike, seems to have made it to Black's at some point in time, and their presence is reflected in the display of photos that take up most every inch of wall space in the dining area. There you'll find 20 years of local football team photos alongside the likes of former governor Ann Richards, with her trademark shock of white hair. "LBJ dined in this room many times," Black said of the 36th president, Texas-born Lyndon Baines Johnson, adding, "Lady Bird's college roommate was from Lockhart."

Look closely and you can also find a collection of photos showing Edgar and Norma Black through the years. That sense of family is what keeps Black's Barbecue together after more than 80 years, even as talk has arisen of a possible second location that would be located in nearby San Marcos.

The Texas Soft Drink Rainbow and Sweet Tea

Juneteenth, the celebration that marks the end of slavery and the granting of citizenship to African Americans, has been a Texas tradition since word of emancipation reached the state. Parades, commemoration services, and parties have since been a part of the daylong festivities, but it's the afternoon picnic featuring huge pits filled with barbecue that has served as the centerpiece. Mollie Evelyn Moore Davis's Texana classic, *Under the Man-Fig*, published in 1895, captures the euphoria of the day, though the author's fairly light on details on what was eaten. The folks at the Texas Committee for the Humanities made up for her oversight in their sesquicentennial publication, *The Texas Experience*. In an extended account of Juneteenth's jubilant history that is repeated in the historical cookbook *Eats: A Folk History of Texas Foods*, it is noted that "in keeping with convention men barbecued the meat, and women prepared the remainder of the food . . . fried chicken, potato salad, greens, sweet potato pie, and peach cobbler. Homemade ice cream, 'glassade' (a blend of shaved ice, sugar and fruit syrup), and red and orange soda were also served."

Red and orange soda. In the late 1800s sodas were a special treat, not something consumed every day, and if you could afford them, it meant you had a little extra to spend. All these years later, they're still a major part of barbecue in every corner of Texas you visit, and not just at Juneteenth festivities or strictly in the African-American community. It doesn't matter if you're in Longview or Brownsville, you'll find chilled-down bottles of Big Red and some brand of orange soda—Fanta, Orange Crush, Sunkist, Jarritos Mandarin, you name it—waiting to be paired up with a plate of ribs or sausage.

Black's Barbecue in Lockhart sells as much Big Red as it sells beer. Think about that: The volume of sales of one brand of soda equals the volume of all beer labels combined at one of the state's busiest barbecue joints. Is it any wonder that the walls of the men's room at Black's are decorated with Big Red bottle caps?

Big Red is a pure Texas creation. It began life in Waco back in 1937 and was first christened Sun Tang Red Cream Soda. It earned that cream soda name because of the almond flavor it features. But it doesn't stop there. One legend has it that the drink is a combination of orange and lemon oils. If that's true, it really is a cousin of orange soda, despite its red color. The drink's brush with immortality came when Texas singer-songwriter Robert Earl Keen included a reference to it in his song "Barbeque," in which he places that neon-red beauty on equal footing with the rest of the feast: sliced beef, ribs, sausage, and "a cold Big Red."

Other sodas, from Grape Nehi to root beer, have their champions among barbecue lovers, and Texans have a soft spot for another local product, the cherry-flavored Dr Pepper, which you sometimes find in a tangy mop for pork ribs. If you're a fan of any of these drinks, you may want to check out the lineup at Gonzales Food Market while you're there; the rainbow-colored selection of sodas in the refrigerator cases includes many made with real sugar instead of corn syrup, including Mountain Dew Throwback. What's the difference? You'd be surprised, first off, at how pristine the fruit flavor comes through in the soda made with sugar. Then you'd be amazed at how much brighter the acid in that soda becomes, which means it cleanses your palate in between bites of meat, making you ready for another bite. Yes, it works in the same way that wine does when you pair it with the right food.

And the right food, of course, is barbecue.

If soda were a sign of affluence back in the late 19th century, then tea would be thought of as merely an everyday drink, one that was, by and large, consumed hot until the early part of the 20th century. Nowadays both are consumed day and night throughout the state. You may hear an adult knock soda pop as being just for kids, but few see a problem in downing gallon after gallon of iced tea, especially that Southern favorite, sweet tea.

At the County Line chain of barbecue restaurants, sweet tea sells right up there with beer and margaritas, founder Skeeter Miller says. "Any given day, you can mix that order up, but it's always those three." Sweet tea is considered a healthy choice by many, in his opinion, because tea itself is considered healthy. It also has a generational hold on us, because so many Texans remember drinking it as a child when their grandmother or mother made it. In Texas, that makes it almost as sacred as barbecue.

Chisholm Trail Bar-B.Q. & Hot Sausage

1323 S. Colorado St., Lockhart, TX 78644; (512) 398-6027
Founded: 1978 **Pitmaster:** Floyd Wilhelm **Wood:** Post Oak

Floyd Wilhelm will tell you he learned his pitmaster skills the best way possible: He worked at Black's Barbecue for 18 years. He left more than 35 years ago because he had the chance to start his own place in Lockhart, which he named Chisholm Trail in honor of the town's place along the historic cattle drive.

Since then his barbecue joint has become something of an anomaly. Though it's located in the Barbecue Capital of Texas—meaning the barbecue capital of the entire world, to some—the restaurant hasn't achieved the fame of the other barbecue hot spots in town. Until recently, that is.

"In the last few years, we've started catching up a little and getting some national press," he says on a tour of Chisholm Trail's massive kitchen, where you'll find a small army of employees hard at work. Some are preparing potatoes for either salad or for smoking. Others are tending the loaves of bread rising in a not-too-drafty walkway or keeping an eye on the massive pots of pinto beans bubbling away. Several are back at the pits, where everything from brisket to chicken to ribs is cooking. Chisholm Trail uses both pits with indirect

heat from flaming post oak coals and a giant rotisserie, a cooking method that may be controversial to barbecue cognoscenti but not to Wilhelm's customers.

These regulars keep the lines long indoors and out, where a drive-thru window stays particularly busy with those who just want to get enough 'cue for the big game or share with the family. Convenience keeps the locals coming back, for sure, but so does the fact that Chisholm Trail has some of the best prices in Lockhart. Never underestimate value in the equation people use when choosing where to dine out. Wilhelm hasn't, and it's helped earn him Best Barbecue in Lockhart accolades from the local crowd for years.

The restaurant goes beyond the barbecue features of Certified Angus brisket, hand-stuffed sausages, ribs, chicken, and turkey and offers a few dishes to appeal to those locals who occasionally want something that isn't smoked. Now, that may seem heretical, but Wilhelm's staff puts as much effort in their fried catfish, chicken-fried steak, fajitas, and even salads as they do in what comes from the pits in back. The hefty array of side dishes goes beyond beans and potato salad to include cucumber-tomato salad, broccoli slaw, greens, fried okra, and, in a nod to the city's German heritage, sauerkraut with sausage in it. The latter is something that Wilhelm tried out because he wanted to see what the customers thought of it. It's a simple dish, served elsewhere in the region, so it's one that the locals have a taste for. They've liked it so much that it's found a permanent spot in the Chisholm Trail lineup. (See Chisholm Trail's recipe for Sauerkraut with Sausage on p. 240.)

The sauerkraut with sausage is a simple side dish that's sure to appeal to more than just those with a German or Czech background.

What all this means is, if you want to check out what the Lockhart locals think of barbecue in their own hometown, make sure Chisholm Trail is on your itinerary.

City Market

633 E. Davis St., Luling, TX 78648; (830) 875-9019 **Founded:** 1958
Pitmaster: Joe Capello Sr. **Wood:** Post Oak

If you go on a weekday and get there early, it's likely there won't be a long line at this renowned barbecue joint. Take our word for it, sausage, ribs, and brisket for breakfast at City Market will beat bacon and eggs almost any day.

To get to the meat-ordering area, one walks through the dining room to the closed-off room toward the back. The atmosphere in here is warm and cloistered, almost blue with smoke. Men move meat around from the grill over a warming pit to the counter, taking orders, bringing in smoked briskets from the pits out back, slicing sausages and ribs. The customers form a line outside the door, then come back out a second door with their meaty treasure.

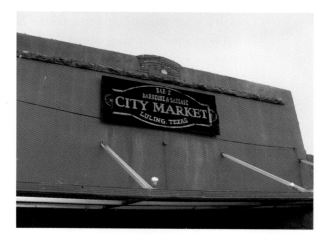

On our way back to the pit room, we passed two women picking through a small hill of pinto beans at one table. It was an early morning job—by the time we left, they'd finished with the sorting of beans and had moved on to covering the cash register at the front of the room, where side dishes are ordered and paid for. We made sure to have some of those beans, too.

This long-revered restaurant is now using a gas-fired rotisserie for at least some of its barbecue, says manager and pitmaster Joe Capello Sr. The gas-fired Southern Pride smoker is there to help them handle the big weekend push.

Capello has been there 45 years or so. He says the business has picked up over the years, attributing that to word of mouth and the Internet rather than advertising or food coverage on TV. Plus, "We're real easy to find," he says.

"We used to wait until the slow part of the year to take vacations," Capello says. That "slow part of the year" isn't easy to come by these days, though.

As do many pitmasters who've made this a longtime or lifetime career, Capello loves his job. "I still enjoy coming in to work every day, lighting up the pit, watching the briskets," he says. That means coming in at 6 a.m. every morning during the week, and for Saturday's business, arriving in the wee hours, 3:30 to 4 a.m.

Whichever pit our brisket had come from, it was flavorful, a little crusty from the salt and pepper rub, sliced relatively thin, and chewy-tender rather than fork-tender. The pork spare ribs were better than just good, taking the right amount of effort to pull the meat off the bone. The pork was succulent and a little chewy. Meat that falls apart or off the rib at a touch isn't what you want in good ribs. You want it to be tender and perfectly seasoned.

Try the mustard sauce on your barbecue, even if you're not a sauce devotee. It's good. We also recommend the homemade all-beef sausages—dunk a couple of slices cut from one of those juicy, handmade rings of sausage into the sauce as well. It's one of the best tastes to tell you why so many customers come back to City Market. Closed on Sunday.

Kreuz Market

619 N. Colorado St., Lockhart, TX 78644; (512) 398-2361; www.kreuz market.com **Founded:** 1900 (original Kreuz Market), 1999 (Rick Schmidt at Colorado Street location) **Pitmaster:** Roy Perez
Wood: Post Oak

Lockhart's reputation as being the heartland of Texas barbecue is due in part to the family that owns Kreuz Market. This building, with its spacious interior,

ample dining area, and cavernous pit room, was opened by Rick Schmidt, who moved the business in 1999 from its longtime downtown home (Smitty's Market, page 137).

The walk into Kreuz sends you past a dining room on both the left and right sides of the building. There's a rustic look to the one on the left, and a more cafeteria-style area on the right. But, look on the wall of the latter and you'll see a sign that is one of the Kreuz signatures: "No Sauce, No Forks, No Kidding."

"You'd be surprised how many people come in here and actually are upset by this [policy]," says Keith Schmidt, who now owns Kreuz Market. The policy goes all the way back to the original Kreuz Market, owned by Charles Kreuz, before he sold it to Edgar "Smitty" Schmidt in 1948.

The theory goes, barbecue sauce isn't needed to hide any off-flavors or enhance the meat.

"My father and I agreed. Sauce covers up plenty of mistakes. That's why Roy [Perez] has to stay on his game. What you want to taste is the flavor of the meat," Schmidt says.

The notion of sauce versus no sauce is controversial in Texas, he says: "There are people who firmly believe if there's not sauce, it's not barbecue."

Forks aren't needed either because the meat is tender. And, really, they're not kidding.

The best room in the building is the awe-inspiring pit room. This is where you'll go first to order your barbecue. Fires burn brightly near the heavy pits, sending up a smoky, atmospheric haze. Out back are stacks and stacks of seasoned post oak.

Most of the time, you'll also encounter Kreuz Market's pitmaster, Roy Perez. Perez, a stocky, handsome man, has become one of the most-photographed and popular pitmasters in Texas. His trademark sideburns, rolled-up T-shirt sleeves, and white apron, as well as a calm, friendly demeanor, are not only appealing to cameras, but also provide a welcoming presence in the heart of the restaurant.

He's a quiet person, who once painted houses for a living and enjoyed that for its solitude. But he says he now enjoys talking to people as he stands at the cutting station in the pit room.

The barbecue that Perez and his team put out of this room is excellent, judging by our visits. The brisket, lavish with crust and pepper, was tender and full-flavored, with a nice ribbon of smoke ring. We suggest getting a little bit of the fatty brisket as well as lean. The beef-and-pork sausages (85 percent beef) are a specialty here. They were firm and juicy—picking up slices to eat with our fingers only made it taste better. We did not miss barbecue sauce.

Slices of beef clod, a cut that gave way in popularity years ago to brisket, are another way to get your beef fix at Kreuz. We also recommend the prime rib. We asked Schmidt how it was that Perez managed to keep the meat on the big ribs at just the right rare-to-medium-rare throughout the day. The answer: "Well, it doesn't last long enough to get to medium."

While the smoky flavor doesn't penetrate deep into the interior of the prime rib, the seasoning and smoke on the outside still flavors just about every forkful (sorry, fingerful).

Also, ask Perez to slice you some pork chops fresh off the rack. They were excellent, and we highly recommend them as well as the pork ribs. Side dishes, drinks, crackers, and bread are served in the dining room—but other than picking up a cold beer to go with your 'cue, you might not pay any attention to things like the mac and cheese or German potato salad. And, that'll be all right. Try them on your next visit. Closed on Sunday.

Luling Bar-B-Q

709 E. Davis St., Luling, TX 78648; (830) 875-3848 **Founded:** 1986
Pitmaster: Gary Blevins **Wood:** Mesquite

Luling Bar-B-Q is just a short walk down Davis Street from the other barbecue place in Luling—City Market. Visitors to Luling often go to both places
because both have good reputations, though there are differences in atmosphere as well as menus. Our recommendation would be to make a day of it,
share and compare the food at both places, then take a look at the farmers'
market across the street, if it is open.

Luling Bar-B-Q is bright, with fresh paint, polished pine tables, and an
almost squeaky clean appearance. This is certainly no drawback, though we
did miss seeing the pits—or in this case, a gas-fired rotisserie—and the experience of walking into a smoky room to watch our meat being sliced. However,
you can watch your servings being carved up at the counter near the cash
register.

Manager Gary Blevins, whose mom is owner Patricia Chambers, strolled
over after we'd taken food to a table and talked to us about his preference of
wood to use in his Ole Hickory smoker. "Mesquite. I like the flavor better than
oak. Mesquite is just a little stronger,"
he said. The rest of our conversation
touched on a matter that often con-
cerns owners of long-lived barbecue
restaurants: Who is going to take
over when mom, dad, or whoever
does the hard work is ready to hand it
over? Blevins has a 17-year-old son—a
good boy, he said, but he has a car
now and "just wants to go."

The shiny nest of cooked sausages was appetizingly displayed
behind a glass partition. The food
looked and smelled good. The bris-
ket was tender and the mesquite flavor didn't overwhelm the taste of beef,
adding its own rustic perfume. The all-beef, handmade sausages were firm in
texture and particularly good with a little of the barbecue sauce drizzled over
fat, juicy slices. Turkey, pork loin, chicken, and ribs are also on the menu as
well as sandwiches.

All is not barbecue here, as there are hamburger and cheeseburger bas-
kets as well as a fish plate offered. The side dishes include the usual coleslaw,

Farmers' Markets in Texas:
There's an App for That

To say Texas is big on agriculture is like saying the Grand Canyon is big on scenery. In his salute to the state's farmers and ranchers in March 2014, Agriculture Commissioner Todd Staples mentioned that agriculture contributes "more than $100 billion to the Texas economy each year and supports approximately 1.8 million agriculture-related jobs, ranging from journalism and advertising to commodity trading." Farmers' markets, such as the one across the street from Luling B-B-Q, offer just-picked produce, fresh eggs, and packaged products, including jams, pickles, and even barbecue sauce. If you didn't bring a cooler with you to pack home a few pounds of brisket or sausage, a jar of pickles or a half-bushel of peaches might be just the right souvenir. There's now an app to help you find a farmers' market in the area where you're living or exploring. Check it out at the GO TEXAN website, gotexan.org/ LocateGOTEXAN/iPhoneApp .aspx.

potato salad, and pinto beans, but also new potatoes, fried okra, broccoli salad, and pea salad. We'll vouch for the fried okra, nicely breaded and crunchy. Fried okra, like fried green tomatoes, is a real Southern treat and fits quite nicely into the relatively few Texas barbecue places that carry it.

End a meal with a thick, heavenly looking slice of coconut meringue pie or whatever flavor is offered. The pie isn't made in-house, but it tasted as fresh and homemade as the rest of the food. As your mom said more than once, "Save room, there's dessert." Closed on Tuesday.

Smitty's Market

208 S. Commerce St., Lockhart, TX 78644; (512) 398-9344; www.smittys market.com **Founded:** 1948 (original Kreuz Market), 1990 (Nina Schmidt Sells) **Pitmasters:** Jim Sells, Pablo Garcia **Wood:** Post Oak

Smitty's is an institution in Lockhart, and history is what you will feel when you step through the doorway at the Commerce Street entrance. Ahead of you is a long, dimly lit hallway with a long bench down one side. At the end of the hall, a fire burns low toward the floor.

However antique this property might seem, it is neatly appointed and polished by owners Nina and Jim Sells. It retains its old-time atmosphere throughout most of the building. The dining room to the right of the entrance has a newer shine, though.

Inside and to the left of the Commerce Street entrance is a fresh meat market, with refrigerated cases and freezers, old butcher blocks, and vintage iceboxes. Fresh meats, as well as smoked breakfast sausages and more, are available in this part of the old building.

At the other end of the market, the flames mark the proximity of the pit room, burning unscreened. The warmth is welcome in midwinter, but in Sep-

tember it can be a blast furnace. Not that we minded this sign of a good Texas barbecue joint. It runs on fire and smoke—and flame around food has an elemental appeal any time.

Smitty's Market, long revered as one of Texas's top barbecue joints, was founded in 1948 by Edgar A. "Smitty" Schmidt, when he purchased the old Kreuz Market, which had been in business since 1900. When he died in 1990, Nina Schmidt Sells, his daughter, inherited the building and property. Her brothers Rick and Don had purchased the Kreuz Market business and name in 1984 from their dad. After their father's death, Sells and her brothers were unable to reach a lease agreement on the property. Don Schmidt retired, but his brother, Rick, left the historic downtown market and moved into a spacious building on N. Colorado Street (Kreuz Market, page 132).

Nina Sells changed the name of the Commerce Street business in honor of her dad. "Dad worked here in this building for 50 years. It's a tribute to him to call it Smitty's," she said.

At the end of the hallway, near the fires, a battered door takes you into the business area of barbecue, a smoky pit and serving room where you'll get meat to eat in or take out. Swift, practiced hands cut the brisket, pork ribs, sausages, pork chops, and pieces of beef clod, then pile them up on doubled pieces of waxed butcher paper, weigh it, and send you on your way to a big adjacent dining room to pick up your sides and drinks.

Sampling brisket from our opened package first, we found our slices tender and juicy, with ample fat-soaked crust and the red smoke ring. (Ask for a mixture of lean and fatty brisket, if you want the full experience.) The hand-tied sausages' coarsely ground meat was perfectly seasoned. We recommend the beef clod, too, as a prime example of Texas pit-smoked meat, tender throughout with a good lacing of fat. It's a cut that was once popular, before brisket entered the scene. Pork chops cut off the rack are another specialty here, and along with the beef clod, brisket, and sausage, we'd recommend adding a pork chop or two to your trove of meat.

Texas barbecue joints rarely hire pastry chefs. But, if there's someone who will make desserts, the sweets range from peach or blackberry cobblers to pies to any number of variations on banana pudding. Smitty's keeps it simple, however. The dessert they have available is Texas's famous Blue Bell ice cream out of big tubs. And, if you're not acquainted with Blue Bell, give yourself that pleasure!

Our favorite side dish at Smitty's is the pinto beans, which are modestly seasoned, leaving the delicious earthy taste of beans the main flavor in a thick, velvety broth. In fact, says Nina Sells' husband, Jim, sometimes people just ask for the broth—without the beans. (He brought us seconds on the broth.)

When you talk about any of the Schmidt family businesses, barbecue sauce is given careful consideration. Kreuz Market and Lockhart Smokehouse in Dallas steadfastly carry on the family tradition of no sauce. Ever. (Or forks. Fingers are fine.) The relatively new Schmidt Family Barbecue in Bee Cave has sauce. No apologies.

Smitty's has a sauce available. People asked for it and so they got it, says Nina Sells, just a tad grudgingly. So, don't feel bad if you don't use any. There are lots of people in Texas who don't.

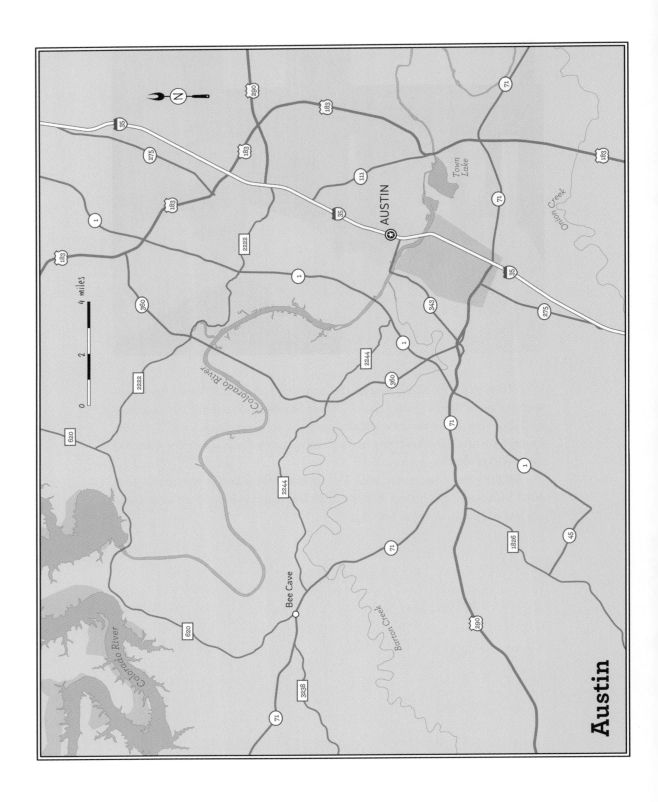

Austin

Austin

When it comes to barbecue, Austin is playing a game of follow the leader—and no one seems to mind. The leader in Texas's capital city is Franklin Barbecue, which has received international attention for its brisket. It's been featured in a national credit card commercial, a feature film, and nearly countless stories. Lines start forming at about 8 in the morning, even though the opening is not until 11 a.m. And there's no guarantee that you'll get a slice of brisket if and when you do make it to the head of the line.

The intense focus on pitmaster Aaron Franklin and his popularity has forced many other barbecue joints in town—at least those who pay attention to such trends (and not all do)—to step up their game. At numerous places we heard pitmasters and general managers alike invoke his status as the measure they strive to achieve. The best thing for customers is that Franklin now has a healthy crop of competitors who are producing barbecue of such a high quality that many barbecue lovers have said Austin has surpassed the Barbecue Capital of Texas, Lockhart, as the place to eat smoked meat.

Of course, there are drawbacks to the situation. The biggest could be Austin itself. The city, known for its diverse music scene and its tech scene, lives by the motto "Keep Austin Weird," which means you have to put up with a place that operates on its own terms, sometimes with little care for visitors. A great many locals walk or bike to their destination, because they can. They know that their city has the worst traffic flow in the state. But if you're a visitor, crossing Texas on the barbecue trail, you're more than likely stuck with your car. So, if you have to travel 5 miles during rush hour, plan on giving yourself at least an hour to get there—and you may want to add more time to find a parking place. Weekends are not an exception.

But when you settle down to your plate of oak-smoked meat, you'll soon forget the stress you endured to get there, whether you're at a food truck, a casual eatery that mingles music and barbecue, or a white tablecloth place like Lamberts Downtown Barbecue, which offers what it calls "fancy barbecue," Austin's barbecue scene runs the gamut of presentations, but more and more places are all about giving you some of the best barbecue you've ever had in your life.

Franklin Barbecue

900 E. 11th St., Austin, TX 78702; (512) 653-1187; www.franklin
barbecue.com **Founded:** 2009 **Pitmaster:** Aaron Franklin **Wood:**
Post Oak

So much has been written about Franklin Barbecue—and a good chunk of those
words has hailed the place as having the best barbecue in all of America—that
it's hard to approach your first visit without expectations, some reasonable and
others not. First, you have to be prepared to stand in line quite a while before
you get served. If you don't, you stand a good chance of not getting any food.
Then you have to ask yourself the question: Can any food live up to the hype
that has surrounded it? If you have serious doubts or you grumble too much
at what you have to invest in order to eat barbecue on butcher paper, then skip
it. It's doubtful that you'd be satisfied with anything you'd be served. But if you
embrace the whole package, enjoying your hours spent in line and then greeting the food with open mouth and mind, you'll discover this is the ultimate in
Texas barbecue experiences.

Nowhere else will you find lines forming three hours before the doors
open. Weekday waits are a little less, but on the Thursday we visited, more
than a dozen people were ahead of us at 8:30 a.m. By the time 11 a.m. rolled

around, the line had snaked
along the patio and down
past the building. By that
time, too, we had talked
with the women in front
of us and the firefighters
behind us about their favorite moments on the Texas
barbecue trail. We mar-
veled at the patience of the
dogs that had been dragged
along. And we enjoyed the
cool of the Texas morning.
When the doors opened, we
felt as if we'd been shot into
the building and around to the counter like a pinball spinning up its chute.

Why would anyone wait that long? Brisket, if you really need to ask. Brisket so tender, so beefy, so rustic that it's hard to comprehend how the thick
slabs of the fatty cut could contain that much flavor. (Go with the fatty cut. The
lean lacked the sublime salty rub and crust, not to mention the moisture that

put its marbled cousin over the top.) The fatty brisket fairly defies description. Words can take you only so far before Aaron Franklin's pitmastery takes over and, after hours of exposure to the indirect heat and smoke of post oak, what emerges is a whole new brisket experience.

Pork ribs, pulled pork, sausage, and turkey do their best to shine, as do the side dishes, limited to beans, potato salad, and coleslaw. But nothing can eclipse the brisket, though the Tipsy Texan sandwich, with chopped brisket, sausage, and a mound of slaw, makes its own case for stardom.

Franklin's espresso barbecue sauce loves smoked beef. And it's readily available at Texas supermarkets, so you don't have to wait in line to get a bottle of it.

If you're not a sauce fan, you might be tempted to overlook the three that appear on each table. Don't. Dip a little of the brisket into the espresso sauce, and see how well the coffee flavor supports and improves the already stellar brisket. Or shake a little of the sweet vinegar sauce on the shreds of pulled pork. Though Franklin's meats do not need sauce, all three, including the tangy Texas Style, do their best to enhance the meats' natural flavors without swamping them.

The brisket may take top honors, but attention must also be paid to the bourbon banana pudding pie. It is almost startling what just a touch of bourbon—as well as a buttery crust in place of the usual Nilla Wafers—does to elevate this already beloved dessert. It is yet another example of how this kitchen can take barbecue classics and make you taste them in a whole new way. Closed on Monday.

Freedmen's

2402 San Gabriel St., Austin, TX 78705; (512) 220-0953; www.freedmens bar.com **Founded:** 2012 **Pitmaster:** Evan LeRoy **Wood:** Oak
In 1869 a former slave named George Franklin built an impressive brick building that, through the years, has been used as a church, a publishing house, a grocery, and a private residence. Late in 2012 it became an upscale, laid-back barbecue restaurant that offers live music in the beer garden and some fine craft cocktails no matter where you sit.

Executive chef Evan LeRoy and his sous chef, Diego Abreu, hold most everything on their menu to the fire, including the cabbage used in the grilled slaw and the beets with herbed chèvre. The bananas get a hit of oak before ending up in the Smoked Banana Pudding. There's even a plate of smoked and grilled vegetables for the vegetarians in the house—and since Freedmen's is in Austin, there's a great likelihood of that happening.

The Smoked Banana Pudding is more like a panna cotta. It is layered with whipped cream inside a jelly jar and topped with an opulent amount of freshly grated nutmeg. The aroma alone is a heady experience.

But it's the meats that command attention, and the best way of discovering that is with the Holy Trinity, a three-meat plate featuring—you guessed it—brisket, ribs, and sausage. The brisket had just the right amount of give to your fork, with plenty of beef flavor coming through each moist bite. A peppery crust added both flavor and texture, making it an exceptional example in a city that treasures its brisket. House-made beef sausage with plenty of snap to the casing was pure comfort on the icy day we visited, while the pork ribs had a welcome sweetness as well as a good give when you bit into them. (Expect specials, including pork belly, specialty sausages, and beef ribs, we've been told; but that's for another visit.) There are sauces, both sweet and hot, but the meat didn't need either.

The smoke has landed at Freedmen's bar area, too: The Ol' Schmokey is a potent blend of Old Forester, smoked pecan bitters, and smoked orange that is both sweet and nutty—and refreshingly different.

On a quick tour of the pit out back, Abreu said that the success of Franklin Barbecue had made most everyone on the barbecue scene want to do better. If that's the reason for Freedmen's being so good, that's great for everyone. We're all the better fed as a result. Closed on Monday.

John Mueller Meat Co.

2500 E. Sixth St., Austin, TX 78702; (512) 524-0559; www.johnmueller meatco.com **Founded:** 2013 **Pitmaster:** John Mueller **Wood:** Oak

John Mueller says on his own website that he doesn't call himself a pitmaster. "I'm a cook—I cook for a living," he says. He can, however, claim his heritage as a third-generation barbecue master and meat merchant.

He and siblings LeAnn Mueller (La Barbecue, page 146) and Wayne Mueller are at this time all carrying on the legacy of their grandfather, Louie Mueller, founder of the renowned Louie Mueller Barbecue in Taylor, and their father, Bobby Mueller. LeAnn Mueller is also a photographer for *Texas Monthly* magazine; Wayne Mueller has taken over Louie Mueller Barbecue (page 98).

John Mueller left Taylor and set up shop in Austin in 2001, establishing John Mueller's B-B-Q. After going through a period of tribulation, he's now back in business, smoking up some of the best barbecue in the state.

John Mueller Meat Co. (JMMC) is set on a large lot with a trailer for ordering and picking up sides, a big indirect-heat pit, and a collection of picnic tables under a blue-and-white awning. Longtime faithful customers and those eager to join their ranks line up for the great hunks of smoky beef ribs, salt-and-pepper-crusted brisket, pork ribs, sausage, and even turkey breast—good and moist enough that you won't consider it an afterthought. (Which is a good thing, because if one wanders in late to JMMC, as we did one day, it's likely to be one of the few things left to order.)

Have beer with your barbecue, take the meat wrapped up to go, and actually use Mueller's thin, peppery, onion-and-tomato-based sauce. Even if you don't usually go for sauce, try this one.

Mueller took some time on our first visit to talk, discussing the role social media has come to play in the world of Texas barbecue—it's important, as Facebook and Twitter are ways for smaller businesses to build a following and get the word out.

Brisket, he mentioned in a moment of near heresy, is really a pretty "horrible" cut of meat.

"It used to be trash, used to go into hamburger," he says. His method of turning this trash into tongue-tingling pleasure is to pit-smoke it hot and fast, rather than adhering to the low, slow method of many a Texas pit wrangler. "I was taught to look at the flame, keep the flame right, and judge [the cooking] by that," he says.

As for the vicissitudes of the barbecue business in general and the current rage for smoked meats in Texas, Mueller, at 44, has been around long enough to see it as cyclical.

"The market will get saturated and the strong will survive," he says. "That's the fascination with barbecue." Closed on Monday.

La Barbecue

1200 E. Sixth St., Austin, TX 78702; (512) 605-9696; www.labarbecue .com; @la_Barbecue **Founded:** 2012 **Pitmaster:** John Lewis
Wood: Mixture (mostly oak)

If the words "free beer" don't pull you into this East Austin enclave of trailer, pits, and picnic tables, the barbecue will, starting with the prime-beef brisket and award-winning beef rib.

The trailer/pit setup has worked for a collection of Austin's best barbecue joints in the past few years. La Barbecue, one of the most popular, is co-owned by pitmaster John Lewis and LeAnn Mueller. The name started out as LA Barbecue, using LeAnn's initials, but when it was too often mistaken as L.A. barbecue (and who knows what that is?), the LA become La. Or, as it explains on their Twitter profile, *la Barbecue*—Spanish for "the barbecue."

The owners' street cred was gained by virtue of their product. Then, there's history. Mueller's grandfather was Louie Mueller and her father was Bobby Mueller, which gives her a solid grounding in the meat-smoking as well as the restaurant business. Louie Mueller Barbecue in Taylor, now run by her brother Wayne,

has stayed firmly on or near the pinnacle of most "best-of" lists touting Texas barbecue.

John Lewis, pitmaster, general manager, and therefore almost always on-scene at La Barbecue, is self-taught. He worked in Denver for a while and went to work for Aaron Franklin when Franklin opened his first trailer in 2009. He built the pit he cooks on, and it's a sturdy-looking, cylinder-shaped, indirect-heat smoker. This is the brisket cooker. The oak he usually uses (along with pecan and hickory at times) burns brightly in a square steel fire box that he also built. (He doesn't claim to be a welder but figured it out and got the job done. He had, in fact, built a few smokers before La Barbecue's.)

La Barbecue's beef ribs won second place in Mick Vann's First Annual Austin Chronicle Invitational BBQ Beef Rib Smackdown in January 2014. (First place went to Thomas Micklethwait of Micklethwait Craft Meats, page 148.) These massive, peppery cuts of delectable meat on caveman-style bones are rapidly growing in popularity on the Texas barbecue trail. So, we naturally suggest tackling one of these. The satisfaction of this glistening moist meat under its crusty, pull-apart exterior is hard to match.

We suggest ordering some of the spicy homemade sausages, too, before heading to sit down at one of the long lines of picnic tables. The side dishes are also good, and we recommend the potato salad.

But brisket is king, and Lewis uses prime Black Angus beef briskets and gives them his exacting attention. The results show it. The higher fat content gives the meat a smooth and silky texture and a full, beefy flavor; the traditional addictive blend of smoke and salt-and-pepper crust combine with that meat for a superior, tantalizing flavor that you won't mind standing in line for. Music is often included in this outdoor environment, which seals the deal for a fine, Austin barbecue experience. Closed on Monday and Tuesday.

Lamberts Downtown Barbecue

401 W. Second St., Austin, TX 78701; (512) 494-1500; www.lamberts austin.com **Founded:** 2006 **Pitmaster:** Zach Davis **Wood:** Oak
Lamberts bills itself as having "fancy barbecue," which may seem like a marriage of opposites, but the chef here, Zach Davis, manages to make it work.

You have to do some work yourself, mainly in the form of making reservations. Without them, you're not too likely to get a seat. The restaurant is housed in a magnificent brick edifice that dates back to the 1870s. On the main floor, folks crowd into the chummy dining area, while the second story is for live music.

There's an open kitchen, where those seated at the nearby tables can watch the staff put together much of your meal, though the pit itself doesn't seem to a part of the scene. The main courses are divided between oak-smoked and oak-grilled items. While the Gulf shrimp and grits with house-cured Canadian bacon or the hangar steak with Cholula butter, both on the grill side, sounded great, we stuck with the smoked items for our visit and enjoyed fatty cuts of brisket that had been rubbed in brown sugar and espresso as well as the pork ribs with some maple in their glaze. The ribs were accompanied by an apple, walnut, and roasted fennel slaw, sort of a deconstructed Waldorf salad that threatened to upstage the ribs.

The macaroni with three cheeses gained a bit of tang from goat cheese, a velvety smoothness from American, and a sharpness from cheddar, all of which blended together into a satisfying whole. You won't find the fancy brussels sprouts with brown butter and house-cured bacon on too many other barbecue menus, and it's a shame, because this side was as satisfying as anything we tasted at Lamberts. The desserts are also gussied up. Instead of banana pudding, it's Caramelized Banana Pot de Crème. Don't settle for vanilla ice cream when you can have a scoop of pumpkin or buttermilk.

Brussels sprouts, brown butter, and bacon — they're the Bach, Beethoven, and Brahms at this tony barbecue spot.

The barbecue at Lamberts is fancy, and so are the prices. If that's a concern of yours, you may want to check the prices online before planning your trip.

Micklethwait Craft Meats

1309 Rosewood Ave., Austin, TX 78702; (512) 791-5961; www.craft meats.com; @craftmeats **Founded:** 2012 **Pitmaster:** Thomas Micklethwait **Wood:** Post Oak

Not long after Micklethwait Craft Meats opened in late 2012, word spread quickly about the little yellow trailer set off the street on Rosewood Avenue in East Austin. And, that word was as good as any pitmaster might crave.

The pitmaster and owner, Tom Micklethwait, had previously worked making sausage in a restaurant, but taught himself how to pit-smoke meat well enough to open his own shop. He says he "learned on the job" by cooking for friends and catering house parties. When we met Micklethwait a year after opening, he was finally training an assistant to help with the smoking of the briskets, pork shoulder, and other meats that have drawn a faithful clientele.

We recommend both the brisket and sliced pork shoulder, with simple salt-and-pepper rubs that emphasize the good, meaty flavors. Beef ribs are also on the menu, and these monsters won a first-place prize for Micklethwait in Mick Vann's First Annual (2014) Austin Chronicle Invitational BBQ Beef Rib Smackdown. If you thought Texas barbecue was all about the brisket, it's time to get acquainted with the beef rib—a carnivore's dream.

Micklethwait's craft of making sausage is not only his specialty, but part of the heritage of Central Texas barbecue. So, finding, say, a fat German knockwurst on the day's sausage menu is not unusual. He makes different sausages every day, and his use of fresh herbs and seasonings makes them stand out. We'd also attribute their firm, meaty texture to Micklethwait's practice and experience, and the unique blends of spice and seasonings to sheer creativity. A spicy lamb sausage with orange, a duck sausage with tart cherry, a pork belly andouille, or a sausage spiked with Thai chiles and kielbasa are a few examples to seek out.

Another hospitable feature of Micklethwait Craft Meats is that there are picnic tables out front, and even on damp, nippy days, guys (on days like this, it is usually guys) will be there, huddled over a very good lunch or dinner. Also, across the parking lot, next to a house that sells

We love barbecue; we also like to have a few good carbs on the side. Micklethwait's Jalapeño Cheese Grits would be one of our first choices from the whole Texas barbecue trail. They weren't fiery hot, but the warm flavor of the green chile, the creaminess of the cheese, and perfectly cooked grits combined into something sensational. Also, if you've never had a Moon Pie (dessert) or a Big Red (soda), these are on the Micklethwait menu as well, with sweetness there to remind you that Texas does have a good dose of the South in its heritage.

vintage clothing, is a tiny gray box. It's just big enough for a barista and equipment for making some good, hot coffee.

Sometime in 2014, Micklethwait plans to have moved to a brick-and-mortar restaurant. It, too, will be in East Austin. We expect the excellent barbecue and great sausages to survive that move just fine. Closed on Monday and Tuesday.

Sam's Bar-B-Que

2000 E. 12th St., Austin, TX 78702; (512) 478-0378 **Founded:** 1940s
Pitmaster: Brian Mays **Wood:** Oak

We arrived at Sam's Bar-B-Que on a Labor Day Monday when far too many other barbecue joints and trucks across the city were taking the day off (so

plan your own holiday trips wisely). But from one taste of the mutton chops, talk of the rest of the city's fabled barbecue vanished. The slabs of tender meat were not too fatty and they weren't too gamey either, which means that even the lamb hater in our group loved what she tried.

Sam's has been operated by the Mays family since it opened in the 1940s, and mutton has been a part of the menu for its entire run. In fact, mutton used to be fairly prevalent on the state's barbecue scene, much like *cabrito* is in West Texas, but you don't see it much anymore because the price of the meat can get too high for some places. Pitmaster Brian Mays swears by the family tradition of serving it, though, so you can always expect to sink your teeth into a moist helping of mutton.

Actually, Sam's has always prided itself on the tenderness of its meat, which is where the joint's now-legendary saying about its brisket came about: "You don't need no teeth to eat my beef!" The same holds true of the chicken. (You can get that slogan on the back of a souvenir Sam's T-shirt, though the memory of the mutton is what we'll treasure more.)

Brian Mays takes great care to point out that his recipes are health-conscious because he doesn't use salt, which many of his older customers have shunned. So, his pinto beans are seasoned with cayenne pepper to give them a little heat.

On weekends Sam's is open until 3 a.m., which has made it an East Austin draw for anyone in the area with a case of the late-night munchies. On that lengthy list you'll find plenty of famous musicians and actors, many of whose pictures adorn the walls of the small dining room. The area, which seats only about 20 people, was experiencing a little indirect cooking action from the nearby pit, as the window air conditioner wasn't operating on full speed the day we visited. But an icy cold root beer and some smoking 'cue made everything right with the world.

Schmidt Family Barbecue

12532 FM 2244, Bee Cave, TX 78378; (512) 263-4060; www.schmidt familybarbecue.com **Founded:** 2013 **Pitmasters:** Chad Franks, Bryan Garcia **Wood:** Oak

If the Schmidt family name rings a bell with you, you've done your barbecue homework well. Yes, this is the Schmidt family of Lockhart, but don't show up in this Austin suburb expecting a carbon copy of Kreuz or Smitty's. First off, you get a fork to eat your slaw with, and there is a barbecue sauce that regulars buy extra to take home with them.

The meats are largely the traditional cuts that you'd expect to find. There's prime brisket, for example, cut thick and rippling with a fine layer of moist fat. But the rub on that bark isn't the same, and it does change the meat's flavor profile somewhat. "I like to use a little more pepper than salt in mine," says pitmaster Chad Franks, who once worked at Kreuz and is married to Susie Schmidt Franks. He also adds a little garlic powder and onion powder to liven it up a bit, but the real recipe is—you guessed—a secret.

The couple has partnered in the venture with her cousin, Keith Schmidt, who manages Kreuz Market. And you'll find ties pointing out the connection in the form of Kreuz signs lining the walk back to the counter where you'll have your meats cut for you. But the connection isn't overwhelming, because, as Franks says, "Half the people who come in here have never heard of Kreuz."

That's right, folks. There are some of you out there who don't have the genealogy of every multigenerational Texas barbecue family tattooed on your brain. So, for you, we'll leave the comparisons largely behind and concentrate on what Schmidt Family Barbecue is. It is a large meat market with a vast, open dining area that is modern and cool, an inviting oasis away from the heat of a Texas day. It seats about 300 people, and it can fill a good portion of that during the daily lunch crowd, Franks says.

Beef clod used to be the barbecue cut before brisket asserted itself. Give this well-seasoned beef shoulder a try.

They're showing up for the brisket, of course, but also the beef clod, the pork ribs, and the handmade sausage that comes in from Kreuz. And they're trying pulled pork and even the burnt ends served in sauce. They're also enjoying the selection of side dishes, which includes the usual suspects, of course, along with a regular and a spicy mac and cheese, the latter with choice bits of ham and jalapeño melted in the mix. Expect more to come as the restaurant grows. "We try to keep it simple," Franks says, adding that his interests are in making sure every detail is addressed. "I'm here for the quality." And he knows his customers will hold him to that.

Stiles Switch BBQ & Brew

6610 N. Lamar Blvd., Austin, TX 78757; (512) 380-9199 **Founded:** 2011 **Pitmaster:** Lance Kirkpatrick **Wood:** Post Oak

Shane Stiles's hometown of Thrall, located between Taylor and Rockdale, used to be known as Stiles Switch, and it was the name he co-opted for his new venture, because of the taste of home it carried. But Stiles Switch wasn't originally meant to be a barbecue joint. The businessman had wanted to open a brewpub, but he just couldn't find the right space. So, he decided to go the barbecue route and make sure beer—Texas craft beer, in particular—was a part of the setup. He placed the pit in the hands of Lance Kirkpatrick, who'd learned his trade at the famous Louie Mueller Barbecue in Taylor, while the management of the restaurant went to James Jackson, who'd worked at the equally well-known Southside Market in Elgin.

Great pedigrees both. So, is it any surprise that the

barbecue is as good as it is? Not really. Still, the richness of a fatty cut of brisket is always welcome when you bite into it and it practically melts into your tongue. Pork ribs mingle smoke and sugar for a toothsome treat, while the beef chuck ribs are overwhelming in size and flavor down at the bone. Don't settle for one type of sausage; order up a tasting of all three: jalapeño-cheddar (made with beef and pork), Thorndale (beef), and Switch Original (beef and pork). Pork loin, chicken, and Frito pie round out the meat menu.

Opening a new barbecue joint brings a set of lessons in paying attention to even the tiniest of details and listening to customers, Jackson says. When too many complained that the coleslaw wasn't sweet enough, the recipe underwent a thorough revision. Now there are two coleslaws, one with a creamy mayonnaise dressing (and plenty of sugar) and another with a lemon vinaigrette that's tartly refreshing.

The coleslaw with the lemon vinaigrette is light, refreshing, and tangy without an excessive amount of sugar bogging it down.

Why get banana pudding when you can end your meal with Stiles Switch's chocolate and banana pudding? This recipe, which is from Jackson, upends the classic in a way that's as comfortably old-fashioned as any dish you might find at a church potluck. Yes, there are fresh bananas, wafers, and vanilla pudding, but they're layered atop Oreo crumbs, chocolate pudding, and Cool Whip. It all adds up to a dish that's practically guaranteed to please most everyone at your table. And that's the goal of the folks at Stiles Switch, whether you're talking brisket, brew, or anything else. Closed on Monday.

Stubb's BBQ

801 Red River St., Austin, TX 78701; (512) 480-8341 **Founded:** 1995 **Wood:** Post Oak

The legendary "Stubb," born Christopher B. Stubblefield, is no longer with us, and neither is his original restaurant in Lubbock. But his fame, his barbecue, and his love of good music live on in the Austin location. Everyone from Willie Nelson and Dwight Yoakam to James Brown and Metallica has played in the music venue out back. And Rachael Ray, who loves throwing a party, has rented out the place for her own music and food extravaganza during the annual South by Southwest festival. Music is also key to the popular Sunday

A Musical Legacy from a Barbecue Legend

BY DEBORAH ORAZI

On a small, tree-lined plaza in Lubbock, a bronze statue stands as a testament to one man's love for barbecue and Texas music.

The statue is of Christopher B. "Stubb" Stubblefield holding a tray of his famous barbecue, and it marks the spot where his original restaurant once stood: 108 E. Broadway. It was an address as well-known to Lubbock musicians as it was to the town's barbecue lovers.

Lubbock was a fertile breeding ground for musicians in the 1950s, '60s, and '70s, and there weren't many who didn't know Stubb and his restaurant. For years local and visiting musicians congregated there to eat, play music, and socialize.

"It was a safe haven for musicians," said legendary musician Joe Ely, who along with his wife, Sharon, became close friends with Stubb in the 1970s. "It was just a little, tiny barbecue place that held about 70 people."

Lloyd Maines, Jesse Taylor, Ponty Bone ("He was a vegetarian, but he sure loved Stubb's," Sharon Ely said), Don Caldwell, and artist/musician Terry Allen, creator of the Stubb statue, were just a few of the Texas regulars.

It may have been physically small, but the restaurant and its owner had a huge impact on the town culturally, as well as musically, according to Joe Ely.

"Stubb's place was like a bridge between the several cultures of Lubbock," he said. "Lubbock was a big cotton town with a lot of workers from Mexico and blacks. There was a cotton gin behind Stubb's place. But there was never any trouble at the restaurant because he was a big, imposing man."

The story of Stubb and his connection to music really began in the mid-1970s with yet another of Lubbock's great musicians, the late guitarist Jesse Taylor. He was hitchhiking in Lubbock when fate stepped in and Stubb gave him a lift. After feeding the guitarist some barbecue at his establishment, the cash-strapped restaurateur offered him a place to play. It was an offer that would prove beneficial to both.

"Jesse called me up and said, 'I found this great place on East Broadway that we can jam at,'" Joe Ely recalled. "I was just getting a band together. I had left the Flatlanders and had been in New York for six months. We called all our friends up. We were, basically, just passing the instruments around."

"I was there that first night," Sharon Ely recalled. "The place was packed."

That first Sunday jam session brought in enough money to keep the restaurant afloat for weeks, Joe Ely added. "We kept the tradition going about six or seven years."

The restaurant would inspire several songs over the years, the most famous a top 20 hit written by Tom T. Hall. "The Great East Broadway Onion Championship of 1978" is about a game of pool that really took place at the restaurant with Joe Ely and Hall, who were supposed to be performing that night, and Stubb.

"While we were turned around talking, Sharon took the cue ball," Joe Ely said. "Leaning up against the wall there was a 50-pound sack of white onions. I grabbed one and used it as a cue ball. Tom T. went along with the gag. Every once in a while someone would scratch—put one in the pocket—and it would get stuck under there. I would grab another onion.

"Three weeks after the game, there was a foul smell coming from the pool table. Stubb pulled out eight onions that had gotten stuck in there."

There was a lot of fun had at the barbecue joint, but also some financially hard times for Stubb. He closed his Lubbock restaurant in 1985 and headed to Austin, where he served up his barbecue at famed blues club Antone's before eventually opening his own place in Austin in 1986.

During one of those rough spells when he was short of money, Sharon Ely came up with the idea of bottling and selling Stubb's barbecue sauce.

"The first few batches were made in our kitchen and [singer/songwriter] Kimmie Rhodes's place," Joe Ely said. "Stubb oversaw the operation."

"Kimmie Rhodes had the canning knowledge, and we needed to know how to can it properly, how to get it hot enough," Sharon Ely said. "Joe designed a label on his 2E computer. After we got all the sauce into the jars, we all sat and put those labels on the jars. Stubb drove him and me in his old Cadillac and delivered the sauce. At the end of the day, we had collected $200."

At one point Stubb suggested moving the "factory" into Joe Ely's studio while he was on tour. That idea was quickly nixed, but he had plenty of others.

"Stubb didn't like the Mason jars we were using," Sharon Ely said. "He wanted to put the sauce in whiskey bottles, so he went and found all the bottles behind the Continental [Club]. He'd bring them home and wash them. Then he got his grandsons to put blue electrical tape around the top [once they were filled].

"He had different ways he cooked the barbecue sauce. We have a video of him making it from scratch. It was not as sweet, and it was spicy. It had a little heat."

"He would say love and happiness were the secret ingredients," Joe Ely added.

Today, the first bottle of sauce produced in their kitchen sits under glass at the Ely home.

The production experience proved valuable for Sharon Ely, who, in 2009, started marketing her own brand of soup called Holy Posole, currently available in supermarkets around Texas.

Stubb's fame and reputation grew after a 1991 appearance on *Late Night with David Letterman*, where he cooked for the host and his audience.

"He went to Nashville and visited the Grand Ole Opry, and he always brought barbecue to the backstage area for the musicians," Sharon Ely said. "All those great stars were there and everybody turned and looked at Stubb when he came in, Johnny and June, Tom T. . . ."

His original sauce recipe may have varied from batch to batch, but he, himself, never changed.

"Stubb was a very large personality with a lot of compassion," is how Sharon Ely remembered him. "He was a great storyteller. He loved music and would always sing 'Summertime.'

"When Joe and I had our daughter, Marie, in 1983, he announced he was going to be the godfather. Then he asked, 'What does a godfather do?' The first year Marie was born, he had saved all the change people dropped and at Christmas time gave her a gunnysack full of coins."

Stubb passed on in 1995, but there are plenty of enduring reminders of him, especially in Austin, where a giant jar of his barbecue sauce on W. Sixth Street marks the headquarters of his product line (which has grown to include sauces, spice rubs, and marinades). A Stubb's restaurant and outdoor music venue, with a capacity of around 1,400, continues to host concerts and feed musicians at its location in Austin's new Red River Cultural District.

In 2009 Stubb was inducted into the Austin Music Memorial on the terrace of the Long Center for the Performing Arts. And in 2014 the Elys plan to release a documentary about their friend.

"Three or four years ago we began gathering interviews," Joe Ely said. "We have so much footage and pictures. A lot of it is Stubb himself, telling the story."

"There was a real man behind the barbecue," Sharon Ely said. "The film will show who he really was."

Deborah Orazi is the publisher of the Austin Music Journal *and producer of* Austin Music Journal TV.

gospel brunches, which raise the rafters with their joyful noise and smoked meats.

As big a role as the music plays, the food is what brings people in day after day. They want the moist Angus brisket with a fine bark, the pork ribs that boast a pepper-rich rub, the jalapeño-cheddar

Serrano cheese spinach balances spicy and creamy elements in ways so exceptional that it could overshadow the barbecue (recipe inspired by Stubb's serrano cheese spinach on page 241).

sausage with a kick, the pulled pork, or any of the other meats. Among the vast array of Southern-style side dishes, which include fried okra, collard greens and mashed potatoes, don't miss the serrano cheese spinach. It's worth a trip by itself, no matter who's playing that night.

Valentina's Tex-Mex BBQ

600 W. Sixth St., Market District, Austin, TX 78701 (truck, behind Star Bar); (512) 363-8520; www.valentinastexmexbbq.com; @valstex mexbbq **Founded:** 2013 **Pitmasters:** Miguel Vidal, Elias Vidal
Wood: Mesquite

The smell of smoking meat and the spicy-hot flavors of a salsa verde (green chile sauce), smoky *carnitas* wrapped in a homemade tortilla, guacamole topping your brisket taco—these are just a few of the homespun pleasures one finds at Valentina's Tex-Mex BBQ.

This bright sheet-metal truck is trimmed with colored Christmas lights and named after the young daughter of co-owner Miguel Vidal. It's tucked into a space behind the Star Bar and shares the bar's covered-patio seating close by. Get a beer from the bar and watch sports on TV outside, or head indoors for protection from weather, if needed. On the other side of the trailer, an offset smoker burns mesquite which flavors the very good brisket with well-

seasoned and blackened crust. It is also the magic that sears the pork shoulder for pulled pork, skirt steak for beef fajitas, and chicken for pulled chicken.

"We wanted a country-downtown feel, an outdoor place that's right in the middle of town," said Vidal. His brother, Elias Vidal, also works at the trailer. Both brothers man the pit.

The menu, posted on the truck, is divided into "Tex" and "Mex." The "Tex"

side lists the sandwiches. The "Mex" side of the menu is tacos, and the rounded balls of tortilla dough proofing inside the trailer prove this part of the equation. His business partner—who manages the books, not the pit—is Michael Lerner, and his wife, Modesty, helps out, too.

This Tex and Mex marriage has worked for Valentina's. Miguel Vidal was born and raised in San Antonio, Tex-Mex capital of Texas. The smoked meat his dad and uncle made often went into his mom's tortillas.

Miguel moved to Austin when he was a teenager, and played soccer for St. Edwards University. Both he and his brother, Elias, have built a solid history of restaurant experience. Both have climbed the hospitality-related work ladder, from valet parking to dishwashing to cooking. Miguel parked cars at the Four Seasons—and eventually became general manager at Ranch 616 in Austin. He traveled to Colorado for five years for the Aspen Food & Wine Festival.

Despite this experience, it was a passion for home-style cooking that led him to open Valentina's in 2013. The tacos, sandwiches, and side dishes, such as charro beans, guacamole (which tops some of the tacos), chips and salsa, Mexican rice, and smoked corn, are all part of the business's success.

A brick-and-mortar version of Valentina's could be in store, too. "I always had a deep-down feeling that people would like my food," said Vidal. "It's inspiring us to work hard and to reach our goal."

West Texas

If your image of Texas is empty spaces filled with sand, sky, and plenty of scrub, then you've got a fairly good take on the back roads and sandhills of West Texas. This is the least populated area of the state, the least cultivated, and the driest.

Once upon a time in the 19th century, in the days when cowboys and Indians were still fighting for control of the land, West Texas served as home to Apache and Comanche, Mexican and white settlers, and Texas rangers alike. Myth and legend grew taller than crops back then, thanks to characters as colorful as Judge Roy Bean, but that didn't stop some people from trying to scrape out a modest living off the land. When cattle drives were at their peak, there were more heads of cattle than heads of people in the territory.

In the 20th century the region, which stretches from El Paso up to the Panhandle and down to the Chihuahuan Desert, was marked by oil booms and busts. With each geyser, largely in the Midland-Odessa area, came plenty of money, but only if you knew how to pick the right spot. That money, however, never seemed to stay in the area for long. So, not every blink-and-you'll-miss-it town has enough people to keep a barbecue joint solvent, but that doesn't mean these Texans live without. Drive around and you'll find plenty of smokers set up around people's homes. Some are store-bought, but others are welded pieces of motorcycle parts, barrels, and whatever is needed to make sure that meat gets smoked to perfection. It's a situation you'll find across the state.

You'll find plenty of fire pits, too, because West Texas is a haven of mesquite cooking. That's what those scraggly looking trees that dot the landscape are, so the wood is plentiful. But mesquite burns so hot that many pitmasters let it burn into charcoal, practically into ash, before they let it come into contact with the meat. This is often done with the meat placed over direct heat with a few feet of space in between. Call it cowboy barbecue because of its history, if you like. But most people you'll meet in the region call it the real thing.

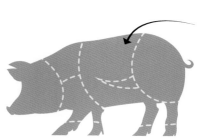

FRESH
BEST IN TOWN!

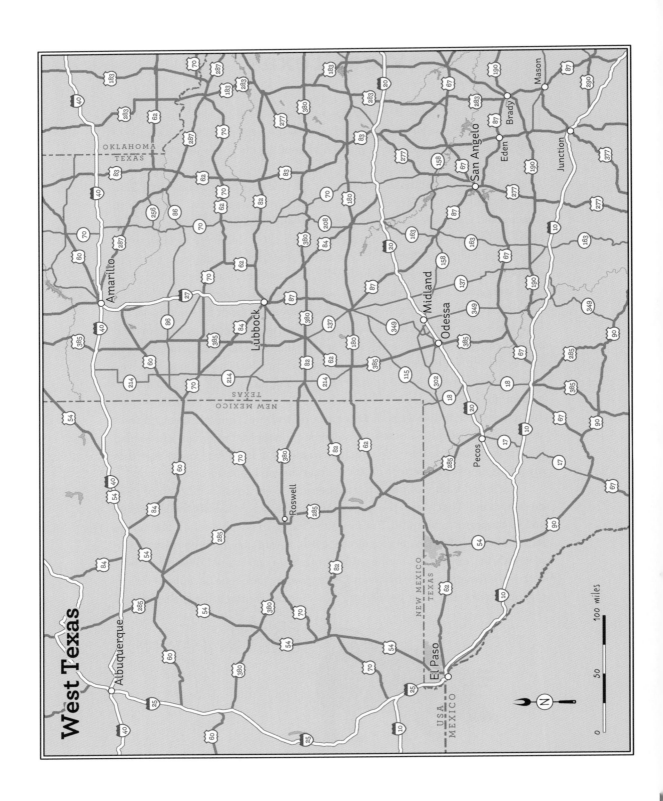

West Texas

Chubb's BB-Q

5810 Dyer St., El Paso, TX 79904; (915) 471-8019 **Founded:** 2011
Grillmaster: Curtis Vaughn

Chubb's is an anomaly is the Texas barbecue world. It's a barbecue joint where the meats are grilled Midwestern-style over Kingsford Charcoal instead of smoked. No mesquite, oak, or any other kind of wood is used, and sauce is as essential to the success of your meat as how it's prepared. That's the way owner Curtis "Chubbs" Vaughn wants it—and so do his customers.

"I've got 30 years in the food business," says Vaughn, who grew up in Illinois and moved to El Paso after his four sons were grown. "I've been a restaurant person my whole life . . . I cook what I know."

Vaughn got his start in the barbecue business when he made some for his church, True Holiness. The response was so great that people began asking for it again and again. So, he started handing out fliers selling plates by order. He got a huge cooler and loaded it with "ribs, pork steaks—anything barbecue and soul food," he says, and he sold it to anyone who placed an order. That eventually led to his taking out a storefront near Fort Bliss, where soldiers from all over the country seem to find a taste of home in his food, whether you're getting ribs or fried catfish with collard greens or fried okra on the side.

Entering the restaurant, take special care to watch your step. There's a warning painted on the sidewalk outside, and Vaughn's voice rings out with another alert as soon as the door opens. That's because the steps inside seem to go up and down at the same time. If you're not paying attention, you might easily trip into the sparsely decorated space with tables up against the walls and a wide walkway in between.

Once inside, you get table service, which is also different from many Texas places where you immediately head for the counter to place your order. A quick look at the menu shows that Vaughn does offer a two-meat plate ($2 extra for brisket) as well as brisket in several forms, including in a mixture with peppers, onions, macaroni, and cheese. The ribs are the centerpiece, and you can get them either regular or "on fire," which means loaded with habanero heat and fruitiness plus an aroma that greets you before the plate reaches the table. The meat is listed on the menu as falling off the bone, but it's not that overcooked. It has a good give to it. Just remember not to rub your eyes if you eat these sauced beauties with your fingers; the chiles in that sauce can sting. Slivers of brisket are served dipped in a jus with a bowl of sweet-smoky hickory sauce on the side. ("It's in the sauce" is Chubb's motto.)

Chubb's also offers soul food, and Vaughn will take special orders for anything from ham hocks to gumbo, if you call a day in advance and place a deposit. The multiple side dishes also show a real Southern touch. Fried cabbage, spicy cheese potatoes, corn bread, baked beans, and fries are all there, but the No. 1 seller, Vaughn says, is the macaroni and cheese, which has a healthy dose of pepper in the creamy mix.

Vaughn got many of his recipes from family members who have cooked before him. "My mother—she's the real cook," he says. "My mother taught me everything I know about Southern food." And an uncle taught him about grilling meat until it's tender but still juicy. He insists they could cook rings around him, but the customers at Chubb's know Vaughn has learned his lessons well.

Don't go to Chubb's expecting Texas barbecue. But don't miss it for the same reason. It's true to its Midwestern roots, and it's good—and that's what matters. Closed on Sunday.

Chuy's BBQ and Catering

606 W. Broadway, Eden, TX 76837; (325) 869-5200 **Founded:** 2010
Pitmaster: Chuy Constancia **Wood:** Mesquite

Chuy's claim to fame is the *cabrito*, which has won its pitmaster, Chuy Constancia, the top prize at the 2008 Labor Day Cabrito Cook-off in nearby Brady. It's still listed on the menu. Trouble is, it's only available on weekends, and you have to get there early to try it, because it sells fast. We missed it on two Saturday afternoon visits, which was sad for us because this is the region where barbecued goat has been a longstanding tradition, and good *cabrito* can be a real treat. "I know, I'm the one who has to listen to all the complaints from people who miss out," Nancy Constancia, Chuy's stepmother and manager of the dining room, says with a laugh.

Most people don't seem to mind. They love Chuy's mesquite-smoked brisket, either in slices, on a sandwich with a grilled-toasted bun, or atop a stuffed baked potato. "That's our No. 1 bestseller," Nancy says. "This is Texas and they love brisket." Ribs, sausage, and turkey sell well, too, but nothing touches the beef.

Still, Chuy's wins over its customers in ways that go beyond the

meats. "We have homemade bread and corn bread," Nancy says. "They're all made here. We just wanted to be a little bit different." It works, especially for those who want to come in and make a meal out of brisket, corn bread, and a helping of beans from the pot in the corner, next to a stand that features Chuy's three sauces. (Try the spicy on that corn bread.) There's also a help-yourself bar with fresh jalapeños, onions, and pickles. They all help to make you feel as welcome at Chuy's as the locals. One of these days, though, we'll get Chuy's goat. Closed on Tuesday.

Cooper's Bar-B-Q & Grill

2423 N. Main St., Junction, TX 76849; (325) 446-8664 **Founded:** 1999
Pitmaster: Mark Cooper **Wood:** Mesquite

Junction is a tiny speck on the map, and yet it has two barbecue joints, both within yards of I-10. Cooper's Bar-B-Q & Grill is the new kid on the block, relatively speaking. But if you're a fan of lineages, it might mean something to you that Cooper's is the last of the various Cooper's restaurants in Texas that is still operated by a member of the Cooper family. (It is no relation to the Cooper's in Mason or the Cooper's in Llano, New Braunfels, or Fort Worth.)

Owner Mark Cooper is a grandson of legendary pitmaster George Cooper. But if you're merely a driver along I-10 through West Texas, you're more

likely concerned with getting a good meal that won't take you too far off the track. Sure, the Cooper name still carries clout, but even that wouldn't keep a restaurant open for 15 years unless the food pleased its customers. Cooper's does that, especially when the meat is hot from the smokers, such as at the 10 a.m. opening time.

Beneath a host of family photos that show Cooper barbecue over the decades, you'll find moist brisket (let them know if you want the dryer end), sturdy ribs, and, if you can take the heat, some fine jalapeño sausage. The meats are all arranged under a heating lamp in a glass box by the counter, so the sight of all your choices together is a temptation that you can hardly refuse. The usual sides of beans, potato salad, and coleslaw fill out your meal. Just make sure you save room for the blackberry cobbler, a Cooper family tradition.

Beyond the food, Cooper's pleases with its family-friendly atmosphere, which has almost the feel of a barbecue theme park. It includes a pleasant outdoor dining space under some shady trees. The pit area is fairly open, so you can walk back to see the mesquite burning into charcoal. The pits themselves, in which the meats are cooked slowly several feet over the hot coals, are fascinating to kids of all ages because of the fun that comes when the counterweights lower at the moment the pit door is opened. Smoke erupts, engulfing the pitmaster, and out comes the meat wrapped in a cloak of mesquite.

Doug's Hickory Pit Bar B Que

3313 Georgia St. South, Amarillo, TX 79109; (806) 352-8471
Founded: 1958 **Pitmaster:** Doug Henks **Wood:** Hickory

Doug's is a hole-in-the-wall in the best sense of the phrase. It's housed in a bright red shack right behind a former Blockbuster. The once-mighty chain store has gone out of business, but the mom-and-pop barbecue joint is still here. That doesn't always happen in the business world, but it's nice when it does happen to a place like Doug's, which is known for its excellent, old-fashioned barbecue sand-wiches.

Yes, you can get sliced beef (it is bris-ket; it's just not sold as such), ribs, sausage, and even ham, all suggesting an East Texas barbecue style right down to the use of hickory, but the real fan favorites are the sandwiches, which you can get with any of the meats mentioned or a combina-tion thereof. Another hit is the Frito pie loaded with beef, beans, cheese, and sauce poured over the corn chips. It comes in two sizes, a whole and a half, both of which are large enough to share.

There's a low-key, old-fashioned ambience that really makes Doug's a pleasure. It's easy to see why so many of the regulars have been coming back for years. Closed on Sunday.

Jack Jordan's Bar-B-Que

1501 John Ben Shepard Pkwy., Odessa, TX 79761, (432) 334-6934;
2631 N. County Road West, Odessa, TX 79761, (432) 362-7890; www
.jackjordansbarbq.com **Founded:** 1952 **Pitmaster:** Jimmy Jordan
Wood: Hickory

The Jordan family has been serving barbecue to Odessa for more than 60 years now, no matter what the city's fortunes may be. The restaurant's name-sake died a few years ago, but his son, Jimmy Jordan, has been running the show since the late 1980s and has overseen its expansion to a second location. There are stories behind every recipe the place serves, says Danny Rodriguez, who is general manager of the John Ben Shepard Parkway store and has been with the Jordans for about 30 years.

The place began during one of Odessa's booms. At that time it was Jack Jordan's goal to offer barbecue on china along with fine service for breakfast, lunch, or dinner, and he continued that service while the restaurant was in its original location on Kermit Highway. During that time he developed the recipes that are still in place today, including the dry rub mix, which only his son knows. "Jimmy comes in on Sundays when we're closed and makes the rub," Rodriguez says. "He sometimes comes in on a Saturday if he's going out of town and he'll be mixing it up. He'll see me and go, 'What are you looking at?' 'Oh, nothing,' I'll say."

That rub is one secret to Jack Jordan's fine barbecue. It's used on all of the meats, including brisket, ribs, and chicken. On the brisket, it creates a dense crust that does its job of sealing in the juices to keep it moist. The ribs, meanwhile, are tender and full of pork flavor that draws you back for bite after bite. Plenty of smoke infuses the sausage, which has a good snap to the skin, but it's more judiciously applied to the turkey breast. The sauce has a tang of vinegar mingled with a dash of sweet.

Side dishes are fairly numerous, with macaroni and cheese and fries offered in addition to solid beans, coleslaw, and a potato salad that has a devoted following. One regular customer, who does business in both Seattle and Odessa, is said to be so devoted to the potato salad that he has to have it every time he arrives in town. Once, his crew didn't have time to go to Jack Jordan's, so they picked up another potato salad, but the customer knew the difference and threatened to make the plane go back for the genuine article, says Rodriguez.

Cobbler is the name of the game for dessert lovers, with peach, apple, and cherry each offered. (Go for the cherry.) Your meal is served either cafeteria style inside the restaurant or in a to-go container picked up at the drive-thru. Having two lines, indoors and out, somehow seems to keep the pace at the counter moving quickly, so you can sit down and enjoy your meal without fuss or frills.

Odessa was going through a boom again at the start of 2014, which benefits most everyone in the community. Jack Jordan's catering was having a good year, with bookings for parties feeding up to 1,000 people. "But it doesn't matter what size the party is, we want to do our best for every customer," says Rodriguez, whose sons now work there as well. "We're a family-oriented restaurant." Closed on Sunday.

Lum's Bar-B-Que

2031 Main St., Junction, TX 76849; (325) 446-3541 **Founded:** 1978
Pitmaster: Rich Lumbly **Wood:** Mesquite

Lum's Bar-B-Que, just off I-10, has been a Junction fixture for decades now, as you can tell from taking a look at the smoky crust that covers the pits. There's a smoky crust on the brisket, too, which is more important. It helps seal in the meat's natural moisture, so that each juicy bite has enough natural beef mingled with mesquite, the way folks in West Texas want it.

You can tour the pits, if you'd like, before entering Lum's and stretch your legs a bit if you've been driving a while. (And who in West Texas hasn't?) They're down at one end of the lengthy building, and even though they're not often open, except when someone is checking on the meats, you can also get a good look at the surrounding stacks of mesquite that'll soon be used.

When you enter Lum's, named after the Lumbly family that runs the place, you'll see the general store merchandise, including a few foodie gifts as well as fishing supplies, on the right. To the left is the counter where you can watch your ribs get cut apart or you can fixate on the array of mouthwatering pies awaiting you for dessert. (Get the coconut cream.)

You'll also notice that Lum's has a generous variety of side dishes, including deviled eggs and the signature spicy spaghetti salad, made with thin noodles flecked with bits of vegetable, garlic, and a mildly spicy vinaigrette. A similar dressing, but without the spice, is used on the refreshing cucumber salad, while the beans are in a well-balanced broth featuring both chili powder and brown sugar.

You don't have to load up on everything at once. In the middle of dinner, you may decide you want some more potato salad. Just go to the counter and get it. You don't pay until you leave, and then all of your meats, extra side dishes, and that third slice of coconut cream pie will all be included before you head back to I-10.

Mac's Bar-B-Q

1903 S. Bridge St., Brady, TX 76825; (325) 597-6227; www.macstexas
bbq.com **Founded:** 2013 **Pitmasters:** Wesley Webb, Clayton Sykes
Wood: Oak, pecan, and mesquite

Mac's had been a fixture on the Brady scene for years, but it fell into disrepair a few years back and finally closed. That's when Wesley Webb and Clayton Sykes stepped in. They took over the joint, cleaned it up, added a knotty pine interior, and made a few changes, including a switch from mesquite only to a mix that includes oak and pecan as well as the West Texas favorite. It's a gutsy move in a community that has grown up solely on mesquite. But the moistness of the brisket, the tenderness of the chicken, and the snap of the sausage skin (try the jalapeño for a real kick) have all won fans in its first few months. The side dishes, especially a macaroni and cheese with hot green chiles and some crunchy onion rings, have worked their magic as well.

Perhaps Mac's biggest challenge is the neighboring barbecue joint, the Spread, which is across the street and only a couple of blocks away. To separate itself, Mac's offers a few items such as burgers to vary the menu. Saturdays bring steak night, in which your cut is cooked to order over direct mesquite flame. Enjoy that with a beer or two while listening to some live music.

Mac's was far from a finished product when we visited, but owners Webb and Sykes appeared to be headed in the right direction, which is good for Brady and barbecue lovers alike. Closed on Monday.

Mail-Order Barbecue

Not everyone can live in Texas. But that doesn't mean people from the other 49 have to do without Texas barbecue. Plenty of mail-order places are glad to ship the meat to you.

Don Baucham operates the Rustic Iron out of Odessa. Since 2009 he's been offering a combination food truck and online barbecue business (www .rusticironbbq.com) when he's not occupied with his other day job, which is working in the oil business offshore in places as far-flung as Angola and, currently, Brazil. It's a schedule that rotates every 28 days.

So, when he's in Odessa, he can be found filling his pit largely with mesquite wood. He uses indirect heat to cook his meats slowly. It's a practice he learned in Elgin using oak, but he's adapted for the West Texas climate, where mesquite grows everywhere. He also doesn't trim too much of the fat from his brisket before he smokes it either. "My fat tastes as good as the brisket," he says. "It's almost like jelly. I don't cut mine unless a client wants it. It helps with the tenderness."

Word has spread about Rustic Iron's meats, and Baucham has developed a regular clientele of people across the country who order his ribs, smoked sausage, whole chickens, or even whole smoked turkeys in addition to his brisket. "This is my passion," he says. "I love it." And people will attest that it comes through in his food.

The Internet is filled with Texas barbecue places that ship. Here are 10 more places, listed alphabetically, that are glad to feed your barbecue hunger, no matter where you are in the US:

Angelo's Barbecue (www.angelosbbq.com)
Black's Barbecue (www.blacksbbq.com)
Cooper's Old Time Pit Bar-B-Que (www.coopersbbq.com)
The County Line Air Ribs (www.airribs.com)
Kreuz Market (www.kreuzmarket.com)
La Barbecue (www.labarbecue.com)
Meyer's Elgin Sausage (www.cuetopiatexas.com)
The Salt Lick (www.saltlickbbq.com)
Snow's BBQ (www.snowsbbq.com)
Taste of Texas Barbecue (www.tasteoftexasbarbecue.com)

Packsaddle Bar-B-Que

6007 Knickerbocker Rd., San Angelo, TX 76904; (325) 949-0616;
www.packsaddlebbq.com **Founded:** 1987 **Pitmaster:** Marshall Gray
Wood: Mesquite

Chopped beef sandwiches are the star of the show at this spacious strip-mall
joint on the outskirts of San Angelo. Packsaddle has developed a dedicated
local following for its barbecue as well as dishes such as its chicken-fried steak,
fried catfish, and grilled cheese sandwiches with meat. Thin slices of brisket

have a good smoke ring and plenty of
smoke flavor, though it can occasionally be dry. Spare ribs have a good give
to them, and the sausage boasts a nice
amount of spice. But the sandwiches,
which can also be had with sliced brisket or sausage, are what regulars recommend most often. It could be the
reasonable price or the addition of either
sweet or spicy barbecue sauce. The end
result is a satisfying, old-fashioned, and
occasionally messy treat. If you don't
mind painting the sides of your face with
a little extra sauce, take a big bite and
wait for a smile to spread.

Get yourself a side order of onion rings and a little extra sauce to enjoy
with your meal, then finish everything off with a taste of house-made ice
cream. Daily specials are worth keeping track of, if you're hankering for a certain meat. For example, Sundays brings pulled pork and smoked turkey.

Packsaddle puts on no airs. The space is clean if slightly faded from years
of use. Yet NASCAR lovers, take note: One dining area has been transformed
into a tribute to all things Dale Earnhardt, both senior and junior, and they're
fun to study while you're munching away on that large chopped beef sandwich
or a po'boy made with brisket and sausage. Closed on Tuesday.

Pody's BBQ

1330 S. Cedar St., Pecos, TX 79772; (432) 448-4635 **Founded:** 2011
Pitmaster: Israel Campos **Wood:** Mesquite, Oak, Cherry, Pecan

Pecos is the home of the world's first rodeo, as a roadside sign in front of the
town's arena announces. It's also the home of some world-class barbecue,
thanks to Pody's. One taste of the brisket, smoked with both mesquite and

oak, will convince you of that. Under a black crust is beef both moist and fork-tender with just the right level of smoke to bolster its natural meaty flavor.

You might not think that's possible judging from the outside of the building, which looks like something right out of an old Western. You can almost picture yourself tying your horse to the railing on the front porch. The inside isn't too fancy either, though the corrugated metal gives it a clean and polished look and the shades block out the intensity of the midday sun. (Pody's is only open for lunch, so arrive early because some items will sell out.)

Pody's isn't putting on any pretensions, and neither is pitmaster Israel "Pody" Campos, who is as genial and down-home a barbecue master as you'd ever want to meet. His excitement is as overwhelming as his menu is limited. It's brisket, ribs, and sausage with a few side dishes, the best of which is a green chile pozole. The name alone tells you that you have definitely left Central Texas and headed into the Southwest.

Pody's sense of simplicity carries over into its drink selection: tea. No sodas, no beer, nothing else. If you're lucky, some banana pudding will be available at the end of your meal. Closed on Sunday and Monday.

Rockin' Q Smokehouse

3812 Penbrook St., Odessa, TX 79762; (432) 552-7105
Founded: 1998 **Wood:** Oak

When you pull up to Rockin' Q, your first impression is that it looks like a chain restaurant. Step inside and take in the murals, the logo-topped tables, and the smiling staff in the order area, and that feeling is enhanced: There's something almost too clean about it for it to be a barbecue joint. But that's okay. Cleanliness, even near a smoke pit, is welcome. And so is the food that Rockin' Q serves up.

Brisket sells the best, and you can have it in a host of ways, such as rolled up with beans in a burrito, in Frito pie, atop a baked potato, or on top of a salad, if sliced or chopped has no appeal to you that day. Any way you order it, you'll be rewarded with solid beef flavor, a pronounced smoke ring, and a

well-seasoned crust. The various people who mind the pit put their effort into making sure the sliced brisket is as good as can be, but chopped brisket in all its various forms actually sells better, says manager Lance Hubbard.

The ribs were what captured our attention—and the attention of anyone who drops in on all-you-can-eat rib night, which is Thursdays from 5 to 8 p.m. These seem to be cut as uniformly as possible, but you can sink your teeth into each one and enjoy the primal thrill of ripping meat from a bone while a wave of pork flavor mingled with smoke overtakes your taste buds. Ham, pulled pork, chicken, turkey, and two types of sausage (regular and jalapeño) fill out the meat menu.

But Rockin' Q doesn't end there. Want a side salad with your barbecue instead of slaw? The kitchen will gladly oblige. You can even get *queso*, which goes well with the sausage, or macaroni and cheese, which would be great with some unsauced chopped brisket stirred in. Nacho fries or french fries, green beans, and two types of pintos, smokehouse and ranchero—all seem to convey a range that aims to please all tastes.

Sam's Mesquite Cooked Bar-B-Que

1112 E. Scharbauer Dr., Midland, TX 79705; (432) 570-1082 **Founded:** 1983 **Pitmaster:** Lee Hammond **Wood:** Mesquite

Lee Hammond has seen his share of oil booms and busts in the Midland-Odessa area. His family's own business, Sam's Mesquite Cooked Bar-B-Que,

has had its ups and downs, too. At one point there were a number of Sam's in the area, but now only two sites remain, one in Midland and another in Odessa, which is part of a market. And neither appears to be in a heavily trafficked area. But that hasn't stopped the folks at Sam's from turning out some fine West Texas–style barbecue.

The Midland location is essentially a nondescript cinderblock box, covered with a layer of smoke that bears witness to its history and the thousands of briskets and racks of ribs that have passed through the heavy metal smoker out back. There is little decoration in the place, and the green-and-white-checked table coverings add a splash of color. Only an antique wood bar behind the counter is of any interest to those looking for decor.

But such touches of finery are not needed in the face of the food. Brisket, which has been in the smoker for at least eight hours, has a bark that really does resemble a tree, with streaks of various browns marbling across it. The flavor is simple but effective, a combination of beef, smoke, and only salt and pepper used in the rub. Ribs, cooked for two or three hours, are toothsome, requiring a pleasant workout as you tear the pink-smoked flesh from the bone. House-made sausage is largely beef with some pork fat to keep it moist. In a combination plate, the whole array will arrive in a bath of sweet and spicy sauce unless you ask for it on the side.

Hammond doesn't seem to mind an audience willing to listen to stories from the past, such as his remembrance of the original Sam, an uncle who died shortly after the first location opened. Or he'll talk about his barbecuing techniques, which have been honed over the decades. The continued business at the last two Sam's has shown him there's no need to change. He's like many of his fellow barbecue lovers in West Texas, who swear by their mesquite, a flavor they've known since they started eating solid food. "I like mesquite because it burns clean," he says. "Oak and hickory, they don't. You can eat meats cooked with that stuff and really get indigestion. But mesquite goes down easy." Closed on Sunday.

The Spread Pit BBQ

2010 S. Bridge St., Brady, TX 78625; (325) 597-1111; www.thespreadpit bbq.com **Founded:** 2012 **Pitmaster:** Clinton Tinney **Wood:** Mesquite
If you'd like to have a little meat before you get to the big meat on your plate, start your visit to Brady's with a quail popper. A large nugget of boneless, tender quail is tucked inside a jalapeño, then wrapped in bacon and cooked over mesquite until everything comes together, crispy on the outside, hot and juicy at the center. When it's ready to serve, that rather large nugget is dropped in a cup and then bathed in a ladle of melted lemon butter. A shrimp version is also available, in case you're looking to increase your seafood intake.

Do you need another reason to visit the Spread? Perhaps news that this friendly joint always has another regional favorite, *cabrito*, on weekends will get you to stop by. You can also dip it in the lemon butter for an added richness (recipe on page 233). Or, if you're looking for more standard fare, such as brisket, ribs, and 1-inch thick-cut pork chops, then the Spread is ready to serve. When you walk up to the covered patio, you'll find a large and lengthy menu covering everything from a 14-ounce rib eye to a stuffed potato. It hangs to the left of the pit, which your carver will open so you can examine the meaty treasures inside. You just point to what you want and it'll be cut to order before being weighed inside. If you're not sure how much a slab will cost, just ask.

The Spread used to be a Hard Eight Bar-B-Que until it closed in 2011. New owners Shaun and Mandy Geistweidt took over the property and renovated the interior with wood and corrugated metal that gleams. The inside serving

line is filled with sides, such as jalapeño sweet corn, corn bread salad, and mac and cheese as well as potato salad and slaw. The sight of the desserts—pecan pie, banana pudding, and cobbler—will make you even hungrier before you sit down at one of the comfortable picnic tables in the ample dining space.

When you go to fill your drink cup, you'll also see the three sauces set out, one hopefully to please your tastes, whether you want sweet, sweet and sour, or simply vinegar-based. That area is also where you can help yourself to all of the beans, bread, pickles, and onions you can eat. Though the staff spends most of its time behind counters, at the pit, and inside, they manage to serve up some good hospitality to go along with the fine spread that the Spread sets out.

Tom and Bingo's Hickory Pit Bar-B-Q

3006 34th St., Lubbock, TX 79410; (806) 799-1514; www.facebook
.com/tomandbingosbbq **Founded:** 1952 **Pitmaster:** Dwayne Clanton
Wood: Hickory

This small restaurant with a rustic, log
exterior has been around for more than
six decades and is usually included in any
account of the city's history and restaurant
lore. If the outside is rustic-quirky, lined with
logs, the inside is as well. Benches line the
wall, with school desks on which to put your
plates, but Tom and Bingo's is probably best
for takeout, so you can pick up your sandwiches and eat them in the car or take them
back to work with you.

Brisket sandwiches and smoked ham are the specialties here. And as one
diner says, you can use your fries to mop up the sauce. Closed on Sunday.

Tony's The Pit Bar-B-Q

1700 Myrtle Ave., El Paso, TX 79901; (915) 546-9140; www.tonysthe
pitbbq.com **Founded:** 1958 **Pitmaster:** Christina Vargas
Wood: Mesquite

"Since 1958, we're doin' it right." That's the motto Tony's operates under, and
you can watch it in action when your meat is carved for you at the counter.
That beautiful, black-encrusted brisket on the cutting board produces fatty
or lean cuts with plenty of juice. Plus, extra care is taken so the meat matches
your order. If you order a burrito, you'll get bite-size pieces. Chopped meat, of
course, works best on a sandwich, while lean cuts are sliced, and shreds, almost
like pulled pork, are served to those who want a fattier cut.

Tony Vargas Sr. opened his barbecue joint more than 55 years ago. Today,
the place is run by his granddaughter, Christina Vargas, who pays tribute to
her family's heritage while keeping a good eye out for dining trends. "Grand-
pa's original menu was brisket, ham, chili, potato salad, and coleslaw," she says,
emphasizing that she has kept everything just as he offered it, though some
additions have been made. The brisket is still marinated for three days before
it's placed in a pit with indirect smoke from burning mesquite. After a night in
the pit, it's ready to be carved.

The meat selection now includes sausage, chicken, and pork, as well as
Tony's signature hash, made with brisket, peppers, onions, and more. You can

sample a couple in a two-meat platter, which comes in two sizes (½-pound and ¾-pound, depending on your appetite). The sauce, which appears in squeeze bottles on the table, is a pale orange mixture of sweet, smoky, and a touch of spice that goes well with the sausage.

Side dishes include potato salad and coleslaw, but you won't find beans, per se. You can find plenty of them, though, in the chili bowl, which is one of your choices. It's not too spicy (you can add your own hot sauce for that), but there are good bits of brisket flavoring the broth along with the beans. Other sides include an old-fashioned carrot salad with raisins, as well as fries, chili cheese fries, and macaroni salad.

Whenever you visit any restaurant that has survived this long, it's interesting to consider the reasons for its longevity. In the case of Tony's, survival—and growth even—seems to have happened while the neighborhood around it has become somewhat deserted. Christina Vargas attributes part of the restaurant's staying power to a sense of consistency that has come with adhering to the recipes her grandfather handed down. The original Tony's was located a block away near the railroad tracks. Back then, you'd often see a train parked in front of the restaurant, blocking traffic and bringing things to a standstill until the people who worked aboard could get their barbecue fix, Vargas says: "Those people still come in here for their barbecue fix." Her old neighbors on the street stop by or call Tony's for catering. Plus, she has seen several generations of customers bringing their children in and introducing them to the sandwiches loaded with mesquite-smoked meat, a bit of sauce, and some pickle slices.

Vargas has kept the ambience welcoming and largely the same, which gives it a retro feel to visitors but just seems like Tony's to everyone else. If you want to stroll through the restaurant's history, check out the series of black-and-white photos that line one wall. Other reasons can't be so easily defined, except to go back to that slogan: Tony's is simply "doin' it right." Closed on Sunday.

Tyler's Barbeque

2014 Paramount Blvd., Amarillo, TX 79109; (806) 331-2271; www.tylersbarbeque.com **Founded:** 2010 **Pitmaster:** Tyler Frazer **Wood:** Mesquite

If the shape of the building that houses Tyler's Barbeque looks a little familiar, it's because the place was once home to a Long John Silver's. But don't worry—any trace of corporate-produced food has vanished from the premises. Instead, Panhandle native Tyler Frazer proudly proclaims that he and his staff do everything from scratch, including chopping the cabbage for the coleslaw and soaking the beans. Such attention to detail, not to mention Frazer's sure hand with mesquite, has helped make Tyler's into a barbecue lovers' destination.

Frazer, most often seen sporting a Stetson and a wry smile, displays a Texas-size charisma that naturally draws his customers into a conversation. It helps put folks at ease and makes them feel mighty welcome. But it's the meats he's personally carving for you that will make you want to come back for more. The brisket is rubbed in a lively combination of salt, pepper, and cayenne that helps create a bark over the meat; tender, thin cuts display plenty of meat juices with a good layer of mesquite smoke. You can have this chopped on a sandwich by itself or stuffed into a roll with sliced hot links. As good as the brisket is, the ribs have their own set of fans. One reason for this is the sweet-hot combination of sugar and plenty of black pepper in the rub, not to mention the great porky goodness that fills each bite.

Sides are the standards you expect, but the freshness of flavor may surprise you whether you are eating the potato salad, the coleslaw, or the beans. On Thursdays the special is macaroni and cheese, which sells out quickly, so get there early if that's an added attraction for you.

Tyler's motto is simple and direct: "Support Texas Barbecue." One bite of Frazer's meats, and you'll be convinced that's the right path. Closed on Sunday and Monday.

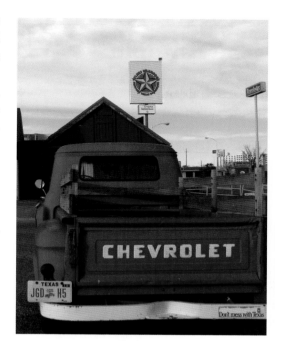

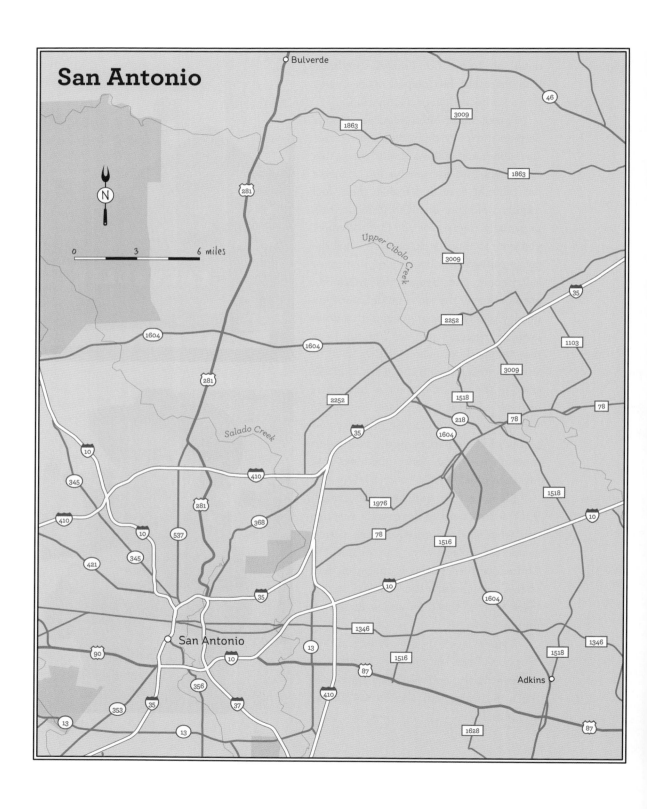

San Antonio

The Alamo City has never been known as a barbecue town. One reason is that it has no clear-cut style that it can call its own. You'll find a little bit of every Texas regional style here, plus an influx of other styles from other states, which can be somewhat confusing as you taste your way around.

But good food is good food, no matter where it comes from or what style it uses. So, you might do like we do and go to one joint for the brisket, another for the pulled pork (or pork butt, as Two Bros. BBQ Market calls it; for recipe, see page 234). Or you might visit Ed's Smok-N-Q when you want mesquite-smoked meats, such as their massive turkey legs, while the Barbecue Station is always good for the beef ribs.

If you have friends visiting from out of town, you may have to toss a coin between Tejas Rodeo Co., where you can watch locals attempt to ride bucking broncos or rope steers while you eat your 'cue, or Texas Pride Barbecue, where you can enjoy a bucket of ice-cold longnecks while listening to live music on a massive outdoor patio and sampling the smoked meats.

The Granary 'Cue & Brew takes barbecue, not to mention microbrews, to a whole new level. It's not just slabs of brisket, it's smoked brisket in a bowl of ramen with noodles made from the house-brewed brown ale. And, yes, you want a mug of the brown ale right alongside it.

The city's population is almost 60 percent Hispanic, so, of course, you'll find Latin and Tex-Mex touches in the rubs, the beans, and occasionally the potato salad. But you'll also find South Texas ranch-style barbecue, meats grilled quickly over mesquite charcoals, at Pollos Asados Los Norteños, which serves mostly chicken. And while the menu is bilingual, be prepared to hear more Spanish than English. Plus, there is a seemingly endless number of taquerias offering *barbacoa*, especially on Saturdays and Sundays.

San Antonians are also very loyal to the two barbecue chains that started here, Bill Miller Bar-B-Q and Rudy's Country Store and Bar-B-Q. Rudy's, in fact, is responsible for San Antonio's signature barbecue side dish: creamed corn. After 25 years, Rudy's sweet version remains the most popular, but you'll also find any number of variations, including a spicy version at The Smoke

Shack and the lobster creamed corn at the upscale Bohanan's Prime Steaks and Seafood, which cooks all of its steaks over mesquite. While you're at the latter, you can also relax with a Texas Gold Rush, a bourbon-based cocktail enhanced with house-made barbecue bitters (recipes begin on page 254).

Augie's Barbed Wire Smoke House

3709 N. St. Mary's St., San Antonio, Texas, TX 78212; (210) 735-0088; www.augiesbs.com **Founded:** 2000 **Pitmaster:** Augie Cortez **Wood:** Mesquite, Oak

Augie's Barbed Wire Smoke House, as colorful outside as inside, is well within view of the spacious, green reaches of San Antonio's Brackenridge Park. The dining area next to the ordering room features this sunny outdoor view, but if it's peak time and open tables are scarce, head for two other spacious

areas to set down your plates of mesquite- and oak pit-smoked brisket, chicken, pork and beef ribs, sausage, burgers, pulled-pork sandwiches, and foot-long hot dogs.

The interior is barbecue classic, and the music is country. The line can get long, but the ordering counter is short; check the menu and know what you want ahead of time, if possible. Smoked burgers are an Augie's specialty, either with or without a healthy drenching of melted cheese. The pulled pork, though, is probably the top-selling item—tender, salty, with a bit of crust for texture. It's not served in sauce, but they'll add it if you ask, and there's more pour-your-own sauce available.

Side dishes deserve more than a passing word. Augie's fresh-tasting creamed corn is one of the best we've tasted, as are the green beans, long-cut and cooked (not overcooked) and also made fresh. If a quarter-pound chocolate chip cookie seems a little much after your meal, save one for later.

Augie's also caters and sells meat by the pound and "foil-pan sides" for takeout, as well as Pig-Out Packs for 4 or 5 people ($33.99) or 8 to 10 people ($64.99).

The Barbecue Station

1610 NE Loop 410 (inside Loop 410 near the Harry Wurzbach exit), San Antonio, TX 78216; (210) 824-9191; www.barbecuestation.com
Founded: 1992 **Pitmasters:** Freddy Freeman and Zac Freeman
Wood: Oak, Mesquite

Before Bobby Peacock opened his barbecue restaurant, his well-thought-out plan was to fashion his product on the best. To find the "best" example, "I went to every barbecue place that was credible," he said. He found it in Lockhart, at Kreuz Market (in its old location at what is now Smitty's). He also found a pitmaster, Eric Mack, and located the restaurant in what was a former Exxon station just off busy Loop 410 East.

Mack, whom Peacock calls "the poster boy for barbecue—he could cook anything," left after a couple of years, but Peacock's good fortune continued when he hired brothers Freddy and Zac Freeman, who are with him still; Freddy for 20 years, Zac for 19.

The Barbecue Station's meat is cooked with an equal mix of oak and mesquite in the restaurant's brick pit and smoker. "It's all wood smoke, that's the key," Peacock says. The low, slow cooking method yields a consistent product that has maintained the Barbecue Station's standing as a favorite among San Antonio barbecue aficionados.

You can eat in or take out by the plate or pound as well as in family-pack meals. Pork and beef ribs, pork loin, brisket, sausage, chicken, turkey, and chopped meats are served on butcher paper. A menu for children and seating for 50 are inside the restaurant. Barbecue Station caters.

Eat in, and you can have refills from the pot of excellent beans, tasting lightly of chili seasoning, at the end of the drinks bar in the dining room. (Be sure you pay for that first order, though.) Side dishes, all made on-site, include potato salad, which uses Peacock's wife's closely guarded recipe, as well as pepper-dotted creamed corn, green beans, fries, and more. Two salads, a chopped meat–stuffed potato, and a buttery baked potato are extras. Closed on Sunday.

The Big Bib

104 Lanark Dr., San Antonio, TX 78218; (210) 654-8400; http://thebigbib.com **Founded:** 2010 **Wood:** Aged Oak, Mesquite

Who doesn't love thick slabs of marbled brisket with an obsidian crust that just crackles with plenty of salt and black pepper when you bite into it? That's the real reason to visit this easy-to-miss spot in the corner of a derelict shopping center. There's not a thick smoke ring visible to the eye, but a combination of mesquite and aged oak in the pit adds a light flavor that will have you eating every last bite in a hurry.

Sure, there are other options on the menu, ranging from turkey breast and chicken leg quarters to baby back ribs and sausage, but the brisket eclipses them all—and most of the side dishes as well. If you want to vary things up a bit, the Big Bib offers smoked turkey legs and fried catfish on weekends. (But, really, get the marbled brisket.)

The peach cobbler is the winner among the desserts, which also includes banana pudding and sweet potato pie.

Sides include the standards as well as collard greens, green beans, and a baked potato casserole. Chili beans have plenty of chili powder mixed in with the pintos plus little bits of brisket stirred in for added flavor and texture, making for a fine complement to your meat.

The flavor of things leans toward the sweet—so much, in fact, that you might mistake the sweet potato casserole for a dessert. All four house sauces, including the one marked hot and spicy, have a pronounced sweetness, too. Closed on Monday.

Blanco BBQ

13259 Blanco Rd., San Antonio, TX 78216; (210) 251-2602; www.blancobbq.com **Founded:** 2013 **Pitmaster:** Arthur Mayo **Wood:** Oak, Pecan

Blanco BBQ is open and bright, filled with plenty of warm wood tones that seem to invite you right on in. Wend your way past displays of wine bottles and longnecks on ice to place your order. Fall-off-the-bone ribs are the biggest sellers here, but a case could be made for the moist brisket, which is Certified Angus Beef. The whole array of meats, including chicken and handmade Polish sausage, are prepared using oak and pecan in the kitchen's Ole Hickory and Southern Pride smokers. Want to try a little bit of everything? Blanco BBQ goes beyond the three-meat plate with its house special, which features brisket, ham, sausage, and a couple of ribs. The mixed platter adds pulled pork to that meaty lineup.

Macaroni and cheese is pure comfort, while the excellent green beans feature both bacon and a touch of vinegar. The coleslaw, potato salad, and creamed corn are all on the sweet side. And the steamed broccoli is, well, just what it says.

Don't miss out on the condiment bar, which is located at the far end of the vast main dining area. It's loaded with dilled onions, pickled carrots, and *pico de gallo* in addition to the usual pickles, onions, and jalapeños.

If someone in your crowd wants to venture beyond barbecue, don't threaten to leave them on the side of the road. Have that person check out the variety of fresh salads, from Greek to Asian, as well as the cheesecake with strawberry sauce. It's not your standard barbecue joint fare, but each of those items has its fans, says Mark Rios, head operator.

Your food is generally served up quickly, but you don't have to be in a hurry to eat it and hit the road. Live music is featured about three nights a week, and the styles of the bands vary from traditional country to Southern rock. So, grab another beer or a second glass of wine, and kick back while enjoying the company you're with. "What we've created here, it'll make you feel right at home," Rios says. Closed on Monday and Tuesday.

Dilled onions on the condiment bar are refreshing, tangy, and a good complement to the smoked meats.

Dixieland BBQ

(210) 845-5428; www.dixielandbbqsa.com; www.facebook.com/ DixielandBBQ; @DixielandBBQSA **Founded:** 2013 **Pitmaster:** Chris Rincon **Wood:** Mesquite, Hickory

Chris Rincon grew up in Corpus Christi, which he readily admits is not a booming barbecue area. Still, he learned to use mesquite, following the tradition that runs in his family, and that's how he's preparing the brisket he sells from his food truck, which can be found at various places around San Antonio. But he wasn't finished there. His wife, NaCole, is from the Deep South, and she wanted her pork smoked with hickory, a flavor she grew up with. So, Rincon

The ribs are outstanding, but don't overlook the sausage with plenty of snap to the skin and plenty of spicy juice in every bite.

obliged and now he's at the point where he prefers that wood lending its aroma to his pulled pork, which is served with a tangy mustard sauce on the side.

But Rincon's pork ribs are the star attraction of the truck, as the couple's growing body of followers has discovered. These are large, meaty ribs with firm, smoky, pink flesh that make each bite a pleasure to tear from the bone. To him, biting into one of his ribs reminds him of the satisfaction you get from taking a big bite out of a steak. They go well with the red cabbage slaw, which is also piled onto the pulled pork sandwiches.

If you're after the ribs, you'd better find Dixieland BBQ early in the day, because they sell out quickly. The best way to follow them is on Facebook, Rincon says, adding that his wife keeps up with the truck's social media daily. NaCole also gets the credit for coming up with Dixieland's sassy motto: "We like pig butts and we cannot lie!"

Ed's Smok-N-Q

902 S. WW White Rd., San Antonio, TX 78220; (210) 359-1511
Founded: 2005 **Pitmaster:** Ed Ashford **Wood:** Mesquite

Ed and Waldean Ashford started Ed's Smok-N-Q in a food truck on San Antonio's East Side. In the cramped space, they did everything from smoke their meats over mesquite to fix the sweet Southern-style potato salad with pimiento in it. After several years they settled into a restaurant space that also has a cramped kitchen, but they've made do by parking the truck out back and using it still as the smoke pit.

Ed Ashford, who hails from Alabama, learned what he knows about barbecue from a neighbor who was willing to share his pit

methods. What he picked up was largely what you'd call a West Texas–style of barbecue, with its mesquite smoke and a lively sauce that complements the meats. If you want something else, though, say, coleslaw on your pulled pork sandwich in a Memphis style, the couple will be happy to accommodate you as much as they can. But they believe in mesquite, which the sign on the door calls "The Original Texas Bar-B-Q."

Not many places serve turkey legs. These are not only delicious, but their size is gargantuan.

The meat board is a bit different from what you'll find in other barbecue joints in the area. In addition to the brisket and ribs, there are massive turkey legs that have cultivated a following, smoked beef bologna, and sausage rings, which you don't see too often outside of the Lockhart area. It turns out those rings are from Lockhart, but most customers would swear otherwise.

Ashford laughs when he watches people's response after their first bite: "They say, 'Those aren't from Lockhart,' and I say, 'Oh, yes, they are.' 'But they don't taste like Lockhart's. They taste better.'" The secret, he says, is that he smokes them differently so they don't dry out as much. What you're left with is juicy sausage, but without the grease.

Also popular are the smoked potatoes and sweet potatoes. Both can be had loaded, which means they come with butter, cheese, and a half-pound of your choice of meat (recipe on page 242). And if you're a bean lover, you can have your pick of pintos, baked beans, ranch-style kidney beans, and Southern-style green beans with a drop or two of vinegar added for a good, light tang.

Barbecue is Ed Ashford's second career. He spent 35 years in the Army, retiring as a sergeant first class. He and his wife have dreams of expanding their place, adding a bigger kitchen, enlarging the dining room, and installing a drive-thru. Right now, there are times when Ed's has so many customers that people have to take their orders to go because the tables inside and out are filled. "We're trying to take it a step higher," Waldean Ashford says. Closed on Monday.

The Granary 'Cue & Brew

602 Avenue A, San Antonio, TX 78215; (210) 228-0124; www.the
granarysa.com **Founded:** 2013 **Pitmaster:** Timothy Rattray **Wood:**
Oak (most often)

In its first year of business, the Granary 'Cue & Brew found itself being lauded
in *Esquire* magazine for taking smoked meats to new frontiers. Articles in the
Wall Street Journal and on *Huffington Post* soon followed. Then, in January
2014, the place landed at No. 5 on Steven Raichlen's top barbecue joints for the
year. So, brothers Tim and Alex Rattray had all of the pressure of living up to
the acclaim while working out the inevitable kinks that come with any new restaurant, from refining the menu to making sure the plumbing works properly.

So, what kind of barbecue does the Granary serve?

"We've been called everything in the book," says Tim, who handles the pit
and the kitchen. "I've heard our food being described as 'modernist' and 'high-
end.' I think of it as just delicious food."

What makes things different for the person who hasn't been to the Granary before is that the place is actually two restaurants in one, located in a
historic building on the Pearl Brewery campus, which has become a haven for
numerous restaurants as well as the Culinary Institute of America's San Antonio campus. At lunch the Granary is a traditional Texas barbecue joint with
metal plates of oak-smoked, moist brisket; well-seasoned pulled pork that's
juicy even without sauce; and delicate, delicious turkey breast. Ribs are small,
but toothsome, while the sausage has a lively spice blend that's both bright
and hot.

On Friday Rattray pulls out all the stops with his cured and smoked beef
pastrami, which occasionally is made with short ribs. We understand that one

cooking process takes time, and two
require even more time. So, you won't
likely see this signature creation copied
at too many other places. But you should
go out of your way to try it at least once,
if only to savor the magenta-colored
beef with the black pepper crust. You've
never had pastrami like it before, and if
you like that cured flavor, the addition
of smoke will likely haunt you long after
your visit, especially when you bite into
the citrusy coriander seeds included in
the crust. Arrive early; it sells out quickly.

"It's developed a cultlike following," Rattray admits.

The lunch sides sound traditional—beans, German potato salad, coleslaw—but the flavors are not what you're probably expecting. The burnt-ends beans feature a colorful mix of pinto, black, and kidney beans with a vinegar base. New potatoes and tarragon fill the lightly dressed potato salad. And the refreshing coleslaw seriously downplays the sugar. But it's the buttermilk bread that you'll remember the most; made in-house, it is both light and dense—and pure comfort food. You'll never want a slice of white bread out of a plastic bag again.

In the evening, when the lights from the modern chandeliers create a cozy glow in the wood-covered dining areas, Tim Rattray lets his culinary imagination run wild. The chef—who trained under two of San Antonio's finest, Bruce Auden of Biga on the Banks and Andrew Weissman

of Il Sogno—draws on a wealth of influences to create spectacular combinations of flavors, such as his smoked brisket ramen made with a smoked shoyu broth and collards. The brown ale noodles filling the bowl are made from one of the beers that Alex Rattray brews on-site.

Leg of lamb is cold-smoked for 20 hours before being poached and served in a curry-saffron sauce with couscous and charred eggplant. It's a dish inspired by one of Tim Rattray's memories of the nine years that the brothers spent in England when they were younger. "It reminds me of when I was a kid," he says. "It's just one of those great food memories." And the smoke flavors from both the meat and the eggplant will remind you that this is still a house of smoked foods.

No smoke was used in the buttermilk chess pie or the outrageous banana pudding made with handmade vanilla wafers (it's available on Saturdays only),

Brew and 'Cue:
Made for Each Other

Barbecue and beer go great together. Ask anyone over the age of 21.

But there's beer and there's beer.

Some barbecue lovers have ventured beyond the world of their Lone Star lager and want to drink their way around the more than 70 breweries active in Texas these days. So, how do you know what kind of barbecue is going to pair up best with your can of Karbach Weekend Warrior Pale Ale? Or if that Shiner Hefeweizen is made for a mess of ribs smothered in sauce?

Of course, half the fun is in the trial-and-error phase. That way you get to drink beer and eat barbecue until your taste buds start to crack the code.

We tried to make a little sense of it with two Texas brewers: Mark McDavid, who makes the Mesquite Smoked Porter and the rest of the impressive lineup at San Antonio's Ranger Creek Brewing & Distilling, and Alex Rattray, who's in charge of the brew half of the Granary 'Cue & Brew at San Antonio's Pearl Brewery complex.

"Beer is pretty versatile," McDavid says. And that makes finding pairings so enjoyable.

The first rule is to relax. "There's always a ton to think about, but beer pairing is a lot of fun and there's no wrong answer," Rattray says. "If you're overthinking it, it probably won't be as good. Sometimes you try something and it doesn't work, but it's rarely bad. You've got to experiment and be willing to try stuff, even if it doesn't sound good. Sometimes those are the best pairings . . . There are also a lot more flavors to work with on beer, including the carbonation factor. Carbonation is a huge mouthfeel factor that can change everything on your palate."

One of the easiest rules, both men agree, would be to start by pairing similar or complementary flavors. So, if you're having the Friday pastrami at the Granary, try it with the Rye Saison and imagine you're having pastrami on rye.

Or, if you know that coffee is used in the rub on your beef, you may want to reach for a Real Ale Coffee Porter.

But, if the meat is too fatty, a dark beer might prove to be too rich. So, think about how opposites attract, too. Hoppy beers, such as India pale ales, go well with marbled brisket.

"You generally don't want a thick, heavy beer to pair with a big, rich piece of fatty brisket," Rattray says. "It's just too much heaviness together." A bitter IPA with plenty of carbonation can cut right through the fattiness and provide the balance your meal needs.

"Fatty foods with hoppy beers generally work really well together," McDavid says. "Our Oatmeal Pale Ale with sausage or fatty brisket is great."

Another pairing that might not be the best is mixing hops and spice, both men say. That brisket taco with *pico de gallo* and plenty of habanero salsa needs a little sweetness to stave off the pepper burn. So, think about a light, crispy Saint Arnold Fancy Lawnmower instead of an IPA.

Rubs have so many flavors going on that you might find an endless array of possibilities. "I tried a mesquite-smoked porter from Ranger Creek with our brisket the other day and it was fantastic," Rattray says. "The smoky flavors complemented each other, but the beer was fairly dry, so it didn't feel too heavy even though it was bursting with flavor. If I'd been eating a sweeter style brisket or pork, I'm not sure that big smoky flavor of the beer would have complemented it. It might have overpowered it. I would choose something more like a Saison or a dry Oktoberfest that has milder flavors with a touch of malty sweetness."

Does all that seem a little too much to process? Then just grab a bottle, pop the cap, and take a big, long swig with whatever you're eating. If you don't like it, grab another style of beer from the ice bucket and finish the first one after your food's gone. "At the end of the day, beer should be social and beer should be fun," McDavid says.

For more on what's brewed in the Lone Star State, visit the Texas Beer Guide at www.texasbeerguide.com.

but these desserts show a kitchen as serious about its baked goods as it is about every other detail (pudding recipe on page 249.)

While Tim is minding the pit and kitchen, Alex is monitoring the beers that he brews. They include the Rye Saison, which tastes like liquid rye bread,

The snow-white, house-made buttermilk bread is so good, you may have to order seconds.

making it a perfect partner for the pastrami. The Brown Ale, of course, works well with the brown ale noodles in the ramen bowl. And, well, all of the beers work. That includes the root beer, especially when sampled with the seasonal favorite of root beer–glazed scallops.

Yes, you can expect to pay more for your food at the Granary. Humanely raised meats come with a heftier price tag than conventional meats do, and both Rattrays insisted before they opened that they would serve nothing else. But if you are interested in seeing how someone uses smoke in new and wonderful ways, a trip to the Granary for dinner should be on your list.

Somehow, Tim Rattray has managed to absorb the national attention he's received without letting it go to his head. In fact, he's more humbled by the praise than anything. "Alex and I are really thankful for everything that's been written," he says. "It's more pressure for us . . . But there are so many things that we haven't done yet that we'd like to do. We want to keep pushing the envelope and using smoke to enhance everything. Barbecue is timeless." Closed on Sunday and Monday.

Morton's Barbecue

(210) 279-9412; @mortonsbarbecue **Founded:** 2010 **Pitmaster:** Rashad Morton **Wood:** Mesquite, Hickory

Morton's is a barbecue food truck and catering company that rolls from as far north as Spring Branch in the Hill Country, through San Antonio, and down south into the Eagle Ford Shale basin. So, you have to keep track of it on social media to find out where it's parked that day.

Owner Rashad Morton keeps his focus tightly on his meats, which are cooked in a pit at the back of the truck and fired largely with mesquite, though some hickory is used for flavor. The star of the show is the brisket, which arrives with a dense black crust. Thick slices are firm with not much fat but a good deal of beef juices. Morton uses the commercial Salt Lick rub in order to get that dark, even crust. He had originally used his own rub, but he'll admit it just wasn't as good.

Pulled pork is just that, well-seasoned meat and nothing else, unless you want the sauce on it. Taste it first. You probably won't need it. The ribs had a

good balance of sweet and heat in the rub, and Morton held them to the heat until they were this side of falling off the bone. The expected side dishes—ranch-style beans, potato salad, and coleslaw—are not likely made on Morton's truck, but you might not pay too much attention to them if you order enough meat to keep you busy.

Morton's family moved to Texas when he was a year old, so he's close to being a native. He's used his first few years in the truck doing catering jobs and serving oil workers as well as staking out promising lots where customers could find him. In that time, he's built a good following, so he doesn't plan on trading in the vehicle anytime soon for a sit-down spot. The economy would have to get a lot better, he says. Plus, he sees more potential in having several barbecue trucks rolling to different areas. So, do a little homework before you set out.

Well-marbled brisket with a black crust has the right amount of salt to make each bite excite your taste buds.

Pollos Asados Los Norteños

4642 Rigsby Ave., San Antonio, TX 78222; (210) 648-3303
Founded: 2011 **Pitmaster:** Frank Garcia **Wood:** Mesquite
You can smell the smoke from the mesquite charcoal at Pollos Asados Los Norteños long before you reach the restaurant. It's almost like a siren's call,

There's a burger that comes with a cheese-stuffed sausage on top. Go for it.

drawing you in for what you know will be a real treat. When you do arrive, you can walk right up to the enclosed pit and watch whoever's in charge of the meat grab a handful of marinated chickens and arrange them neatly on the grill. It seems like it's only a matter of minutes before you have your own half or whole chicken in front of you. It's all been cut up in the meat market at the entrance into easy-to-manage pieces. Squeeze some lime juice over the top and sink your teeth in.

This is the type of barbecue you'll find on the ranches in South Texas. The clientele is decidedly Hispanic in origin, and Spanish is the dominant language spoken here, though the menu appears in side-by-side columns of English and Spanish. The meats offered don't take too long to cook, especially when seared over blazing hot mesquite coals, with all of their juices and some of that tangy marinade sealed inside. The side dishes all impressed, including beans with the addition of *chicharrón*, Mexican rice, and excellent handmade tortillas; a fragrant cooked onion that arrives wrapped in foil; and a grilled jalapeño.

Though chicken is part of the business' name, it's not all that you'll find here. Burgers are heaped high with everything including ham and cheese, while a cheese-stuffed sausage (like a Pittsburg hot link) is served up with a ring of bacon on the outside.

So, is this meat, which has been grilled over direct heat and scented with the smoke that arises from the juices that hit the coals, really barbecue? To some of the people who frequent Pollos Asados Los Norteños, it is (as opposed to *barbacoa*, which is something else entirely). But the bottom line is that it's really good, and that's what makes a trip here worthwhile. Closed on Monday.

The Smoke Shack

2347 Nacogdoches Rd., San Antonio, TX 78209; (210) 829-8448; www.smokeshacksa.com **Founded:** 2010 **Pitmaster:** Chris Conger **Wood:** Pecan, Oak

When the new wave of food trucks began around 2010, the Smoke Shack was one of the first to roll into San Antonio. It quickly developed a following, even though it can be found parked in a ramshackle lot that had been vacant for years.

Folks fell for the lightly sweet pulled pork sliders, which, if you ask for it, can be piled high with coleslaw. This style of barbecue isn't Texas born and bred, but good is good, no matter the pedigree. They also love the decidedly tender brisket and the St. Louis–style ribs, all of which sell out quickly, so get there early if you want any. Add in some turkey or sausage as sliders or as part of a three-meat plate, and all are made even better with the Smoke Shack Mac or the spicy creamed corn on the side.

Chris Conger, who worked for Smoke in Dallas before launching his own truck and catering business, has added a few items over time, including that San Antonio favorite, Frito pie. This version does not feature chili, but it does have brisket, beans, and barbecue sauce over the corn chips. There's also the Big Dog for healthy appetites. It's a hoagie stuffed with sausage, brisket, pulled pork, two barbecue sauces, and slaw. It's a carnivore's dream come true.

Slip back into childhood with the ageless appeal of Frito pie.

As we went to press, Conger had just opened a sit-down restaurant at 3714 Broadway. So, now you can enjoy his barbecue at two locations. Closed on Sunday.

Tejas Rodeo Co. Smokehouse

401 Obst Rd., Bulverde, TX 78163; (830) 980-2205 **Founded:** 2011 **Pitmaster:** Tyler Horstmann **Wood:** Mesquite, Hickory

This compound, seemingly out in the middle of nowhere, offers much more than barbecue. It's a place where several thousand people gather every Saturday for an authentic Texas rodeo. Folks in their cowboy hats, boots, and jeans fill the stands of a large arena out back to watch some riding, roping, and tying. And when they have a hankering for a snack, the Smokehouse stand is there to fill them up.

It's one of four food venues on the site, says Tyler Horstmann, who wears a number of hats around the place, including pitmaster for the barbecue, chef

at the Steakhouse, and food and beverage director for the entire venue. In addition to the Steakhouse and Smokehouse, you'll find the Mercado offers snacks, such as Frito pie and a Kobe beef hotdog, while the Stagecoach Station is largely used for catered events.

But it's the 'cue at the Smokehouse that commands the attention on these pages, and Horstmann's team delivers up plates of mesquite-smoked brisket or hickory-smoked chicken and pulled pork as quickly as possible. Fresh creamed corn, in which you get a good taste of the sweet corn; a tangy coleslaw; and beans are among the sides, though hot-out-of-the-fryer french fries are also a big seller. It's not fancy—this is a concession stand as much as anything—but it is satisfying, which is why lines remain long throughout the evening.

Most of the locals who show up at Tejas are there for the rodeo, to watch their family members or good friends compete. That gives the evening a sense of intimacy you won't find in some of the larger, more professional rodeos. Admission is $12 for adults and $6 for children, and it lets you into the larger parking area as well as the rodeo arena. It also gives you access to the food areas and the cantina as well. You don't need to buy a ticket if you're just going to the Steakhouse or dropping by the Smokehouse for a snack, but you might find parking difficult without it. The place gets that packed.

The Saturday schedule is well choreographed, so that visitors find no lags between one event and another, Horstmann says. The gates open at 5 p.m. with any preliminary events. The rodeo begins at 7:30 p.m. and ends at 9 p.m. A live band in the cantina area begins at 9:01 p.m. It's generally a warm-up band, which plays for an hour or so while people are filing out. The headliners continue until closing time at 1 a.m.

If you've never been to a Texas rodeo before, this is a great place to start. And you can get some good barbecue to snack on while you watch. Open Saturday only except during the winter.

On a cold night, a basket of steaming hot fries is a warming treat.

Texas Pride Barbecue

2980 E. Loop 1604, Adkins, TX 78101; (210) 649-3730; www.texaspridebbq.net **Founded:** 1996 **Pitmaster:** Tony Talanco **Wood:** Mesquite

Tony Talanco's grandfather, Steve Talanco, emigrated from Italy back in the 1920s. After settling in San Antonio, he set up an Italian restaurant and introduced some of his family favorites to the area. In return, the Mexican nationals who worked for him taught him the fine art of Texas barbecue. It's a legacy he handed down and one that can be tasted in the mesquite-smoked meats at Texas Pride Barbecue, located just to the east of San Antonio.

The menu is loaded with old favorites, including brisket, baby back ribs, turkey, and pork tenderloin, but the country sausage made in-house with a good garlic kick may be the standout among the meats. Sides are divided into cold (coleslaw, American or German potato salad, macaroni salad) and hot (green beans, pintos, cheezy potatoes, mac and cheese).

Talanco's tasty menu is only one part of the Texas Pride experience, however, and it is the whole package that draws thousands each week for events such as Thursday's Bike Night or the Friday Fish Fry, which begins during Lent and goes until the high school football season starts.

The fun starts with the main building,

which resembles a 1940s gas station replete with Sinclair signs and plenty of artifacts that Talanco and his family have carefully chosen. You'll see it

If you have a sweet tooth, do not miss the pecan or peach cobbler.

high above Loop 1604 as you approach. It's not until you get into the dirt parking lot that you realize how huge the compound is. Thankfully, there's usually someone on horseback who keeps the parking lot in order and who can guide you to where you need to go. If the weather's good, you'll likely end up out back, where you can escape the sun under a canopied area while an army of fans keeps the air moving. You can two-step to the live music coming from the bandstand or catch up with friends over a bucket of icy longnecks and either ribs or a helping of Friday's fried pollock. There's a huge play area for the kids, and a weekly gospel radio show broadcast from a station that's been set up on the grounds.

Giving you that little something extra is Talanco's way of thanking you for stopping by—and it's why you'll remember Texas Pride long after you head to your next stop. Closed on Monday.

Two Bros. BBQ Market

12656 West Ave., Ste. B, San Antonio, TX 78216; (210) 496-0222; Catering: (210) 289-4955; www.twobrosbbqmarket.com; @TwoBrosBBQ **Founded:** 2009 **Pitmaster:** Emilio Soliz **Wood:** Oak

In just a few years, chef and owner Jason Dady has turned barbecue into unexpected fame. His restaurant group in San Antonio prior to the 2009 opening of Two Bros. BBQ Market had been principally fine dining, including two Italian restaurants named Tre Trattoria. Two Bros. brings on classic Texas barbecue

style, favoring pit-smoked meat imbued with good smoke flavor, handmade side dishes, freshly made pickles, beer and wine, and a nicely kept patio dining area out back.

Jason Dady is one of the brothers mentioned in the name; Jake Dady is the other. Jason says he wanted Two Bros. to be a family-friendly place as well as a good meat market, and that it is. There is a play area adjacent to the outdoor picnic tables, and the shrieks of happy kids playing under some sprawling oaks make a nice accompaniment to barbecue.

Bags of charcoal lie next to the indirect-heat smokers. This stuff is used only to get a good, hot start to the wood, which is always oak, pit-master Emilio Soliz says. And "smoke and time" is the philosophy here.

Two Bros.' bacon-wrapped smoked jalapeños are a signature appetizer and something not to be missed, if you can help it. (They're popular, and the restaurant sometimes runs out. So, try to get lucky.) They're hot both in temperature and spice, but chill them down with a little iced-down Kool-Aid or cold beer.

Indoors, you'll do the usual walk-up ordering, then walk around the corner to pick up your eats and move down the counter area toward the back for glasses with ice and further along, the cashier. That trip takes you past the row of plastic coolers that hold the drinks, including grape-flavored Kool-Aid (a nice change from sweet tea—try it), beer, and a barbecue-friendly selection of wines. Try the beans; they're different. Cut-up peaches might scare purists away, but that little touch of fruity sweetness with the thick, beany flavor doesn't hurt a bit.

The brisket is tender and smoky, with a good blackened crust on thickly cut slices. Sausages are firm-grained and spicy, and the cherry-glazed baby back ribs are tear-apart tender and just sweet enough. The pitmaster won't divulge the recipe for the rub, but Dady tells us the cherry flavor comes from a cane sugar cherry syrup.

At press time, Dady had opened a new barbecue joint, B&D Ice House BBQ & Draft, at 1004 S. Alamo St. in San Antonio's Southtown.

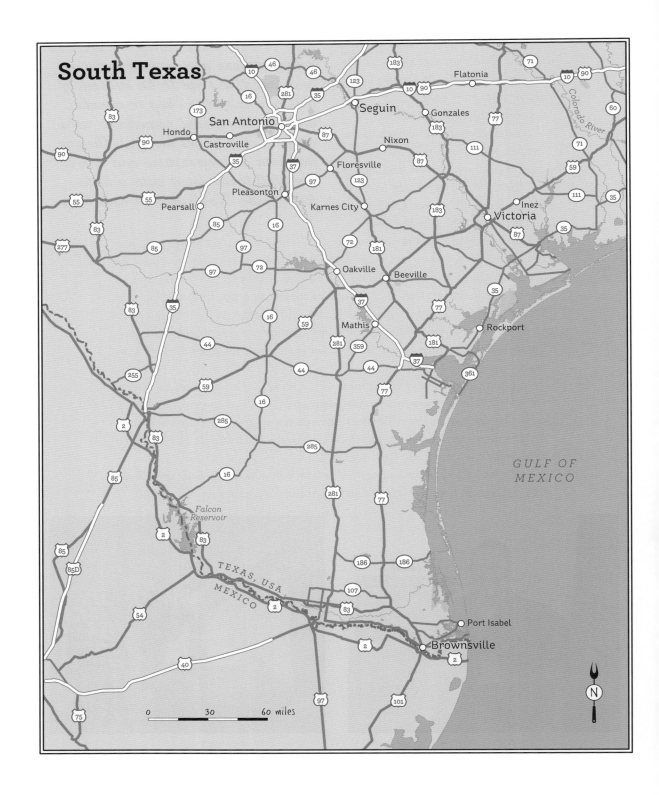

South Texas

South Texas

South Texas is more of a barbecue melting pot than the rest of the state. Some pitmasters use mesquite, others choose hickory or oak. Some places are known for their brisket, and at least one place draws lines of customers for its North Carolina–style pulled pork. In other words, if you've got a hankering for a certain style of barbecue, you shouldn't have to drive too far to feed your needs.

Head further south, along I-37 or US 281, and you enter a land of the unknown. After all, this is a region where you'll occasionally find fruit stands that sell live goats alongside recent crops of grapefruit and Valley lemons. So, you'll discover that people's impressions about barbecue change as much as the landscape. Sure, there are numerous smokehouses offering briskets boasting righteous rings of smoke and beautifully dark layers of bark, hot sausages that spurt forth tongue-searing juices with a touch of wood flavor, and ribs that still cling to the bone in a judicious give-and-take that your teeth just love. But by the time you hit the Valley, you'll have passed countless frack shacks, lean-to barbecue joints set up to feed frackers working in the oil industry, as well as ranches that spread out over one mesquite-filled stretch of land after another. Here, the whole notion of barbecue has been upended. Suddenly, you find several schools of thought over what barbecue actually means.

Go beyond the domain of restaurants and onto the cattle ranches themselves. There you'll meet the vaqueros, modern-day cowboys, and other ranch hands. They use the word *barbecue* in the same sense as folks across the country outside of Texas's boundaries. It's the meat they grill directly over burning charcoal. The smoke isn't there necessarily to flavor the meat as much as the heat is there to cook it. And the meat is not likely to be brisket as much as it is fajitas or something else that cooks quickly when exposed to heat.

Cookbook author Melissa Guerra knows this firsthand. She's an eighth-generation Texan who grew up on one of those ranches before becoming a culinary historian of her native state. Listen to her talk of the barbecues she's taken part in, and you can practically smell the grass-fed beef as it sears over those coals and hear the crackle and hiss whenever a bit of grease drips onto a hot coal. Those campfires weren't started with lighter fluid. Instead, Guerra says, people would use an old magazines or papers drenched in bacon grease, collected in a cup or strainer on top of the stove. It burns cleaner, without carcinogens, and seems a bit safer, too. She also remembers the young children, always eager to lend a hand wherever fire is concerned, loving it when they were allowed to light the tinder that was used to build that mesquite fire.

This is not what you'll find in many restaurants under the heading of barbecue, though you can certainly find grilled fajitas and steaks at places both high end and low. Barbecue joints throughout South Texas are more traditional temples of smoked meat, with mesquite more often than not being the wood of choice because it is what grows in the area.

Taquerias and *molinas*, or tortilla factories, across South Texas are also filled with the delicious aromas of *barbacoa*, which is meat scraped from a cow's head that traditionally was cooked in an underground pit. Meat and coals were both buried underground until the meat was done. Certainly the words *barbacoa* and *barbecue* look similar, and the two are often used synonymously, especially since they share the cooking technique of preparing meat with heat from charcoal, most often using some form of mesquite. But there are distinct differences.

To non-Texans of all backgrounds, the scope of *barbacoa* is something that may take a little getting used to. Yet the tradition common among all poor or struggling cultures of not letting an ounce of meat go to waste is very much alive here. That's why a few *barbacoa* menus will include some of the meats separated into *ojos* (eyeballs), *lengua* (tongue), *cachete* (cheek), *paladar* (palate), and more. Others simply feature *mixta*, a mixture of meats scraped from the skull and chopped up together. One part you won't find any more is *sesos*, or brains. They were outlawed in the US after the breakout of mad cow disease. That hasn't lessened the demand for them, especially among older Latino diners, who remember the soft tissue as being a great delicacy. Diners willing to go across the border to Mexico might be able to find them there.

Home *barbacoas* remain popular, too, which is why you can still buy your own *cabeza de vaca* at most Latin meat markets. You may have to place a reservation at some, but be on the lookout for smaller heads, weighing about 30 pounds or even less. Not only is the meat more tender, but it is also easier to handle. You'll have to dig less to bury it, too, if you're preparing it the old-fashioned way.

But is *barbacoa* really barbecue? The pitmasters who make it nowadays wrap the heads tightly in aluminum foil so that the meat does not pick up any smoke flavor at all. Why? It's not part of the culinary tradition of the Latin customers who eat *barbacoa* faithfully on Saturdays and Sundays. They don't like smoke and they don't equate their *barbacoa* with what comes from a smokehouse. To people like the Hispanic characters in Oscar Caceres's book of short stories, *Brownsville*, *barbacoa* is merely what is eaten after church on Sundays, a snack or meal their mother serves up so she has more time to concentrate on getting the larger Sunday family dinner ready.

So, what is barbecue in South Texas? It's whatever you want it to be. Why quibble? Just find what you like and enjoy.

Cowpokes Bar-B-Que

1855 W. Comal St., Pearsall, TX 78061; (830) 334-8000 **Founded:** 1993
Pitmaster: Sam Hotchkiss **Wood:** Mesquite

The red barn exterior is easy to spot as you exit I-35 into Pearsall (pronounced PIERCE-all), and there is ample parking. Inside is classic modern barbecue decor, which means the tables and chairs are not rough-hewn and not permeated with smoke residue.

Cowpokes opened in 1993, burned down in 1994, and came back the same year. Don't get owner Sam Hotchkiss going about that incident, just appreciate that he persevered and serves good barbecue.

The staff is efficient and quick to answer any questions or craft your order to your request. Daily, they serve beans, potato salad, and coleslaw as sides—though they offer many more for catering. Also on the menu are a tortilla wrap, cobbler, homemade pie, and sandwiches. Before we arrived at Cowpokes, the sandwiches had been praised by a local who provided directions to the restaurant.

But barbecue places are about meat, and Cowpokes offers sausage, whole or half chicken with a beautiful browned skin, brisket with a pronounced mesquite smoke ring, great smoked turkey lightly pinked by smoke, and juicy, tender pork ribs. The sauce is light, with the expected regional tastes of citrus, mild seasoning, and a dash of sweetness. Closed on Monday.

Dziuk's Meat Market

608 US 90 West, Castroville, TX 78009; (830) 538-3082; www.dziuks .com **Founded:** 1975 **Wood:** Mesquite

This family-owned meat market/smokehouse/game-processing emporium has been in operation for almost 40 years, and the current proprietor, Marvin Dziuk (pronounced sort of like "jook"), is following the long-held family traditions of attention to detail and custom quality products.

Entering the market can seem daunting since there is limited floor space, but an expansion was under way when we visited. No matter the space, the friendly staff is quick to greet you and start working on your order. They can answer questions about any item because they are all involved in all aspects of product preparation.

In addition to the fresh meats and game processing, they have a huge selection of mesquite-smoked items, such as sausages in a variety of styles. The jalapeño and cheese pork sausage is worth the visit by itself, but there are

also links made in the Polish style, reflecting the Dziuk family's background, and Alsatian-style sausages from Castroville's heritage. They keep adding new flavors, too, including the Green Chorizo, which is pork with poblano, serrano, and jalapeño peppers blended with some cilantro.

They have amazing smoked bacon, as well as turkey and salami. For the hunters wanting a snack while waiting for a deer to appear, there's jerky made from both turkey and beef as well as dried sausages. The Alsatian influence also manifests itself in the *parisa* offered fresh daily. This traditional cracker spread is a mix of cured (but raw) beef with cheddar, onions, salt, pepper, lime juice, and family secrets, which make it a local favorite.

Since there is no dining area, wave good-bye and know that you'll be back after you enjoy your purchases. Closed on Sunday, except during hunting season (November through January).

El Valle Tortilla Factory

103 W. Queen Isabella Blvd., Port Isabel, TX 78578; (956) 943-2759

This is a small meat market where English isn't the primary language spoken, so you might have to do some pointing if your Spanish isn't so hot. But good food always supersedes language barriers, and the cordial staff is willing to help you find whatever you want, which, for our purposes, is some very good *barbacoa*. It's available only on Saturdays and Sundays, along with *menudo*, a spicy tripe-based soup that more than a few people swear is the perfect hangover cure.

The rest of the week, this meat market offers *carnitas*, tamales, chiles rellenos, *chicharrones*, and other Mexican favorites. Get the thin corn tortillas that are just about perfect, though the flour tortillas are also a fine demonstration of why there is no substitute for handmade. The *barbacoa* is sold by weight, so you might want to grab a half-pound of cheek meat for a few breakfast tacos and enjoy the slow-cooked meat with plenty of salsa, cilantro, and onion to eat on the go while doing your weekend chores or after church on Sunday morning.

While you're at El Valle, do yourself a favor and check out the dried chile selection, which includes guajillos, pasillas, and more fairly uncommon varieties of peppers that can add spice and dimension to your own home cooking. Open Saturday and Sunday.

Hatfield's BBQ

621 W. Market St., Rockport, TX 78382; (361) 729-4BBQ (4227); www.hatfieldsbbq.com **Founded:** 2012 **Pitmaster:** Kenny Hatfield **Wood:** Oak, Mesquite

Kenny Hatfield calls his rotisserie pit "the Big Nasty," which may not sound too appetizing, but it produces some fine barbecue. He smokes his brisket for about 18 hours using indirect heat from a mixture of oak and mesquite. The end result has a fine crust on the outside and a pleasant smoke ring around meat so tender and rich that it practically falls apart at the touch of a fork. That's

The pretzel bun by itself or used as the bread for a sandwich has salt, a good crust, and a soft interior.

what makes his barbecue such a standout in this coastal community known for its excellent birding.

Hatfield's menu also has succulent pork ribs, chicken, and sausage, each worthy of attention. You can try all but the ribs in a four-meat plate that is as generously ample as it is flavorful. Or you could have that pulled pork in a sandwich made on a pretzel bun and the brisket in a wrap made with a flour tortilla. Mix the shredded pork and sausage with jalapeños, cheese, and Hatfield's Maddy Belle Glaze, named after his daughter, and you have a mighty meaty taco.

You can also get your choice of meat included with a triple dairy threat—butter, sour cream, and cheese—stuffed into the loaded baked potato. If you prefer something more cooling, try the baked potato salad, loaded with sour cream. The standout dessert was a bar cookie that was some kind of mash-up of chocolate, caramel, salt, and crushed pretzels; think community bake sale, only better. All of this, not to mention a fine beer selection, is served up in a large, well-lit, utilitarian space that has plenty of dining, a bar area, an arcade, and enough room for a band to offer live music.

Kenny Hatfield has had his share of challenges lately, including a bout with cancer. But Hatfield's keeps going strong. Closed on Monday and Tuesday.

Heavy's Outdoor Bar-B-Que

1301 19th St. (US 90), Hondo, TX 78861; (830) 426-4445
Founded: 2008 **Pitmaster:** "Heavy" Bernal **Wood:** Mesquite

The exterior may seem underwhelming, but the fragrance of smoked meats as you exit the car is entrancing. Inside, you can still smell the smoke, but because the smoker is outside, it's at a pleasant level as you eat. Heavy's opened in 2008, and "Heavy" and Kimberly Bernal do it all. He is the pitmaster and she is chef for the sides.

Heavy's choice of wood for smoking is an easy one. "Mesquite," he says. "Just look around—that is what grows here, so that's what we use." They use it very well on the brisket and the well-peppered pork loin, both showing a lovely smoke ring. The smoked turkey breast is moist, flavorful, and a step above many competitors. The barbecue sauce is lightly sweet and tangy, with a good seasoning level that does not overwhelm the meats. The pork ribs are juicy, and though they pull easily off of the bone, they do not fall off in a heap on the first bite.

The side dishes are what you would expect, though the finely minced egg in the potato salad not only flavors the dish, but adds a nice textural touch.

Most of the people coming into the restaurant were greeted by name, which always makes even visitors feel at home. One man came in and said to Heavy: "Fix me up a to-go deal, would you? I got seven guys out there working and need to feed them." He didn't have to get any more specific. He just paid, picked up his order, and headed out the door. He'll be back. So will we. Closed on Monday.

Lady and the Pit

1401 TX 100 West, Ste. 7, Port Isabel, TX 78578; (956) 433-5855
Founded: 2013 **Pitmaster:** Natasha Smith **Wood:** Mesquite

Natasha Smith, the "lady" of the restaurant's name, is not from South Texas, but she is a native Texan by way of Fort Worth. Still, when she moved to this charming coastal town, she left behind any notion she may have had about her hometown style of barbecue and adapted to the region's preference for mesquite.

An enticing perfume of smoke fills the air around her strip-mall location and intoxicates you before you even open the door. The interior is spacious and Spartan, with few touches decorating the place. Behind the cash register, however, are two word sculptures on display that all good pitmasters take to heart: "patience" and "love."

You can certainly taste both in Smith's brisket, which has an admirable smoke ring and is so juicy that it fairly drips flavor on your tongue. The rib meat falls off the bone in pieces large enough to chew. But it is the sight of the loaded potato that gets customers throughout the joint talking. It is a massive serving of all the wonderful things you can use to fill up the gap when you split a spud down the middle, including butter, cheese, bacon, more cheese, and scallions plus the meat of your choice, such as chopped beef in sauce, chicken, pulled pork, or even sausage or hot links. Sour cream and additional sauce land on the side.

Learning How to Make Barbecue, Texas Style

Yes, there are classes for making your own Texas-style pit-smoked meat. Buy or make yourself a pit-smoker, and you're on your way. Classes are given in educational institutions such as Texas A&M and the Culinary Institute of America, San Antonio. Some barbecue joints like to share tips and pointers, such as Lockhart Smokehouse in Dallas, which offers monthly sessions. Also, check casual courses from community colleges.

The state's barbecue bloggers and writers, *Texas Monthly* magazine, and folks on Twitter will keep you updated on educational opportunities, barbecue competitions, festivals, and more. Finally, search "Texas Barbecue" on You-Tube for some insights into the art of pit-smoking meats and the folks doing it on a daily basis.

Here are three programs for those who want to learn more about what it takes to get in the pit:

Culinary Institute of America, San Antonio Campus: This two-day barbecue boot camp is a grilling and barbecuing extravaganza that focuses on backyard entertaining. Learn how to grill the perfect steak and hot-smoke and barbecue everything from meat to seafood and poultry. You'll also prepare traditional barbecue side dishes such as potato salad and macaroni and cheese. This is a food enthusiast's course and covers barbecue from North Carolina's pulled pork to Kansas City's ribs as well as Texas 'cue.

Visit http://enthusiasts.ciachef.edu/boot-camps, then select Grilling and BBQ Boot Camp.

Texas Foodways BBQ Summer Camp: This meat- and smoke-filled weekend teaches unique barbecue traditions, methods, and styles. It features award-winning professors from Texas A&M's Meat Science Section, well-known pitmasters, and regional barbecue authorities. Also, the seminar provides instruction on cooking and butchery, with demonstrations focusing on the different types of meat, smoke, and spices used throughout Texas and beyond.

In addition, attendees will tour some of the area's legendary barbecue places, learn some barbecue history, and find out how different regions of Texas do things, well, differently. It takes place in College Station. See www.foodwaystexas.com/events/barbecue-camps for more information.

Texas Barbecue at Texas A&M University: The College of Agriculture and Life Sciences' Texas Barbecue at Texas A&M University offers the freshmen class Texas Barbecue, the workshops Barbecue Summer Camp and Camp Brisket, the BBQ Genius Counter, and other educational efforts in the art and science of barbecue.

Visit the website, http://bbq.tamu.edu. It is full of helpful information, from blogs, companion sites, articles, and links to meat science information to lots of tips on making Texas-style barbecue and how it works. It is loosely organized, so click around and you'll be informed—and entertained.

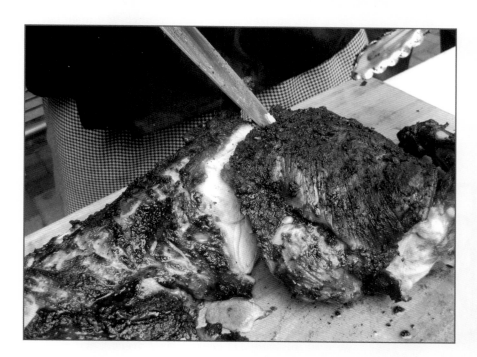

Among the soul food side dishes, the candied yams score, thanks to plenty of brown sugar, cinnamon, and butter.

The Southern side dishes will kick-start your taste buds, whether you're in the mood for collard greens and baked beans or old-fashioned macaroni and cheese and candied yams. As the relatively new restaurant evolves, Smith is working to find out what her customers want, and so it seems more Southern comfort food would likely be added to the menu with time.

Smith, who started as a caterer, has taken up residence in a space that had been occupied by another barbecue joint, R&R Barbecue, which still had its shingle hanging in the plaza sign alongside the road. Just remember to look for Lady and the Pit in front of the Port Isabel Walmart. And don't overlook the oversize potato when you place your order. Closed on Monday.

Lazy J Bar-B-Que

931 10th St., Floresville, TX 78114; (830) 393-0571 **Founded:** 1999 (previously a McBee's Barbecue) **Pitmasters:** Patrick Carillo, Jeff Oltjendiers **Wood:** Mesquite

This town in Wilson County is less than an hour's drive southeast from San Antonio on Highway 181. It leads past farms, hayfields, and stands of wildflowers in the spring. If you find yourself in the area for lunch or dinner, Lazy J Bar-B-Que offers up all-mesquite-smoked meat served with good side dishes, handmade by Patrick Carrillo, the restaurant's head cook and one of the pitmasters. Their steaks are all hand-cut.

At lunchtime the tables are packed with guys who work hard enough to need a hefty lunch, retired couples talking politics, moms with kids, and not too many travelers. We were welcomed, however, coached on the side dishes, smiled at by customers ahead in the line, and comfortably seated in a small but

tidy dining area. We waited for co-owner Jeff Oltjendiers, who was out in the fields getting the hay in (he is also a real estate broker), but there was just no point letting good food go cold.

The pork ribs, brisket, and sausage were all good. The brisket was salty with a respectable amount of black crust, tender enough to pull apart easily with fingers or fork. The meat on the long, curved ribs offered some resistance before pulling off the bone. A light seasoning of cracked black pepper and a little shot of a sugar/vinegar-style barbecue sauce were all this perfectly cooked meat needed, and made us think of coming back some Friday for the all-you-can-eat rib day. The sausage was firm and flavorful, purchased from Pollock's Sausage in nearby Falls City.

The side dishes refused to be ignored, as we sometimes do. The fresh-looking green beans were seasoned with a few bits of bacon, tomato, and onion, while the pinto beans were given some heat with fresh jalapeño or serrano chile. The cheesy potatoes looked great, and one of the servers shook her head when we passed them up. Our eyes were on the warm apple cobbler, which turned out to be a fortunate choice with its sugary sauce, moist apples, and thick bits of tender crust.

When Oltjendiers arrived, he said that while he personally likes to cook at home on direct heat, the Southern Pride rotisserie smoker they use at Lazy J is necessary for the volume of meat they sell and for consistency. He and his father, Charles, also work

the smoker. It's all hands on deck, in fact, when the catering trade is going full steam. Lazy J is one of Floresville's most popular restaurants—and it worked for us, too.

The Market

208 E. Calvert Ave., Karnes City, TX 78118; (830) 780-3841
Founded: 2002 **Pitmaster:** Ruben Cano **Wood:** Mesquite

The folks in Karnes City know that if they want barbecue steaming hot out of the pit on a Saturday, they have to hit The Market by its 10:45 a.m. opening or they might not be able to get some of Ruben Cano's justly praised brisket. It sells that quickly, and the lines are often quite long.

The Market is only open two days a week, Friday and Saturday, because its owner, Jerry Quintero, works four days a week as a music professor at Texas A&M International in Laredo. The rest of the time, he can be found performing as a pianist. "I wear a lot of different hats," he says at the end of a Saturday shift. "Right now, I'm a barbecue man."

Quintero grew up in Karnes City, enjoying both the barbecue and the sauce from the original Smolik's, which was housed in the same building. It's a

focal point of the town's main thoroughfare, along with a pharmacy, a hardware store and the police station. (Two other members of the Smolik family still operate their own, unrelated businesses. For more on the one in Mathis, see page 212.) After the Smolik family sold the business, the space was renamed The Market and served Karnes City for about 10 years before Quintero bought it. He was working at the time as a teacher and band director at the local high school. He sold the place when he started work in Laredo, but he got it back again after a foreclosure in 2009. Things have been going strong ever since.

A mural placing barbecue as a key part of the town's life adorns the front room, and it's a fact of Texas life that cannot be denied. Pass by it and head on back to the counter at the far end of the building to place your order. The meats are available only by the pound, while the side dishes—just beans and a potato salad that's on the sweet side—are sold separately. Pork ribs are a standout, while massive beef ribs make a fine impression. The brisket on the day we visited was on the lean side but had good mingling of beef and mesquite flavors. The real surprise was the lemon pepper chicken, available half or whole. It was moist throughout and steaming hot. It only spends a couple of hours in the pit, so there was no overwhelming smokiness, from breast to thigh, just natural chicken goodness.

House-made beef sausage is boiled first and then exposed to smoke for a short time before serving. You may find yourself back in line to get a second.

Quintero and Cano are essentially the staff of The Market, plus a third person who joins them on Saturday. The work begins at about 5 a.m. Large orders can usually be placed if you call before opening. But if you want only enough for you and your family for lunch, you may have to wait in line. If and when the brisket sells out, the line usually disperses—and that happens most Saturdays long before the posted 1:30 p.m. closing time. Open Friday and Saturday.

McBee's Bar-B-Que
309 Second St., Pleasanton, TX 78064; (830) 569-2602 **Founded:** 1982
Pitmaster: Fausto Rodriguez **Wood:** Mesquite
McBee's is a traditional barbecue dive, complete with low ceiling, picnic tables and benches, rolls of paper towels on the tables for napkins, plastic bottles full

of sauce, and exposed florescent bulbs for lighting. But the place also has moms with their babies, workingmen wearing their gimme caps, and at least one local representative of law enforcement.

Like most barbecue stops in the area, it has an order counter where you make your selections and get your beverage cup. Then step over to the bar for your tea or soda before you grab the plastic forks and go to a table.

Plates are offered by the quarter-, half-, or three-quarter-pound weight of meats—you pick whatever you want—then decide on the side dishes and watch them add the fresh sliced onions, pickle chips, and, if you want, pickled jalapeño slices. They have the usual side dishes, including a fine coleslaw and some wonderful cheesy potatoes, which is like a baked potato loaded with butter, bacon bits, pepper, and cheese. It's all been made into a multi-textured, hot, mashed potato dish.

The lightly salted brisket is juicy with a good, fatty edge; the sausage makes up for the light salt in the brisket and has good seasoning; and the pork ribs are tender and juicy with a great black pepper bite. McBee's also has turkey, chicken, and pork chops—which the locals eat like ribs. The barbecue sauce has a pronounced tomato flavor to complement the sweet-and-sour seasoning and seemed to be popular with the local crowd.

Norma's "Real Pit" Bar-B-Que & Catering

2301 W. Corpus Christi St., Beeville, TX 78102; (361) 254-1075
Founded: 2013 **Pitmaster:** Shad Harper **Wood:** Hickory, Pecan, Mesquite

A few years back, Norma Faye Davis had been working as an independent contractor in the oil and gas industry only to discover that her contract had not been renewed. Still, she kept her home in Beeville because she was hopeful something would turn up. It did—only it was in the barbecue field. A barbecue joint on the edge of town had opened up, and Davis felt God's hand leading her to take the space, which had originally been a Dairy Queen.

So, she opened Norma's "Real Pit" Bar-B-Que as a way of bringing a taste of her native Tennessee to Texas. She brought in Shad Harper, another Tennessean (though he's from the town of Covington and she's from Mason, she's quick to point out), to run the pit. He'd learned the trade from his mother and

sister, who ran their own place back in the Volunteer State. Davis had her own restaurant out in San Diego back in the 1990s.

Yes, Norma's has brisket. It's as moist as you could want it, and it's the best-selling item. It arrives topped with sauce, unless you ask for it on the side, as some of the regulars do. But that's not the most interesting part of the menu. What is likely to surprise people driving through town is that Norma's sells pulled pork and chicken in Memphis-style sandwiches piled high with coleslaw. You don't find that too often in Texas. Yet she has found a market for it. "They love the lemon pepper" on the chicken thigh meat, which is boneless and skinless, she says.

Be early if you want to get the barbecued beans, because they do sell out. These are not baked beans, but beans that are finished off in the smoker, Davis says. The pintos are excellent in a quiet way that sort of sneaks up on you, with their black pepper and thick broth that bring out the real flavor of the bean. There's a secret ingredient in those pintos, she says, but she's keeping it to herself.

Harper's approach to brisket is to keep it simple, using only salt and pepper in the rub. He prefers to smoke it in hickory, but he's worked with pecan and mesquite, too, so he'll use what he gets and adjusts to that. "We cook our meat low and slow . . . makes you want to come back for mo'!" Norma's slogan reads. Closed on Sunday and Monday.

Smolik's Smokehouse

501 E. San Patricio Ave, Mathis, TX 78368; (361) 547-5494; www
.smolikssmokehouse.com **Founded:** 1985 **Pitmaster:** John Rodriguez
Wood: Mesquite

Smolik's sits in the middle of Mathis, a town with little more than 5,000 people. But nothing about the operation seems small. On a busy Saturday you'll find more than a dozen workers doing everything to keep the lines moving at both the counter and the always-popular drive-thru window. Some are minding the sausages, jerky, and other smokehouse meats that are sold on one half of the business; others are carving plates of brisket, ribs, and chicken. There's even someone who makes the rolls and pecan pie in-house.

A sign on a clipboard hanging in the kitchen cautions everyone to "keep calm and pray on." It seems to work because, despite more customers than tables in the dining room, the staff seems focused on doing its best to serve everyone promptly and with a smile. They've handled crowds before, and it shows.

Owners Mike and Gail Smolik opened this outpost of Smolik's in the 1980s. The original, in Karnes City, was started in 1928 by William Smolik and has since closed, while another Smolik's, also operated by family, is in Cuero. The Czech heritage can still be found in any number of areas, but perhaps none as impressive as the sausage-making, which is still done on the premises and includes an excellent jalapeño-cheese variety that is so juicy, it threatens to upstage the rest of a savory three-meat plate with some tender brisket and pork ribs worth sinking your teeth into.

Chopped beef sandwiches are made to order with plenty of tangy sweet sauce and meat that's fresh from the smoker.

Overseeing the food preparation is John Rodriguez, who might be described as a chef in any other type of restaurant. In the world of barbecue, it makes him a pitmaster, and he's fine with that. He knows that Smolik's doesn't live by barbecue alone. Chicken-fried steak, burgers, and fried shrimp fill out the menu, offering the town a little variety. Side dishes include macaroni and cheese, french fries, mashed potatoes, and Spanish rice in addition to the must-haves of pintos, potato salad, and coleslaw. And true to the town's Czech heritage, braised cabbage is a big seller. So are sweet and savory *kolaches*, which are sold on weekends.

"We don't have anything that doesn't sell," Rodriguez says. That's good menu planning, and it was to be put to the test in 2014 when a second Smolik's was due to open on Highway 359 near I-37. Closed on Sunday.

Van's Bar-B-Q

I-37 exit 65, Oakville, TX 78060; (361) 786-3995; second location at Three Rivers, near Love's Travel Stop at exit 72 **Founded:** 1982
Wood: Mesquite

Van's Bar-B-Q is a South Texas tradition. Those traveling south on US 181 toward Corpus Christi are often told ahead of time to "be sure and stop at Van's."

We met longtime owner Ona Van Dorn one afternoon at Van's. She had been in the restaurant business in both Corpus Christi and Beeville years

before she purchased this well-known barbecue roadhouse. In Corpus, after the steak house she owned burned down, she made a vow to leave the restaurant business for good, but she was soon back at it.

She was waiting for us at a table in the center of the dining room with a friend, Terry Reichel. Though she'd had a stroke in February 2013, she showed little sign of it and, at 94, was looking forward to an upcoming trail ride from Corpus Christi to San Antonio, a traditional annual outing for Reichel and her. She talked of how she purchased the building from a man who'd given up on doing business there because, he said, "Oakville is dead," and he was tired of having the building by the side of the highway "doing nothing." Van Dorn brought in the barbecue pit from Beeville and set up shop.

"On an Easter Saturday we put up a sign [on the highway] saying, 'Next exit, barbecue,' and we've never been closed since," Van Dorn said. A second location, at exit 72, near the Love's Travel Stop, has been doing a lively trade as well, she says.

The original Van's Bar-B-Q has a weather-beaten look, with wood paneling and a boardwalk under the front awning, strings of year-round holiday lights festooning the top of the front walls, and a large American flag by the front window. Even at 3 p.m., cars and trucks belonging to travelers or neighbors pulled into the parking lot next to the front door. It was folks taking a break, looking for smoked meat, or maybe just stopping in for a cold drink and a chat.

A waitress came to take our order, then brought it out on a long piece of butcher paper with a couple of pickles and a scoop of excellent potato salad. The brisket had a good, blackened crust; ribs were big and meaty. These and a fat sausage were laden with a generous dose of mesquite smoke and made a satisfying lunch. Not generally sauce users, we liked Van's tangy, not-too-sweet homemade barbecue sauce.

The service was attentive, but another waitress has made a name of her own at Van's. Marty Ellers Taylor showed up from an afternoon break while we were there, wearing a red T-shirt, mismatched socks, and a cowboy hat printed with red chile designs. Her boisterous spirit, genuine love of customers, and colorful dress have helped bring back customers almost as long as Van's has been a stop on the road, her boss says. Stop and say hi and have dessert, too. It's traditional and good—pecan pie and peach cobbler.

Vera's Backyard Bar-B-Que

2404 Southmost Rd., Brownsville, TX 78521; (956) 546-4159
Founded: 1955 **Pitmaster:** Armando Vera **Wood:** Mesquite, Ebony
The sign in front of Vera's Backyard Bar-B-Que says it all. Though the name of the restaurant is in English, the description of the place is strictly in Spanish: *Barbacoa en Pozo con Leña de Mezquite*. That roughly translates into *"barbacoa* from a mesquite-fired pit," and it is what Vera's is all about.

This is the last of an old-school style of *barbacoa* restaurants in which the cow's heads are still buried with charcoal in order for them to cook until tender. Vera's, which has been around since 1955, was grandfathered in by the health department, so owner Armando Vera, or Mando, to his many regular customers, still prepares the meat the way he learned

> *If Vera's has brisket, get yourself a double order and revel in its velvety texture. It becomes even better when wrapped in a corn tortilla with cilantro, onions, and salsa added.*

from his parents about 40 years ago, when he first started out.

He describes the process as beginning with soaking the head in water before wrapping it in aluminum foil, a more modern touch than the old canvas or burlap bags that were used in the earlier days of the 20th century. Meanwhile, a fire is built using mesquite and a related wood that Vera calls ebony. It's a mesquite-like wood that actually burns even hotter than its cousin, he says. Once the charcoal is ready, it is placed at the bottom of the pit. A layer of sheet metal is placed over the coals, and the wrapped heads are placed on top. Then another layer of sheet metal covers it before everything is buried. When the meat is done eight or so hours later, it is dug up, and Vera begins the task of shredding it into the various meats that he sells by the pound.

The meat sign, written by hand on a large sheet of poster paper, is printed solely in Spanish, with *cachete* (cheek) and *cachete y lengua* (cheek and tongue) heading a list that also includes *jeta y mollejas* (snout and sweetbreads) and *ojos y paladar* (eyes and palate). You can buy a stack of 20 thin but sturdy corn tortillas, an incendiary hot sauce in which jalapeños are used to temper the habaneros, a cilantro-based green sauce, and even an *americano* sauce for those who can't handle the heat. Plenty of cilantro and chopped raw onion can be sprinkled on top of your tacos.

Vera's best seller is his *ojos*, which attract an older generation of diner who grew up eating the gelatinous treat. No matter how many cows' heads Vera cooks on a weekend, the *ojos* will often sell out early in the morning. Younger diners seem to prefer the velvety richness of the cheek meat, which is almost buttery. And for the tourists who drop by, such as the parade of writers who have come through in recent years to feast on its last-of-its-kind fare, tender brisket and pork *carnitas* with a crispy exterior are also available. The brisket had just a hint of smoke flavor, but apparently that is too much for Vera's Latin clients, who don't care for a smoke flavor at all. "It's just not to Hispanics' tastes," he says. "Smoke is something whites and blacks like."

Vera says that, God willing, you should be able to find him making *barbacoa* for another 10 or 15 years. But don't expect the tradition to continue. All of his children, except one daughter, are off in college, and while she works at Vera's, she's not likely to take over the place, or at least work the pit. The heaviness of the heads, about 30 pounds apiece, means the work doesn't attract too many women to the pit—or too many men, for that matter. "I think it's probably gone after me," he says. Open Saturday and Sunday until sold out.

Chains

Barbecue joints come in all shapes, sizes, and stripes, as the places in this book illustrate. There's the mom-and-pop place as modest as can be. There's the cultural institution that seats dozens if not hundreds. There's the food truck with its smoker on wheels, ready to move to the next busy corner, catering gig, or private party. And there's the meat market that sells you its smoked treasures by the pound or by the plate.

What we haven't written about too much are the barbecue chains. Yet attention must be paid. That's because a growing number of customers seek out these places, which go by names such as Bodacious, Cousin's, the County Line, Rudy's, Grady's, Bill Miller, Pappas, Soulman's, Dickey's, and Tony Roma's. And the owners of many new places long to join their ranks. It's no different from the way customers want a steak from Texas Roadhouse or Outback (both of which originated in Kentucky, not the Lone Star State or Australia) or a burger from a Red Robin or Chili's. It's a sense of consistency along with a sense of ease; they've eaten at the same place so many times, no matter the city they're in, that they don't really have to think about what they're going to order. They know what they want, and they expect it to taste the same everywhere they go.

In a way, that's anathema to the whole concept of barbecue, which is about having a pitmaster examine each brisket or each chicken on the grill and determining if it's good enough to sell. Trent Brooks of Brooks' Place in Cypress stresses that he doesn't care as much about quantity as he does about quality. If he opens his pit and sees a rack of ribs that doesn't look good enough to serve, he won't serve it.

You'll find some chain barbecue joints place the same emphasis on their product, if you do your research. The County Line, which started in Austin back in 1975, now has seven locations in Texas and New Mexico. Each one has a pitmaster who oversees the meats to ensure that what you get meets their standards.

There are similarities at each County Line location. The meats are all smoked using green oak. "It's still got the leaves on the bark," says co-owner Skeeter Miller. This is desirable because that wood doesn't cook at too high of a temperature, ensuring a low and slow cooking process, and yet it produces a good smoke ring, he says. It also produces an aroma that many regular customers now recognize as the County Line. From the moment they walk in the door, they know they're where they want to be.

The sauce, the smoked pecan vinaigrette on the salads, and the margarita may also be the same at each County Line, but the meats and sides could vary depending on the restaurant's location. In El Paso, for example, you'll find a healthy spice level in the food, reflecting the tastes of the city. But not in Austin. If you used too much spice there, "you couldn't give that away," Miller says.

It's all about listening to your customers. That's why your meat comes without sauce on it these days. "We prefer it that way," Miller says. "And customers now do, too. You don't need to cover up our meat in any way." But the sauce is there if you want it. (Garrett Stephens, pitmaster of the County Line on I-10 in San Antonio shared his take on smoking his Good Ol' Boy Baby Back Ribs. See page 227.)

Not every chain wants to take that time—and many of the customers don't want them to either. A big appeal of some chains is that the service can be quick. That's long been a hallmark of Bill Miller Bar-B-Q, which started in San Antonio back in the early 1950s and has grown to include almost 70 locations across the state. Today the company boasts on its website that, at its kitchen headquarters, it can cook up to 2,500 pounds of brisket at one time, all in pits that Miller designed. That meat is then shipped out to its various restaurants, where the staff will hand you your food as quickly as possible, whether you're dining indoors or using the drive-thru. The family-owned restaurant chain, run nowadays by the namesake's three sons and son-in-law, is known just as much for its fried chicken as it is for its barbecue. But the meat, whether smoked or fried, may be eclipsed by the popularity of its sweet tea, which the chain sells by the quart and by the gallon if you've just got to have that jolt of sugar and caffeine.

The roster of barbecue chains across Texas features a number of names that people grew up with, including Grady's Bar-B-Q, which was established in 1948, and Cousin's BBQ, which has been a Dallas fixture for more than 30 years. And they have their appeal to customers. It could be as simple as the fact that they offer convenience, a good price, and a clean booster seat for a stressed-out parent. Whatever the reason, their flavors left indelible impressions on their young customers' taste buds, and now those children are grown and taking children of their own out for barbecue.

RECEIPES

In the Kitchen
& Around the Smoker

You'll find dozens, if not hundreds, of side dishes and their variations when traveling around sampling Texas barbecue. The most common sides are pinto beans or baked beans, potato salad, coleslaw, macaroni and cheese, creamed corn, and baked or smoked potatoes, along with the occasional salad and lots of desserts. Depending on what part of the state you're in, you'll get barbecue sauce on the side or poured on the meat (sometimes they ask if you want it this way, but if they don't, you can express your preference).

If you want to smoke a brisket or a few racks of pork ribs, the recipe is going to be more of a method. Texas-style barbecue generally uses wood smoke, indirect-heat pits, or rotisseries that also burn wood to impart flavor to meat. Some recipes and, in fact, some barbecue restaurants cook with direct heat, on a grill. Wood chips can also be used with a gas grill, but it's not the most effective way to make wood smoke flavor.

When you get to the rubs (and mops or glazes) for the meat, there are plenty of recipes. Even so, for many of the pros, a good rub contains just salt and black pepper and possibly a heat source such as cayenne pepper for a little added bite.

We could have found hundreds of recipes for all of the above on the Internet, and we wouldn't discourage anyone from doing so. But we sought out recipes from the folks we talked to across the state. This wasn't always easy to do—and we understand the reasons why. First, if the recipes were written down, they might specify portions to feed hundreds of people. Also, many of the barbecue joints we had on our lists were mom-and-pop places that considered these recipes part of the lifeblood and legacy of their restaurants.

In Houston, we spoke to Kathy Brady, whose parents opened their restaurant in the mid-1970s. She is the pitmaster at Burns BBQ on N. Shepherd Drive and carries the family recipes intact at her restaurant to this day. Her family surrounds her, their roles being her loyal support and her conscience. If she were to give away family recipes or if she decided to change them even a little bit, she'd hear about it!

As we covered the highways and back roads of Texas, we discovered that most barbecue restaurant owners are among the most friendly, interesting people we've met in the food business. Not only that, they are also certainly among the hardest-working. If they didn't share a recipe, that was fine with us. Many shared techniques, from which we adapted our own.

As we present our hard-won collection of recipes for sauces, pinto beans, cobblers, and more, we're very grateful to the contributors and to those who provided inspiration. If any side dishes are mentioned for which we didn't get recipes, take that as a challenge to take a drive, visit the barbecue places mentioned, and then sample and enjoy.

How to Smoke

Want to become your own pitmaster? Or make your own barbecue at home? It requires time and either money or a little ingenuity. You could go to a barbecue supply store or a hardware store for a pit that's ready for your first load of firewood and meat. Or you could follow the lead of Ernest Servantes, the *Chopped Grill Masters* winner from the Hill Country town of New Braunfels: He made his first pit out of a refurbished metal barrel.

The Internet is filled with ideas on how to get started, as well as more advanced suggestions for those who've been at it awhile. Just don't expect to become the next Aaron Franklin or Tootsie Tomanetz overnight. It took them years to learn their craft, and they've succeeded because of trial and error. You could apprentice yourself to any legend looking for help. Or you could go it alone.

Here are five sites with advice to give you a good foundation in smoking meat and suggestions on how to take your new skills to places you may not have dreamed of:

www.smoking-meat.com—"Learn to smoke meat with Jeff Phillips" is the motto of this site, which has been going strong since 2004. The basics, from brisket to chicken, are covered, but Phillips doesn't stop there. Smoked turkey with bacon butter, lobster tails, and even a crown roast of pork are covered.

www.smokingmeatforums.com—Network with other smoked meat aficionados across the US and abroad using this expansive site, which offers information for the novice and experienced smoker alike. You'll find plenty of recipes as well as information on home gardening, preserving food, and Dutch oven cooking.

www.thesmokerking.com—The Smoker King shows you how to build your own smoker out of a 250- or 1,000-gallon tank—and then he offers plenty of recipes to make sure you put that barrel to good use. The instructions on how to smoke a chicken for competition are a must-read.

www.the-greatest-barbecue-recipes.com—No false modesty here. This site celebrates "the mystical communion of fire, smoke and meat!" And it does so with plenty of tips, "the 6 secrets" you need to learn, and recipes for all levels of pitmasters.

www.smoker-cooking.com—Your smoker is capable of preparing a banquet of meats, including both hot and cold smoked salmon, apple wood–smoked duck breast, and even what's known as "half smoke." You can also use this site to learn how to make your own bacon out of pork loin.

Tips for Smoking Brisket from Black's Barbecue in Lockhart

Choose a high-quality prime or choice grade, 10- to 12-pound brisket. Avoid the cheap, on-sale briskets at the grocery store. They will taste cheap and on sale no matter what you do to them.

Don't put anything crazy on the brisket. Add Black's Barbecue Dry Rub, which you can purchase at the restaurant or on their website, to the brisket, and only use 2 teaspoons of the dry rub per 1 pound of raw meat. Rub the dry rub onto the top, bottom, and all four sides of the brisket, making sure to rub it into the meat fibers. (*Editor's note*: You can make your own simple rub of salt and pepper or purchase another prepared rub and follow instructions.)

Black's Barbecue in Lockhart, Texas, is one of the top barbecue restaurants in the state. They, as do many other barbecue places, sell their rub as well as other products. For Black's products or to have their barbecue shipped to you, visit them at www.blacksbbq.com/store.

Smoke the brisket for 10 to 12 hours at about 300°F on a pit with a firebox burning oak or post oak. No flames should be under the meat, because that is "grilling" and we want to barbecue!

When you lay your brisket in the pit, you always want to put the fat side up (on top) so the fat juices can soak into the meat.

Don't turn the brisket or poke it too much, because that lets out the meat juices.

Don't rush the brisket. Allow plenty of time for the brisket to cook and become tender. Remember, low and slow is the name of the game.

The brisket is ready when a temperature probe stuck into all parts of the meat goes in and out easily, like a cake that's done.

BBQ-SPICED LOCKHART QUAIL

From James Canter, executive chef at the Victoria Country Club, Victoria TX

For this recipe, chef James Canter prefers to use locally grown quail from Diamond H or any of the other Texas Hill Country farms that raise the tiny, tasty birds. He prefers to grill the birds, but quail can be smoked using indirect heat.

The Country Club is obviously not a barbecue joint, but Canter has held barbecue parties on the golf course, in which the golfers encounter a different item near the green of each hole. It might be a bite of quail, a taste of potato salad, or a martini. No knows until reaching the green. **Serves 8 as an appetizer**

½ teaspoon ground cumin (see note)
1 tablespoon finely ground instant coffee
1 tablespoon smoked paprika
2 tablespoons dark brown sugar
1 tablespoon kosher salt
½ teaspoon granulated garlic
½ teaspoon onion powder
Extra-virgin olive oil
8 semi-boneless quail

Note: Canter likes to use whole cumin seed that he dry pan toasts and grinds as needed per order.

Mix the cumin, coffee, paprika, brown sugar, salt, granulated garlic, and onion powder together until completely homogenized.

Coat the quail in olive oil generously so that the spice mixture will stick to the birds. Be sure to generously coat the quail with the spice rub and then let them sit in the refrigerator for at least 4 hours to marinate.

Before the quail are ready, preheat a grill to about 400°F (I prefer a wood/charcoal mix, usually oak wood and mesquite coals). Make sure to rub your grill with some oil before placing the quail onto the grid. I like to start breast-side down for a quick char and then finish the quail on its back to prevent the breast from overcooking. This can be a quick process depending on the grill, of course, and I prefer to serve the quail so that the outer extremities are slightly charred (to offset the sugar component in the rub) and medium-rare on the inside of the breast.

You can also smoke the quail using indirect heat of about 225°F and letting the meat set for about 1 hour. Check on the meat to make sure it is not drying out. If it is, baste it with a little more olive oil.

BRISKET TACOS

From John Griffin

In the heart of Tex-Mex country, there's nothing easier—and more welcome—than rolling some warm meat into a tortilla and creating a taco. Why not do the same with some barbecue? It's really that simple.

Here are two versions inspired by our travels throughout Texas. Amounts can be adjusted depending on needs and taste.

Corkscrew BBQ-Style Tacos

This recipe was inspired by the tacos served at Corkscrew BBQ north of Houston. Fair warning: The combination of moist, hot brisket and warm corn tortillas can be addictive.

Place 2 tortillas on a plate or sheet of aluminum foil so that they partially overlap. Lay 2 or 3 thick-cut slices of moist brisket in the center. Sprinkle cabbage over the meat. Spoon on *pico de gallo* and then pour ranch dressing over the top. Sprinkle radishes and cilantro on top, if desired. Wrap the foil around the taco, if using, until it's time to eat.

You can use any kind of barbecue you want in this: pulled pork, shredded chicken, turkey, ham slices, or a sausage either split down the center or sliced. As you change the meat, you may want to use barbecue sauce instead of the ranch dressing. The choice is yours.

Corn tortillas, warmed
Thick-cut brisket
Shredded cabbage
Pico de gallo (a blend of chopped tomato, onion, and jalapeño or serrano pepper)
Ranch dressing (Corkscrew makes a green chile ranch)
Radish slivers, for garnish
Chopped cilantro, for garnish

Curly's Carolina, TX–Style Tacos

These tacos, inspired by those served at Curly's Carolina, TX in Round Rock, also use brisket, but the approach could not be more different.

On a warm flour tortilla, layer your brisket slices in the center. Top with cilantro leaves, smoked Gouda, and pickled onions. Wrap in aluminum foil and place in a warmer for a few minutes, if possible, so that the cheese can begin to melt into the brisket.

Flour tortillas, warmed
Thick-cut brisket
Cilantro leaves
Smoked Gouda, cut in strips, at room temperature
Pickled onions

CINNAMON CHICKEN

From Jacob Walbert of Pioneer BBQ in Nixon

You can vary this recipe from Jacob Walbert using the amount of chicken you want to smoke or the amount of each of the ingredients you want to use.

Chicken breasts

Cinnamon to taste

Black pepper to taste

Honey to taste

Texas lager, such as Ranger Creek South Texas Lager or Pedernales Lobo Texas Lager

Prepare your smoker using the wood of your choice. The folks at Pioneer BBQ use oak.

Place each breast on a large piece of foil. Sprinkle the chicken with cinnamon and black pepper. Drizzle honey over it.

Make a boat out of the foil and pour the beer in. Place it in the smoker and slow cook it until the meat reaches an internal temperature of 165°F. The length of time will vary depending on how hot your smoker is and how indirect your heat is, but a general rule is that it takes about 1 hour for 1 pound of chicken smoked at 225°F.

Serve with ripe plantains that have been sautéed with a little sugar, ginger, and honey.

GOOD OL' BOY BABY BACK RIBS

From Garrett Stephens, pitmaster at the County Line on I-10 in San Antonio
Garrett Stephens injects his recipes with plenty of good humor as well as flavor:

Being a good ol' boy from South Texas, and a 20-year vet managing the pits at a Texas barbecue joint, has taught me a thing or two about the art of smoking ribs.

Although beef—and all its glorious cuts—has traditionally defined Lone Star state barbecue, we know the tenets are the same for Mr. Porky, too. By following these principles, you'll find yourself perfumed with smoke and the recipient of adulation and applause. Oh, and there's beer involved, so life just got a little bit better. **Makes about ¾ cup**

1. Skimp on the Veggies, Not the Meat

It's real simple—great barbecue starts with great cuts of meat. Go to your butcher and ask him for fresh (not frozen), high-quality baby back ribs. The meat should be slightly marbled. And if you ask nicely, they may even skin those babies for you.

If you have to skin them yourself, simply get a paring knife and peel back an edge at one of the ends. Once you get a hold of the membrane, peel it off. Also, look for any fat that can be trimmed from both sides and remove. This will help the smoke, rub, and sauce permeate the meat. Be sure to rinse your slabs thoroughly and dry them off.

2. If You Build It, They Will Come

The idea here is to build flavors starting with quality meat. Then, we add another layer with a dry rub, then yet another layer with the wonderful aroma of smoke, and, finally, a nice lacquer of sauce at the end.

You can use any number of rubs that suit your palate. There are as many different retail rubs available to buy as there are stars in the sky. Hint: Be aware of salt content in the rub—and adjust the amount you use to your taste. For our County Line BBQ rub, combine all the ingredients listed to the right, then rub each slab down with 3 tablespoons of vegetable oil and about 4 tablespoons of rub. This combination of oil and rub combined with a low and slow cook will give you the quintessential bark on the outside of the ribs. That's flavor, people. Your ribs are now ready for the smoker, but if you have the time, wrap the rubbed racks in plastic wrap and place in your refrigerator for 6–12 hours before smoking.

¼ cup brown sugar
⅓ cup paprika
4 tablespoons coarse black pepper
2 tablespoons sea salt
2 teaspoons dry mustard
2 teaspoons cayenne pepper
1 teaspoon granulated onion
1 teaspoon granulated garlic

3. Smoke 'em if Ya Got 'em

Let's face it, folks, if you're cooking on a gas grill, at best you can call it "grilling." Barbecuing is a whole different animal that requires coals, wood, smoke, preparation, patience, and time. So, keep that gas grill tucked away under its cover and get yourself a smoker. You can use a large kettle grill and place hot coals on one side of the kettle and your precious ribs on the other. However, it may be time to invest in a smoker with an offset heat box. There are thousands of variations for all sorts of budgets. Google it.

Once you have a nice bed of coals going in your offset box, place a large handful of hardwood chunks on the coals. Good Ol' Boy Ribs require oak. Oak's inherent benefits provide a long burn, a mild smoke and aroma, and a beautiful smoke ring.

Get a foil pan and fill it halfway with water. Place it in the smoker close to the heat box. This will provide moisture and help maintain a steady temp in your pit. Place your ribs as far from the heat source as possible, and rotate the racks closest to the heat halfway through the cook. Adjust the vents at the top and bottom of the smoker to fine-tune the heat to 225°F and do your best to maintain this temp. Here's a hint: Don't keep opening the pit and peeking at those beautiful slabs. They are still there. I advise you to crack open a beer and play some Grateful Dead. You may substitute the beverage and music of your choice.

Add pre-lit coals as needed throughout the cooking, and add another large handful of oak chunks halfway through. Baby back ribs should take 3–4 hours depending on the heat and its consistency (St. Louis–cut pork ribs will take 5–6 hours, if you cheated).

The next step is to put away that digital thermometer. Checking to see if your ribs are done is a snap. Literally. Simply grab a pair of tongs and bounce the ribs. The rack should bend to the point where the beautiful bark you made cracks and "snaps."

JALAPEÑO-CHEDDAR SAUSAGES

From John Griffin

This style of sausage will forever be associated with Easter in my mind because the aroma stemming from a sizzling skillet of these treats caused the conversion of one vegetarian that day. And he's been happily eating meat ever since.

Those sausages were from Green's, a store in the tiny Texas town of Zabcikville—and it is worth the drive to check it out. While you're there, pick up a pound or two of bacon (there are five types), plus five or six pounds of the fingerling jalapeño-cheddar sausages. **Makes about 3 dozen sausages**

Note: You want lard freshly rendered from a pig, not the white blocks sold in supermarkets. The best place to get the lard you want is at Mexican meat markets.

Soak the casings for at least 30 minutes and run water through them from the faucet to see if there are any tears.

Fit your stand mixer with the grinder attachment or set up your hand grinder. Beneath the grinder, set up a bowl partially filled with ice water. Set a mixing bowl inside the ice water to catch the meat.

In a large bowl, mix together the pork shoulder; the fatback, if using (do not add the lard here); and the cheese. Run it through the grinder on a fine plate. If your pork shoulder is too lean, add more fat. You want at least a 75:25 ratio of meat to fat. Remember, you are making sausage, and it's the fat that makes it sizzle.

Add to the bowl the lard, if using, and the jalapeños, garlic, salt, pepper, and beer. Place the mixing bowl in your stand mixer fitted with the paddle and let it run for a couple of minutes to combine. Put the bowl back on the ice and refrigerate for at least 20 minutes. During that time you can fry up a little bit of the sausage to taste the seasonings and to see if you have enough fat.

Remove the ground meat from the refrigerator when it is icy cold and stuff into the casings, if desired, twisting into links at about every 6–8 inches, as desired.

When you're ready to cook the sausage, build your fire and smoke the links the way you would any others. If you're using direct heat over mesquite, they shouldn't take longer than 20 minutes or so. If you're using indirect heat from oak or pecan, they could take about 90 minutes or longer, depending on the size of the links and the temperature in the smoker. For an even richer, smoky flavor, you could boil the links in beer and then finish them off for about 10 minutes in the smoker. Uncooked links will freeze for up to 6 months.

Medium hog casings

5 pounds pork shoulder, trimmed of any gristle or skin, but with the fat remaining, and then cubed

3 cups lard (see note) or 1½ pounds fatback, cubed

1 pound aged, sharp cheddar, cubed

10 pickled jalapeños, seeded and minced

4 cloves garlic, minced

Salt to taste

Black pepper to taste

½ cup Shiner bock

MAC'S BAR-B-QUE PORK RIBS RUB

From Billy McDonald of Mac's Bar-B-Que in Dallas

Billy McDonald doesn't use a rub on his brisket. Not even salt. But he does have a simple rub for his pork ribs, which often sell out before his brisket. And he applies it with a light but sure touch. He creates it in parts, not in cups or tablespoons, so you can scale it to your own needs.

1 part Lawry's Seasoned Salt
6 parts white sugar
½ part garlic powder
A touch of cinnamon
   (optional)

Mix the seasonings thoroughly. McDonald doesn't always use cinnamon, so you can decide by taste if you'd like it included. Remove your ribs from the refrigerator. Sprinkle the seasoning on top and, using a gloved hand, pat it onto the ribs, making sure they are lightly covered. Place in the pit and smoke using your method, your wood, and your temperature.

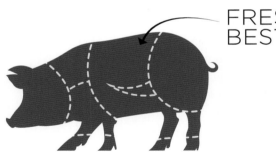

FRESH
BEST IN TOWN!

OVEN BARBECUE BRISKET

From Stephen Paprocki, executive chef at the Grill on the Hill in San Antonio

Smoked paprika is one ingredient that helps give this oven-baked brisket recipe from San Antonio's Stephen Paprocki its barbecue flavor. It's a great way for those without a smoker in back to make their own barbecue at home. The basting sauce, with its tangy mix of tomatoes, sugar, and vinegar, is another. He doesn't bake his first-cut, or flat-cut, brisket as slowly as you would in a pit, but the 3½-hour cooking time is long enough for the meat to tenderize.

Paprocki, executive chef at the Grill on the Hill, has been known to help out at the barbecue cantina at Tejas Rodeo Co., so he knows his way around a pit. **Serves 8–10**

Combine shallots, garlic, chili powder, paprika, cinnamon, oregano, and salt in a small bowl. Rub into both sides of the meat. Set the meat in a 9 x 13-inch baking dish, cover, and refrigerate for at least 8 hours or overnight.

Pour Worcestershire sauce over the meat. Cover the pan with foil and set aside at room temperature while the oven heats to 350°F.

Bake the brisket, covered, for 2 hours. Meanwhile, blend tomatoes, brown sugar, and vinegar in a large blender or food processor until smooth.

After 2 hours, pour the tomato mixture over the meat. Continue baking, covered, until fork-tender, basting with pan juices every 30 minutes, for about 1½ hours more.

Remove the meat from the sauce. Let rest for 10 minutes, then slice against the grain. Skim the fat from the sauce in the pan; pour the sauce over the meat and serve.

2 medium shallots, minced

2 cloves garlic, minced

4 teaspoons chili powder

4 teaspoons smoked paprika or Hungarian paprika

2 teaspoons ground cinnamon

2 teaspoons dried oregano

1 teaspoon kosher salt

1 (4-pound) first-cut brisket, trimmed of fat

¼ cup Worcestershire sauce

1 (14-ounce) can no-salt-added diced tomatoes

¼ cup packed dark brown sugar

¼ cup cider vinegar

QUICK BARBECUE SAUCE

From John Griffin

The mixture of ketchup and mustard, in various proportions, isn't new, and there are variations on this blend at some barbecue joints. So, when you've run out of your favorite store-bought or restaurant-brand sauce, reach into the refrigerator for the ingredients to make this sauce. It works, especially when used on heavily peppered beef ribs, brisket, and sausage. **Makes ½ cup sauce**

¼ cup plus 2 tablespoons
    ketchup
2 tablespoons yellow mustard
¼ teaspoon Worcestershire
    sauce
½–1 teaspoon very finely
    chopped onion

Mix all the ingredients together.

THE SPREAD'S MESQUITE GRILLED *CABRITO*

From Clinton Tinney at The Spread Pit BBQ in Brady

Cabrito, or goat, was once a mainstay of cowboy barbecue in West Texas. If you could find one, it was smaller than a calf, easier to prepare, faster to cook, and generated far less waste. Plus, a goat wasn't part of the cattle drive, so cost was not a factor.

The Spread Pit BBQ in Brady is one of the places that still features *cabrito* on its menu. It's available on weekends, and it's a real treat from the heart of Texas. Brady is also the home of the World Championship Goat Cook-Off, held on Labor Day weekend for the past 40 years. The Spread was honored to serve their version of *cabrito*, moist from the use of their secret lemon butter seasoning, at the 2013 gathering.

"*Cabrito* is only done justice over a bed of mesquite coals cooking on an open pit," says the Spread's owner, Mandy Geistweidt. Her pitmaster, Clinton Tinney, created the recipe.

Prepare a bed of mesquite coals. When the coals are ready, lay all of the pieces of *cabrito* on the pit. Lightly sprinkle with Lawry's Seasoned Salt and pepper on both sides of the meat while it's cooking on the pit. Brown both sides until they're golden brown.

Wrap all the pieces in aluminum foil. If you're cooking one goat, add 2 cups lemon butter and 1 cup water, and let steam for about an hour. Unwrap and serve.

Mesquite wood
Goat (*cabrito*), cut into pieces
Lawry's Seasoned Salt
Coarse ground pepper
2 cups The Spread's Famous
Lemon Butter or your own
version (see note below)
1 cup water

Note: To make lemon butter, melt 1 pound of butter, then stir in the juice of 1 lemon and 1 generous tablespoon lemon pepper (from John Griffin).

TWO BROS. PORK BUTT

From Jason Dady of Two Bros. BBQ Market in San Antonio

Call it pork butt or call it pulled pork—by either name it's one of the rising stars on the Texas barbecue scene. And although brisket continues to reign supreme, more and more customers are demanding this dish, which is actually from the barbecue scene outside of Texas. Its rising popularity can be said to reflect an influx of people from other Southern states, though a few have said it signals an increasing homogeneity on the barbecue scene. Or possibly the rising cost of beef.

In this version, from Jason Dady's Two Bros. BBQ Market in San Antonio, the meat is smoked low and slow. You can get this sandwich Memphis-style, which means coleslaw comes on top of lightly sauced pork, or you can get the meat just by itself with no sauce at all. **Serves 8–10**

1 (5-pound) bone-in pork butt
Your favorite pork rub

Before placing the pork butt in the smoker, cover it moderately with the rub.

Place the meat in the middle of the smoker heated to anywhere from 225 to 240°F and let it smoke for 4 hours. Dady uses oak, and his intent is to give the meat only a medium toast on the outside.

After the 4 hours, wrap the pork butt in foil and return it to the center of the smoker for 2–3 hours. Unwrap the pork butt and smoke for 1 hour more before it is ready to serve. At this point, the meat should come apart in chunks, Dady says, not in the shreds some serve up. He finds that a little too overdone for his tastes.

At this point, you can add sauce to taste. A traditional Carolina-style sauce would be vinegar-based; Dady's version is made with vinegar, a little tomato, and pickle juice. You could also add a little heat if you're using the meat in sandwiches; you can top it with coleslaw, too, also in the style you prefer. Dady suggests serving this with a slaw dressed with a red wine vinegar sauce, because he likes the way the acid cuts through the richness of the meat. If that's too tart for you, use the dressing you want.

BEANS IN A SLOW COOKER

From John Griffin

There are endless ways to cook and season pinto beans. This is a savory version that goes together quickly. Then you just turn on the slow cooker and forget about it while the flavors coalesce during the 8-hour cooking time. **Serves 8–10**

Place the beans in a pot. Cover with water and let sit overnight. When you're ready to put the pot of beans together, half-cook the bacon and render all but about 1 tablespoon of fat.

Drain the beans and place in the slow cooker. Add the bacon and remaining fat, tomato, peppers, onion, garlic, cumin, salt, plenty of pepper, beer, and water. Stir, so everything is incorporated.

Cover and cook on low for 8 hours. If you have time, you may want to taste the bean broth about 4 hours into the cooking process and adjust seasonings as needed.

1½ cups dried pinto beans
6 slices thick-cut bacon, cut up
1 medium tomato, diced
1 red or orange pepper, diced
1–2 jalapeño peppers, seeded and minced, or less to taste
1 onion, minced
3 cloves garlic, minced
¼–½ teaspoon cumin, to taste
1 teaspoon hickory-smoked salt or regular salt
Freshly ground black pepper to taste
1 (12-ounce) bottle Texas lager beer
1 cup water

CREAMED SWEET CORN

From Bonnie Walker

This is a version of creamed corn we found in a number of places—one that is likely to stamp out any memories of creamed corn out of the can.

The cream sauce is smooth, thick, and rich; the kernels of corn taste fresh. We could not get a recipe, as such, but Wayne Kammerl at the Brisket House in Houston gave us a tip or two that sent us in the right direction to develop a recipe that resembles his creamed corn. Cream cheese is the secret, a product that won't break down as you simmer this corn. The milk and cream will thin down the dish if it gets too thick. If you use fresh corn, be sure to scrape the juice from the cob with a knife so you get all that fresh corn flavor, plus extra starch for thickening. **Serves 8–10**

1 pound corn, either freshly cut from the cob or frozen kernels

1 (8-ounce) package cream cheese

¼ cup unsalted butter

¼ cup heavy cream or half-and-half

½ cup milk

1 teaspoon sugar, or to taste

Salt and white pepper (just a couple of pinches each) to taste

If you're using frozen kernels, let them thaw. If using fresh, stand the cob up on the cutting board and hold the top firmly, then cut the kernels off the cob by running a knife lengthwise from the top to the bottom of the cob. After you've cut off the kernels, run the knife down again, pressing down as you squeeze the last of the juice and starch from the cob.

If you're cooking fresh corn, put it in a microwavable dish with a few spoonfuls of water and run it in the microwave for a minute or so. Drain well.

Put the prepared corn kernels, cream cheese, butter, cream, and milk into a heavy-bottomed pot and turn the heat on low. Let the cheese melt and add the seasonings. Cook until the corn is to your liking and the sauce is smooth and hot (15 minutes or so over medium-low heat). Keep an eye on the pot so that you don't burn it. Add a little extra milk to thin, if needed. You want a creamy, smooth, but not pasty-thick texture. Correct seasoning and serve.

CUCUMBER SALAD

From John Griffin

When you're eating substantial smoked meats, a tangy salad composed of raw ingredients offers a welcome contrast and a certain brightness to the meal. Coleslaw fits the bill at many barbecue joints, but the dressing is too often laden with so much sugar that the freshness of the cabbage gets buried.

That's where the cucumber salad comes in, which you can find in places such as Chisholm Trail Bar-B.Q. & Hot Sausage in Lockhart or Lum's Bar-B-Que in Junction. This may be the easiest salad of all to make because it has so few ingredients, but you have to remember to find the balance that you like between the oil and vinegar. You also have to let it rest so the flavors have time to coalesce. **Serves 4**

Note: Look for a cucumber that's not too fat with water and burp-inducing seeds. You could use an English cucumber, which would not have to be peeled.

Toss the cucumber, tomatoes, and onion, if using, in a nonreactive bowl. Splash with a little oil and vinegar (about 2 tablespoons oil and enough vinegar to suit your tastes, maybe 2 teaspoons). Add salt and pepper to taste.

Let sit for at least 20 minutes before serving. Stir and adjust seasoning.

Variations: Use Wishbone Italian Dressing instead of your own oil-and-vinegar blend. Or, if you want a really tart salad, omit the oil and use only a mild vinegar, such as cane vinegar or rice vinegar.

1 cucumber, peeled and sliced about ¼-inch thick (see note)

½ cup grape tomatoes, cut in half, or 3 Roma tomatoes, seeded and diced

¼ red or yellow onion, halved and thinly sliced (optional)

Olive oil

Apple cider vinegar

Salt and pepper to taste

DEEP-FRIED CORN ON THE COB

From John Griffin

Off the Bone pitmaster Dwight Harvey found himself with more fresh corn than he could use. So, he decided to fry it up on the cob and see if people liked it. Months later it was still on the menu at his Dallas restaurant. He swears the method is simple, even if he didn't share the exact method he uses. We've come up with a version that's sure to please in terms of flavor and simplicity. **Serves 4**

4 ears corn, shucked and silk removed
Vegetable oil
Lawry's Seasoned Salt to taste
Cayenne pepper to taste
Lime wedges

Clean the ears of corn. Once the silks are removed, pat the ears dry with a paper towel.

Heat the oil in a deep fryer or Dutch oven to 375°F. Drop in the ears of corn and fry for about 4 minutes or until the kernels start to turn a golden yellow.

Remove the ears of corn from the oil and drain. Sprinkle with Lawry's Seasoned Salt and cayenne pepper to taste. Serve with lime wedges.

KITCHEN SINK TATER SALAD

From James Canter, executive chef at the Victoria Country Club, Victoria, TX

Chef James Canter stages a barbecue party at the Victoria Country Club in which golfers find a different treat at each green. It could be a portable pit filled with meat or a cocktail that'll keep people swinging.

What barbecue—on the golf course, in your home, or at a barbecue joint—is complete without potato salad? Canter's version is mayonnaise-based and gets a lift from the inclusion of an apple. "I love this little gem," the chef says. "It is chock-full of goodies and hidden treasures. I also like to add a little barbecue sauce into the mix for a little more tang, even though it's just as good without it."

Serves 8–10

Cube potatoes and boil with carrot until they are very tender. Remove potatoes and carrot and mash with a fork. A few lumps are okay; they do not have to be mashed potato consistency.

Chop cucumber, onion, eggs, and apple into small pieces. Add to potato-carrot mixture along with barbecue sauce, if using.

Slowly stir in mayonnaise in small amounts and mix well. Continue adding more mayonnaise until desired consistency is reached (salad should be creamy and soft). Add salt and pepper to taste.

Chill well before serving.

6 medium potatoes
1 carrot, roughly chopped
1 cucumber
1 sweet onion
2 hard-boiled eggs
1 apple, cored
1 tablespoon barbecue sauce (optional)
½–¾ cup sweetened mayonnaise (add 1 teaspoon sugar)
Salt and pepper to taste

SIDE DISH RECIPES

SAUERKRAUT WITH SAUSAGE

From John Griffin

Floyd Wilhelm of Chisholm Trail Bar-B.Q. & Hot Sausage in Lockhart gets kind of sheepish when he talks about this sauerkraut. It's little more than a canned version of kraut mixed with a dice cut of his handmade sausage, he says. It's then cooked down to a thick, caramelized mix in which the fat of the meat saturates every strand of cabbage. What's wrong with that?

He wouldn't give us exact proportions of what he uses, but that didn't stop us from making our own.

Serves 5–6

1 (20-ounce) can or bag
    sauerkraut
1–1½ pounds smoked sausage,
    diced (your choice of pork,
    beef, or venison)
⅛ cup brown sugar (optional)
½ cup chopped onion
    (optional)

Rinse the sauerkraut and place in a slow cooker. Stir in the sausage and, if using, the brown sugar or onion, or both.

Set on high and cook for about 2 hours. Check after 1 hour and after 90 minutes to see if any water needs to be added.

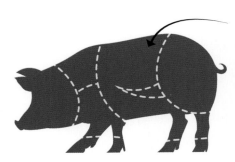

FRESH
BEST IN TOWN!

SERRANO CHEESE SPINACH

From John Griffin

This side dish, inspired by the version at Stubb's BBQ, is a thoroughly welcome surprise. It goes together quickly and actually improves upon classic creamed spinach by adding the welcome punch of pickled serrano peppers. **Serves 3–4**

Preheat oven to 350°F.

Whisk the cream cheese and heavy cream together. Set aside.

Squeeze any excess water from spinach and put the leaves in a baking dish. Stir in cream cheese mixture, ¼ cup Parmesan cheese, peppers, salt, black pepper, and garlic until well incorporated. Sprinkle remaining tablespoon of cheese on top.

Bake for 20–25 minutes or until the top is brown and the cream mixture is cooked through.

Note: Pickled jalapeños can be substituted, but only use 1 large or 2 small jalapeños because of the difference in size of the peppers.

3 ounces cream cheese, cut in pieces, at room temperature

¼ cup heavy cream

1 (10-ounce) package frozen spinach, thawed

¼ cup plus 1 tablespoon grated Parmesan cheese, divided use

4 pickled serrano peppers, diced (see note)

¼ teaspoon salt

Freshly grated black pepper to taste

1 clove garlic, minced

SMOKED POTATOES

From Ed Ashford of Ed's Smok-N-Q in San Antonio
It's easy to smoke a potato, says Ed Ashford of Ed's Smok-N-Q in San Antonio. In fact, it hardly needs a recipe. **Serves 4**

4 baking potatoes or sweet
 potatoes
Melted butter or oil, for
 brushing

First, you clean your potatoes and rub a little melted butter or oil over the skin of each. Second, you wrap each individually in foil. Then you place them in the pit in an area of indirect heat, so that they can cook until done.

Sweet potatoes will cook a lot faster than white potatoes, and both will cook differently depending on the size of the potato and what wood you use in your smoker. Mesquite burns hotter, so the potatoes will cook faster. In Ashford's pit, it takes 2 hours for the white potatoes to cook through.

Of course, you could just throw the foil-wrapped potatoes into the fire and, using the right tongs, retrieve them after they've baked, Ashford says.

You can tell when the potatoes are tender and cooked through by stabbing them with a fork.

Without unwrapping the potato, slice it down the middle and force it open. Then top with your choice of butter, cheese, sour cream, scallions, and bacon. Or, in the case of the sweet potato, you may want to add a little brown sugar with the butter.

For a true Texas loaded potato, such as the ones served at Ed's Smok-N-Q or the Lady and the Pit in Port Isabel, you may want to add a half pound of your favorite smoked meat. It could be chopped beef in a sauce, pulled pork, or chicken. They all help dress up that simple spud in a regal dose of excess that will make you really want to eat your vegetables.

SMOKY DEVILED EGGS

From Bonnie Walker

Deviled eggs have been a welcome find at several places along the barbecue trail, including Lum's in Junction. But then again, deviled eggs are always welcome. **Makes 12 servings (2 halves per person)**

Let the hard-boiled eggs cool well as you prepare the bacon. Chop the bacon into a small dice and fry over moderate heat until it has crisped up well. Drain on paper towels and set aside.

Peel the eggs and rinse to make sure you don't have any bits of shell on them. Pat dry. Using a sharp paring knife, slice eggs in half, putting the yolks in one bowl and the whites in another. If one or two of the eggs don't peel nicely, put the entire egg into the bowl with the yolks. (Or, if you want to make about a dozen deviled eggs, put 1–2 whole peeled eggs into the bowl with the yolks so that you have plenty to use for a generous filling.)

After the eggs are separated, gently wipe the whites with a wet paper towel to remove any yolk that is left on them. Cover with plastic wrap and place in the fridge while you prepare the filling.

Put all of the egg yolks and whole egg, if any, in a wire mesh strainer and press the yolks through. The strainer gives a good, fine texture, though it's a little work.

Add the mayonnaise, mustard, onion, Tabasco, Worcestershire sauce, white pepper, and salt to the yolks. Taste for seasoning and add more mayonnaise if you think it needs it.

If you're not going to serve the eggs right away, cover both bowls and refrigerate them until serving time. Keep bacon covered with a paper towel.

Just before serving, remove both bowls from the refrigerator. Fill each egg white generously with the yolk mixture and place on a plate. Sprinkle each with some paprika or smoked pimentón for garnish, then top with the bits of fried bacon and serve.

8 hard-boiled eggs

3 ounces smoked bacon

2 tablespoons mayonnaise

1 teaspoon Dijon mustard

½ teaspoon finely chopped white onion (or onion juice)

2–3 dashes Tabasco sauce

¼ teaspoon Worcestershire sauce

Pinch of white pepper

Salt to taste

Paprika or smoked Spanish pimentón, for garnish

SPICY COLESLAW

From James Canter, executive chef at the Victoria Country Club, Victoria, TX

Texans love their jalapeños, fresh and pickled. You'll usually find one or the other served up at most barbecue joints throughout the state. Chef James Canter of the Victoria Country Club likes to use the pickled version, also known as *escabeche*, diced up and stirred in his coleslaw for a little extra heat, which he tempers with the addition of blue cheese crumbles. Bright cilantro leaves and basil add a dark green to a colorful array that includes red and pale green cabbage, bright orange carrots, and flecks of black pepper. **Serves 10–12**

1 tablespoon sugar
2 pounds shredded green
   cabbage
1 cup shredded red cabbage
2 whole carrots, shredded
1 cup mayonnaise
2 cups crumbled blue cheese
1 cup chopped pickled
   jalapeño
2 cups rough-chopped
   cilantro
½ cup fresh basil leaves
Salt and black pepper to taste

Mix sugar and a pinch of salt with the cabbages and carrots. Make sure that the spices are well incorporated. Add mayonnaise and thoroughly incorporate into vegetable mix.

Add blue cheese and jalapeños and mix again. Finish with cilantro, basil, salt, and pepper. Mix well and refrigerate for at least 1 hour before serving.

BOURBON PECAN PIE

From John Griffin

Texas's favorite pie is generally made with corn syrup, but it doesn't have to be. Brown sugar is far less cloying. **Makes 1 pie**

Preheat oven to 350°F. Spread pecans on a baking sheet and toast for 5 minutes, stirring once. Let cool while you mix the filling.

In a medium bowl or in your stand mixer, whisk eggs, egg yolk, and water together until frothy. Add melted butter, brown sugar, bourbon, and vanilla. Mix thoroughly, making sure the sugar is well incorporated.

Arrange the pecans in the unbaked crust. Pour in egg mixture.

Bake for 50–55 minutes or until the center no longer jiggles. It doesn't have to be firm; that will happen after the pie cools.

Serve with bourbon whipped cream on top.

1½ cups pecan halves or pieces

3 whole eggs

1 egg yolk

¾ cup water

½ cup (1 stick) butter, melted

2 cups light or dark brown sugar

2 tablespoons bourbon

1 tablespoon vanilla

1 (9-inch) pie crust, unbaked

BUTTERMILK PECAN PIE

From John Griffin

Texans love pecan pie so much that in 2013 the state house of representatives named it our official pie. But you'll find more than a few who love buttermilk pie, too, which some food historians have said came about when fruit was scarce but the taste for something sweet was not. So, this was a perfect way to use up sour milk rather than letting it go to waste.

A handful of barbecue joints have taken things one step further and combined the two into one irresistible pie. It's easy to make, once you've assembled your ingredients, but you don't need to tell anyone that. Just let them enjoy the combination of pecans and tangy custard. (If you wanted to make a regular buttermilk pie, you could add an extra egg and a dash of nutmeg while omitting the nuts entirely.)

Makes 1 pie

6 tablespoons unsalted butter, melted
2 cups sugar
Generous ½ teaspoon kosher salt
4 large eggs, beaten
¼ cup all-purpose flour
2 tablespoons fresh-squeezed lemon juice
1 teaspoon vanilla
1 cup buttermilk
1 cup coarsely chopped pecans
1 (9-inch) deep-dish pie crust or 1 (10-inch) pie crust

Preheat oven to 325°F.

In a large bowl, stir together melted butter, sugar, and salt. Add the following one at a time: eggs, flour, lemon juice, vanilla, buttermilk, and pecans.

Pour into unbaked pie crust. Bake for 55 minutes or until pie sets.

FRUIT COBBLER

From John Griffin

There are a number of ways to make cobbler, from baking a biscuit topping over a fruit filling to creating an open deep-dish pie, according to Adrian Miller, who studied the dish's history in his book, *Soul Food: The Surprising Story of an American Cuisine, One Plate at a Time*. But there's one style you'll find more often at Texas barbecue joints. No matter what fruit is used, bakers prefer their cobblers with a layer of dumpling-like dough in the middle of the fruit filling. It's certainly more economical because it uses less fruit, but it's also richer and silkier. This style is not just found in Texas. It's the style of cobbler my mother makes, and her version inspired this recipe.

You can use this basic recipe for the dough and then use the fruit of your choice. What's interesting about the fruit cobblers in Texas is that they're rarely made with fresh fruit, even though the Hill Country is renowned for its peaches. One reason is that canned or frozen fruit has a greater consistency, which makes it easier on the baker. **Makes 1 (9 x 13-inch) cobbler**

Preheat oven to 375°F.

Stir together the flour, baking soda, baking powder, and salt. Cut the butter in, using a pastry cutter or your hands. Slowly add the buttermilk and stir together with a spoon. This will be sticky.

Flour your hands and pinch off a slight bit of dough. Pat it out into a dumpling and repeat until you can cover the bottom of a 9 x 13-inch dish. (This should be about ⅔ of the dough.) Pinch the pieces together, if you'd like, but the dough doesn't have to cover the entire bottom. Spread about half of the fruit filling over the top.

Flour your hands again and pat out about ⅓ of the remaining dough into dumplings. Scatter the dumplings over the fruit. They will not cover the fruit, but that doesn't matter. Pour in the remaining fruit.

Flour your hands again and pat out the remaining dough, covering as much of the top with dumplings as possible. Brush the top with egg white mixed with water or milk. Sprinkle sugar and cinnamon on top, if using.

Bake for 25 minutes, then check the cobbler. You want a rich, golden brown crust on top. It may need to bake 10 more minutes. This can vary, depending on how thick your crust is.

2¼ cups flour, plus more for rolling out

1 teaspoon baking soda

½ teaspoon baking powder

¼ teaspoon salt

½ cup (1 stick) butter, at room temperature, or shortening

¾ cup buttermilk

Fruit filling (see recipes on next page)

1 egg white mixed with a splash of water or milk

Sugar, for garnish (optional)

Cinnamon, for garnish (optional)

DESSERT RECIPES

Peach Filling:

6 cups canned sliced peaches
   in light syrup
2 tablespoons sugar
2 tablespoons butter
½ teaspoon cinnamon

In a saucepan over medium heat, stir together peaches in their syrup, sugar, butter, and cinnamon. Bring to a boil. Remove from heat and let thicken. Reserve until ready to fill cobbler.

Variation: If you're using frozen peach slices, you'll need to make a syrup, so that the filling thickens. To do that, mix $1/4$ cup water, $1^1/4$ cups sugar, and 4 teaspoons cornstarch melted together over medium heat. Bring to a boil, then add thawed peaches, butter, and cinnamon, stirring until butter melts.

Cherry Filling:

6 cups canned sour cherries
   or sweet cherries, drained
   (see note)
¼ cup sugar, or more, to taste
2 tablespoons butter
4 teaspoons cornstarch
1 teaspoon almond extract
   (optional)

Note: If using sweet cherries, you may want to add a good spritz of lemon juice to add some needed acidity.

In a saucepan over medium-high heat, stir together the cherries, sugar, butter, and cornstarch. Bring to a boil. Add almond extract, if using, and let thicken. Taste and adjust sugar to preference. Reserve until ready to fill cobbler.

Multiberry Filling:

¼ cup water
1¼ cups sugar
4 teaspoons cornstarch
6 cups frozen mixed berries,
   such as blackberries,
   blueberries, and raspberries,
   thawed
Spritz of lemon juice
2 tablespoons butter
¼ teaspoon cinnamon
   (optional)

In a saucepan, make a slurry of water, sugar, and cornstarch. Bring to a boil over medium-high heat. Stir in thawed berries, a little lemon juice, butter, and cinnamon, if using, stirring until butter melts. Reserve until ready to fill cobbler.

THE GRANARY 'CUE & BREW'S BANANA PUDDING

Lightly adapted from *The Granary 'Cue & Brew in San Antonio*
The Granary packs these puddings in individual Mason jars, tops them with a little whipped cream, and keeps them cold before serving. This recipe is for from-scratch vanilla wafers and banana custard. (The fast version uses a boxed pudding mix and vanilla wafers from a box, but it doesn't taste anywhere near as good.) **Serves 8–10**

For the wafers: In a bowl, cream together the butter and sugar. Stir in the egg and vanilla extract and mix well without beating. Fold in the flour and salt and mix until you have a firm dough. Roll dough into a cylinder about 1½ inches wide, roll in plastic wrap, and refrigerate.

Preheat oven to 350°F. When oven is hot, slice the roll of cookie dough into round pieces about ½-inch to ¾-inch thick. Keep the slices of uniform size. Place on a cookie sheet and put on a rack in the center of the oven. Turn the sheet once while they bake. Check in about 5 minutes; take out when they are just starting to color. Let cool.

For the pudding: In a bowl, beat (don't whip or whisk) the egg yolks. In another bowl, blend the sugar and cornstarch, then cream in the butter. Add to the egg yolks and blend well. Set aside. In a saucepan with a heavy bottom, scald (heat but don't let boil) the milk. Stir some of the hot milk into the bowl with the egg yolks and mix well. Put the milk back on the stove over medium-low heat and slowly stir in the sugar and egg mixture. Cut open the vanilla beans and scrape the seeds into the mixture. Let the custard heat and thicken, but don't boil, and keep stirring. If it gets too thick, add a little more milk or cream. When it is thick and silky, add the banana schnapps. Take off heat and let it cool. (Should lumps form, you can put the custard through a strainer.)

For the Chantilly cream: Whip the cream until stiff peaks form. Add the sugar and vanilla toward the end of the whipping. Keep cold if making ahead of time.

To assemble: Peel and slice the bananas as soon as the custard has cooled. In a bowl (or in individual dishes or jars), layer the custard mixture with sliced bananas, wafers, and a bit of the whipped cream. On top, put a little more cream and a wafer to garnish, or sprinkle crumbled wafers on the cream.

Vanilla Wafers:
¾ cup butter
⅔ cup sugar
1 egg, lightly beaten
2 teaspoons vanilla extract
1¼ cups flour
Pinch of salt

Pudding:
6 egg yolks
1¼ cups sugar
⅛ cup cornstarch
3 tablespoons butter
4¼ cups milk
1½ vanilla beans
¼ cup plus 1 tablespoon banana schnapps
2–3 bananas

Chantilly Cream:
1½ cups heavy cream
2 tablespoons sugar
1 teaspoon vanilla

PECAN COBBLER

From John Griffin

Pecan cobbler has begun appearing on a small but growing number of barbecue joints' dessert menus. It's different from pecan pie in that the pastry is sometimes made with oats and it's actually baked into the center, like a giant dumpling that soaks up some of the rich, syrupy filling. The coarsely chopped pecans, meanwhile, form a gleaming, pebbled mosaic on the top. Serve it warm with a scoop of another Texas treasure, Blue Bell vanilla ice cream, on top. **Serves 10–15**

Filling:

1½ cups light corn syrup, such as Karo

1 cup maple syrup

1½ cups sugar

¾ cup packed brown sugar

6 tablespoons unsalted butter, melted

1 generous tablespoon vanilla or more, to taste

5 eggs, lightly beaten

3 cups coarsely chopped pecans

1 teaspoon oats

Pastry:

1 cup oat flour (see note)

1 cup all-purpose flour

Scant ½ teaspoon coarse salt

½ cup (1 stick) cold unsalted butter, cut into pieces

¼ cup ice-cold water, plus more as needed

Note: To make oat flour, place whole oats in a food processor with the knife blade and process until the consistency is like flour.

Preheat oven to 350°F. Butter a 9 x 13-inch pan.

In a large mixing bowl, combine syrups, sugars, butter, vanilla, and eggs. Spread a third into the prepared pan. Bake for about 12 minutes, until it is bubbly. Remove and let cool slightly.

While it is baking, stir the pecans and whole oats into remaining filling mixture and set aside. Then make the pastry.

To make the pastry: In the bowl of a food processor, add the two flours, salt, and butter. Pulse about 20 times, until the butter is incorporated into the flour mixture, leaving everything looking like crumbs. Turn the processor on and add the water through the tube gradually until it is incorporated. Remove blade and turn out onto a flat surface. Form it into a ball and knead just a few times. Lightly flour your surface and roll out the dough into approximately a 9 x 13-inch rectangle. The dough will be more than ¼-inch thick.

Place the dough over the already-baked filling. Top with remaining nut mixture. Bake 40–45 minutes, until the top is a rich, shiny, dark brown. Let the cobbler sit for at least 20 minutes before serving. Top with Blue Bell vanilla ice cream, if desired.

SOUTHERN TEA CAKES

From John Griffin

The South is filled with its culinary traditions, and many have worked their way into the barbecue culture. One such treasure is the old-fashioned tea cake, an airy confection that adds a light touch to the end of a meal laden with substantial cuts of brisket, meaty ribs, or half a chicken.

Most every family has its own take on these cookies, whether they add nuts or buttermilk to the dough. This version features a touch of nutmeg. Grate your own for a little extra kick.

Also, pay attention to the cookies as they're baking. You don't want them to get too brown.

Makes 3-5 dozen cookies, depending on the size

Preheat oven to 350°F.

In a medium bowl, stir together flour, baking soda, and nutmeg. Set aside.

In a stand mixer on medium-low speed, cream butter for about 1 minute, then add sugar and salt, beating until fluffy. Add eggs one at a time, allowing each to mix in thoroughly. Add vanilla. Reduce the speed and slowly add the flour mixture until a dough forms. Stop mixer as soon as you can.

Using your hands, form a ball of dough. Take half of the dough and sprinkle it with flour over a rolling board or large flat surface. Sprinkle a little more flour on your work surface. Roll out the dough until it is between ¼- and ½-inch thick. (If you roll the dough out any thinner, your cookies could become crisp while baking. You want the cookies to be airy.)

4 cups all-purpose flour

1 generous teaspoon baking soda

¼ teaspoon nutmeg

1 cup (2 sticks) unsalted butter, at room temperature

1½ cups sugar

¼ teaspoon salt

2 large eggs, at room temperature

1 tablespoon vanilla

Sugar or candy sprinkles for garnish (optional)

Using a cookie cutter, cut out each tea cake to the size and shape you want. Many that you'll find in barbecue joints are quite large, but you don't have to make them that big if you don't want to. Space each cookie at least 1¼ inches apart on a cookie sheet lined with parchment paper.

Bake the cookies for at least 8 minutes (the time will vary depending on how thick they are), checking regularly to make sure that only the slightest hint of light brown can be seen at the edges. Remove from the oven and immediately sprinkle each with either a pinch of sugar or, during the holidays, candy sprinkles, if desired. Move them to a cookie rack as soon as possible or the bottoms could continue to brown on the hot cookie sheet. Let cool. Store in an airtight container.

SWEET TEA

From John Griffin

Don't mess with Texans' iced tea.

We drink it by the gallon every single day, summer or winter, and we drink it every hour of the day. Just look around Austin, San Antonio, or Corpus Christi and you're likely to find people carrying around orange-capped quart-size mugs from the Bill Miller Bar-B-Q chain. And who knows how many times a day they refill those?

Making iced tea isn't as easy as it looks, at least if you want it to sparkle in the light. Some believe that the way to avoid cloudiness in your glass is to let the temperature of the hot tea drop slowly, instead of pouring it over ice instantly. You might also hear people talk about filtering it twice before serving. Or you could use filtered water.

There are also a number of ways to create what Southerners, including those from all over Texas, lovingly call sweet tea. One is simply to dissolve about ¾ cup sugar into the hot tea, stirring until every last crystal has melted. (This won't work if the tea is already on ice—you'll just end up with a mound of undissolved mess that you'll have to rinse out later.) Another is to add a pinch of baking soda to a gallon of tea, for what reason we don't know, except perhaps to temper the acidity slightly.

Or, you could just whip up a simple syrup, as follows:

Heat the water and sugar in a saucepan, stirring until sugar dissolves. Remove from heat and let cool. You can use this to sweeten both hot and iced teas. And if you like really sweet sweet tea, use 1 cup of sugar.

1 cup water
¾ cup sugar

Variation: If you like the flavor of mint, take 1½ cups fresh mint leaves and tie them in cheesecloth. Add the mint sachet to a saucepan with 1 cup water and 1 cup sugar. Bring to a boil, reduce heat, and stir until sugar dissolves. Let simmer for 2 minutes. Remove the sachet and gently squeeze the liquid from the cheesecloth. (Don't press too hard because the mint can get bitter.) Let cool. You can freeze this for months. In addition to tea, you can also use this in a mint julep.

TEXAS B-B-Q BITTERS

From Heather Nañez of Bohanan's Prime Steaks and Seafood in San Antonio

Now you can drink your barbecue, thanks to the ingenuity of chef Heather Nañez, who created this unique bitters for the bar at Bohanan's Prime Steaks and Seafood in San Antonio. The restaurant's a high-end steakhouse, not a barbecue joint, but the flavor of these bitters in the tangy Texas Gold Rush, created by head bartender Jake Corney, will take you back to your favorite pit. Because of the volume that you're mixing up in this recipe, these bitters could also make a one-of-a-kind gift for all of your cocktail-loving friends. You can share both a small bottle of bitters and Corney's cocktail recipe to get them started on their own series of barbecue-infused drinks.

Thanks to the alcohol content of Nañez's creation, these bitters will keep forever.

2 tablespoons whole black peppercorns
1 teaspoon cumin seed
1 tablespoon yellow mustard seed
1 tablespoon black mustard seed
¼ cup espresso beans
2 dried chipotle peppers
8 sun-dried tomatoes
2 tablespoons dried oregano
1 handful fresh thyme
6 bay leaves
1 (750-milliliter) bottle Everclear
Liquid mesquite smoke

In a medium saucepan, toast the black peppercorns, cumin seed, yellow and black mustard seeds, and espresso beans until fragrant.

Put the spice mixture, chipotle peppers, sun-dried tomatoes, oregano, thyme, bay leaves, and Everclear in a glass container with a tight-fitting lid. Allow to macerate for 10 days. For best results, shake daily.

After 10 days, strain solids and put them in a medium saucepot. Cover with water and simmer for 7–10 minutes. Add to initial maceration (this will drop alcohol content without loss of flavor).

Strain through cheesecloth. Add liquid smoke to taste.

TEXAS GOLD RUSH

From Jake Corney of Bohanan's Prime Steaks and Seafood in San Antonio

Texans love the sweet corn flavor of a fine bourbon, and a growing number are being distilled in the state. So, if you like to drink local, keep an eye out for names such as Garrison Brothers, Ranger Creek, Treaty Oak, Yellow Rose, and Firestone & Robertson. **Makes 1 cocktail**

2 ounces bourbon
¾ ounce lemon juice
¾ ounce honey
2–3 dashes Texas B-B-Q Bitters (recipe above)
1–2 drops vanilla

Add bourbon, lemon juice, honey, bitters, and vanilla to an ice-filled shaker. Shake and serve over ice.

Sharing the Passion

If there is one ingredient that unites bloggers, it is a passion for whatever topic they choose to write about. Needless to say, there are quite a few people who are undeniably passionate about their Texas barbecue, and they blog about it with gusto as they continue in their quest for the next great joint, whether it's in El Paso or Marshall.

Men and women alike ring out their praise and criticism, and they share the stories they find on the trail. The following blogs listed are just a sampling of those that deal largely, if not exclusively, with barbecue made the Texas way. Some will keep you up-to-date on openings, closings, and any juicy tales from the pit, while others will regale you with their impressions of what they've tasted along the trail.

Some of these blogs reference other bloggers. One to check out for links to other sites is Full Custom Gospel BBQ from Daniel Vaughn. He's author of *The Prophets of Smoked Meat* and is *Texas Monthly*'s barbecue editor.

A corps of Texas photographers have captured breathtaking images of the masters in their pits and the tools of the trade from throughout the state. *Texas Monthly* has a monthly review that focuses on one of these photographers at www.tmbbq.com/?s=BBQ+Photographers.

Blogs

Brisket Man, http://brisketman.com
Don O's Texas BBQ Blog, www.donobbq.blogspot.com
Eats BBQ, www.eatsbbq.com
Fed Man Walking, www.fedmanwalking.com
Full and Content, www.fullandcontent.com
Full Custom Gospel BBQ, www.fcg-bbq.blogspot.com
Kevin's BBQ Joints, www.kevinsbbqjoints.com
Man Up, Texas BBQ, www.manuptexasbbq.blogspot.com

Scrumptious Chef, www.scrumptiouschef.com/food
The Smoking Ho, www.thesmokingho.blogspot.com
Texas BBQ Posse, www.texasbbqposse.blogspot.com
TMBBQ (or Texas Monthly BBQ), www.tmbbq.com
Wood. Smoke. Meat., www.woodsmokemeat.com

Photography

Wyatt McSpadden, www.wyattmcspadden.com
Nicholas McWhirter, www.redblank.com
Robert J. Lerma, www.robertjlerma.com
Robert Strickland, www.rsphotography.info

ENJOY
Old Fashioned Restaurant

Glossary: Texas Barbecue Terms to Learn

beef brisket: Many cuts of different types of meat, as well as a big variety of sausages, come out of the pits and off the grills in Texas. Texas barbecue is all about plenty—of everything. But the beef brisket is viewed as the king of Texas barbecue, and getting it right is at the top of the list of "how to succeed at barbecue." It has to be tender and perfectly seasoned (often with only salt and pepper), and be just about the best meat you've ever eaten. Right behind it come the pork and beef ribs, sausage, chicken, lamb ribs, mutton, and other cuts of beef such as clod, or shoulder.

fat or lean: Learn these two terms before placing your order for pit-smoked brisket. (Some places use "wet" or "marbled" and "dry." A handful charge extra for orders of lean meat only.) Some order-takers ask what you want, others don't—but you can always name your choice. If you're not sure which you'd prefer, tell the meat cutter to give you half and half. Watch to be sure they don't trim all the fat off the lean, though. Enjoy that flavor!

barbacoa: An early form of barbecue from which today's barbecue takes its name. *Barbacoa* is served in parts of Texas and considered to be a part of the barbecue genre (pages 16, 200–201).

barbecue sauce: Texas does have barbecue sauce, and in some areas, especially in East Texas, it is served over the meat. You can specify that you want it on the side, if you prefer. Restaurants often have two or more versions of sauce, of which they are not only proud, but also might sell in bottles at their restaurants and even in supermarkets. Texas supermarket shelves are well-stocked with barbecue sauces.

Not everyone loves barbecue sauce, though. The revered Kreuz Market in Lockhart makes the decision for you. A large sign on the wall in the big dining room plainly states, "No Sauce, No Forks, No Kidding."

burnt ends: These aren't exactly burnt, at least most of the time, but rather crusty and blackened from heat and smoke. They are also crunchy and full of flavor. If you see the meat cutter pushing these aside with the knife, ask if you can have some. Sometimes burnt ends are on the menu; sometimes the cooks add them to the beans. Either way, they're good.

cafeteria-style: This is often the way Texas barbecue is served. The first reason, as far as we can tell, is that there is nothing any menu you read at the table can do to whet your appetite like the sight of barbecue being sliced right in front of you, whether it's a big juicy brisket, shiny sausages, or an almost fork-tender pork shoulder. If the meat doesn't look right or isn't being cut the way the customer wants, there's time to make an alternate choice. Plus, if you want some of the crust or burnt ends that you see them pushing aside, all you have to do is ask.

Another tradition in Texas barbecue, though, is to serve meat in a pit room, where you can see the fire and smoke, and the pitmaster is overseeing the business of meat-cutting. The big pit room at Kreuz Market in Lockhart and the smaller, smoky room at City Market in Luling offer the real taste and feel of traditional Texas barbecue.

As for the side dishes, being able to see what you're getting, whether on a steam table or packed into cartons, is good for business as well. Customers might find it harder to turn down an offer of green beans when they see bright green vegetables spiked with a little bacon and onion or fresh tomato.

city cookers: What the competitors on the barbecue competition trail call restaurant barbecue cooks.

crust, or bark: If you see a row of big, uncut briskets sitting inside a cooker on a steel grate, don't worry if they look like dark-brown, or maybe black, bundles. This is the crust, or bark, that forms outside the meat as it cooks—what's inside is going to be (hopefully) tender, juicy, smoke-kissed beef. The barky exterior should not be bitter, but it should offer a well-seasoned crust nestled next to a layer of fat. That crust is desirable on pork ribs as well and needs to be lightly chewy and flavorful rather than brittle, overly salty, or downright inedible. If you want to discard the pieces of melted fat and peppery crust from your slice of brisket, at least take a taste. You might change your mind.

direct heat: This method is all about cooking meat on a grill directly over coals. Some smoky flavor is nevertheless created by the meat juices and fat dripping down onto the hot embers or by the addition of wood chips. Generally speaking, this is grilling, and a faster, hotter method for cooking meat and getting some smoke in the flavor. Some barbecue restaurants, such as Cooper's in Llano, use direct heat for their cooking.

indirect heat: "Low and slow" describes a popular method and much-used term for this type of cooking, where the meat is kept away from direct heat and is cooked by the heat and smoke from a wood fire at one (or two) ends of a pit. The pit might be made of brick or steel, but the principles are generally the same. A steady-burning fire brings the smoky pit to the desired temperature; meats will slowly (or more quickly, depending on who's managing the pit) reach the state of perfect, smoke-imbued tenderness as the meat, fat, and collagen seem to almost melt together.

Maillard reaction: Food is browned by way of a chemical process that occurs when amino acids and sugars are heated. It's named for the French scientist Louis-Camille Maillard. The crust, or bark, on barbecued meat is an example of this chemical reaction.

rest: In the cooking process, whether it's grilling or roasting, protein fibers in the meat shrink and the juices are forced toward the middle of the cut. Just as a cook lets an oven-roasted prime rib or turkey sit and rest for 15 to 20 minutes, so does a good pitmaster. The natural juices in the meat have time to redistribute, adding both flavor and moisture to the final product.

rub: Mix together salt and pepper—with a significantly higher ratio of pepper, of course—and you've got one of the simplest, as well as most widely used, rubs found in Texas barbecue. Add a little sugar, some cayenne pepper, and other spices of choice, and that is a rub, too. Personal spice blends in rubs are sometimes carefully protected secrets, but use just salt and pepper, and you'll be in some very good company. One of the top barbecues in the state, Louie Mueller Barbecue in Taylor, sells its rub, but the ingredients are no secret: nine parts pepper to one part salt.

side dishes: Beans, potato salad, coleslaw—this trinity of side dishes is found in most every barbecue joint, and as one might expect, their quality varies. You'll find green beans with bacon added, as well as pinto beans seasoned with "burnt ends." Pinto beans might also be prepared baked-bean style with a sweet tomato sauce, or made in a more traditional ranch style with bacon and a touch of chili seasoning. Or, they might be just plain pintos cooked with a little salt, pepper, and bacon fat, developing a velvety thick broth that some like better than the beans themselves.

If you're lucky, you might also find creamed corn that was scraped off the cob, homemade pickles, deep-fried onion rings stacked high on a plate, steak fries, baked potatoes, mashed sweet potatoes, macaroni and cheese, collard greens, mixed vegetables, or even a Tater Tot casserole, such as the good one served at Opie's BBQ in Spicewood. Traditional and rarely absent are sliced dill pickles, sliced raw onion, and pickled jalapeños.

smoke ring: We thank bbq.about.com writer Derrick Riches for this description of the pink-to-red band of meat that is under the surface of the crust, or bark: The smoke ring "can be just a thin line of pink or a rather thick layer. A good smoke ring is around ¼ inch in thickness. The smoke ring is caused by nitric acid building up in the surface of meat, absorbed from the surface. This nitric acid is formed when nitrogen dioxide from wood combustion in smoke mixes with water in the meat. Basically it is a chemical reaction between the smoke and the meat."

stick burners: Pitmasters who only use wood—no charcoal, gas, or other fuels. Competitive cookers who use wood are proud of the "stick burner" appellation.

white bread: Now and then we see a complaint online that a Texas barbecue joint had the audacity to serve them white bread. And we are amused. White bread is part of the tradition. It's always been that way—and sometimes it's served along with saltines. Some restaurants are doing it a little differently, such as the homemade buttermilk white bread at the Granary 'Cue & Brew in San Antonio. It's a whole other kind of white bread, and it's delicious. There are a number of ways to use the cottony, mass-produced white bread that comes on your tray of barbecue. Eat it, use it as a napkin, use it to soak up meat juices, or make an impromptu sausage wrap. And remember, you can always just say no.

Bibliography

Barbecue Any Old Time: Blues from the Pit, 1927–1942. Raleigh, NC: Old Hat Records, 2011. CD.

Byres, Tim. *Smoke: How to Build Flavor with Fire on the Grill and in the Kitchen*. New York: Rizzoli International Publications, 2013.

Caceres, Oscar. *Brownsville: Stories*. New York: Little, Brown and Co., 2008.

Davis, M. E. M. *Under the Man-Fig*. Houston: Riverside Press, 1899.

DeMers, John. *Follow the Smoke: 14,783 Miles of Great Texas Barbecue*. Houston: Big Sky Press, 2008.

Englehardt, Elizabeth S. D. *Republic of Barbecue: Stories Beyond the Brisket*. Austin: University of Texas Press, 2009.

"The 50 Best BBQ Joints in the World." *Texas Monthly*, June 2013.

Keen, Robert Earl. "Barbecue." *The Party Never Ends*. Durham, NC: Sugar Hill Records, 2003. CD.

Kelton, Elmer. *Sandhills Boy: The Winding Trail of a Texas Writer*. New York: Forge Books, 2007.

Linck, Ernestine Sewell, and Joyce Gibson Roach. *Eats: A Folk History of Texas Foods*. Fort Worth: Texas Christian University Press, 1989.

McSpadden, Wyatt. *Texas BBQ*. Austin: University of Texas Press, 2009.

Miller, Adrian. *Soul Food: The Surprising Story of an American Cuisine, One Plate at a Time*. Chapel Hill: University of North Carolina Press, 2013.

Reid, J. C. "The Ten Best Barbecue Joints in Houstonia." *Houstonia*, March 2013. www.houstoniamag.com/eat-and-drink/barbecue/articles/the-ten-best-barbecue-joints-in-houstonia-march-2013.

Riches, Derrick. "Smoke Ring." About Barbecue & Grilling, About.com. Accessed January 13, 2014. http://bbq.about.com/od/barbecuehelp/g/gsmokering.htm.

Texas Barbecue. Texas A&M University. Accessed January 13, 2014. http://bbq.tamu.edu/bbq-science.

Vaughn, Daniel. "The Best Barbecue in Dallas (That's Not Really in Dallas)." *D Magazine*, February 2010. www.dmagazine.com/publications/ d-magazine/2010/february/the-best-barbecue-in-dallas.

———. *The Prophets of Smoked Meats: A Journey Through Texas Barbecue.* New York: HarperCollins, 2013.

Walsh, Robb. *Legends of Texas Barbecue Cookbook: Recipes and Recollections from the Pit Bosses.* San Francisco: Chronicle Books, 2002.

———. *The Texas Cowboy Cookbook: A History in Recipes and Photos.* Berkeley, CA: 10 Speed Press, 2007.

———. *Texas Eats: The New Lone Star Heritage Cookbook with More Than 200 Recipes.* Berkeley, CA: 10 Speed Press, 2012.

Index